Photoshop® Elements 4 FOR DUMMIES

Cheat Sheet

Getting Familiar with the Elements Workspace

Shortcuts bar   Menu bar   Make creations

Tools palette   Image window   Go to Organizer

Foreground and Background colors

Photo Bin   Status bar   Palette Bin

- Open an image in the Elements Editor by choosing File⇨Open.
- Get information about your image by looking at the Status bar. Click the right-pointing arrow to get more details regarding your document.
- Need to see detail in your image? Zoom into your image by pressing Ctrl+spacebar and clicking. Zoom back out by pressing Alt+spacebar and clicking.
- Easily switch between open documents by clicking images in the Photo Bin.
- Access palettes as needed by selecting them under the Window menu or in the Palette Bin.
- Execute common tasks, such as Open, Save, and Print, by clicking buttons on the Shortcuts bar. You can also jump into making creations or dive into the Elements Organizer by clicking the buttons shown in the figure above.

For Dummies: Bestselling Book Series for Beginners

Photoshop® Elements 4 FOR DUMMIES

Toolbox Shortcuts

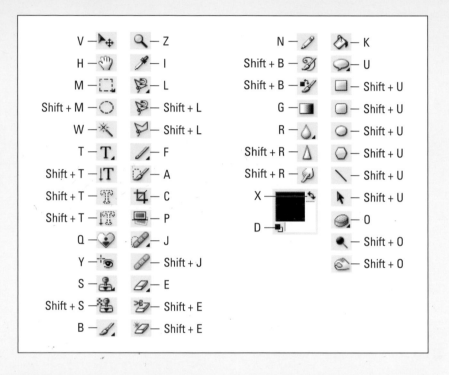

V —	Z	N —	K
H —	— I	Shift + B —	— U
M —	— L	Shift + B —	— Shift + U
Shift + M —	— Shift + L	G —	— Shift + U
W —	— Shift + L	R —	— Shift + U
T —	— F	Shift + R —	— Shift + U
Shift + T —	— A	Shift + R —	— Shift + U
Shift + T —	— C	X —	— Shift + U
Shift + T —	— P	D —	— O
Q —	— J		— Shift + O
Y —	— Shift + J		— Shift + O
S —	— E		
Shift + S —	— Shift + E		
B —	— Shift + E		

Selection Tricks

Add to selection	Shift+drag	Copy selection	Ctrl+C
Deselect from a selection	Alt+drag	Paste image last cut or copied	Ctrl+V
Deselect all but intersected area	Shift+Alt+drag	Paste into a selection	Ctrl+Shift+V
Deselect	Ctrl+D	Adjust levels	Ctrl+L
Reselect last selection	Ctrl+Shift+D	Adjust hue/saturation	Ctrl+U
Select everything	Ctrl+A	Image Size	Ctrl+Alt+I
Hide selection outline	Ctrl+H	Free Transform	Ctrl+T
Cut selection	Ctrl+X		

For Dummies: Bestselling Book Series for Beginners

Photoshop® Elements 4

FOR

DUMMIES®

Photoshop® Elements 4

FOR

DUMMIES®

by Barbara Obermeier and Ted Padova

WILEY

Wiley Publishing, Inc.

Photoshop® Elements 4 For Dummies®

Published by
Wiley Publishing, Inc.
111 River Street
Hoboken, NJ 07030-5774
www.wiley.com

WILEY

About the Authors

Barbara Obermeier: Barbara Obermeier is principal of Obermeier Design, a graphic design studio in Ventura, California. She's the author of *Photoshop CS2 All-in-One Desk Reference For Dummies* and has contributed as author, coauthor, or technical editor on numerous books. Barb is also a faculty member in the Visual Communication Department at Brooks Institute.

Ted Padova: In addition to writing several books about Adobe Photoshop and Adobe Illustrator, Ted is the world's leading author of books on Adobe Acrobat. He is a coauthor of *Adobe Creative Suite* and *Adobe Creative Suite 2* (Wiley Publishing, Inc.) and spends most of his time writing and speaking at conferences and expos nationally and internationally.

Dedication

Barbara Obermeier: I would like to dedicate this book to Gary, Kylie, and Lucky, who constantly remind me of what's really important in life.

Ted Padova: For Arnie.

Authors' Acknowledgments

The authors would like to thank our excellent project editor, Becky Huehls, who kept us and this book on track; Bob Woerner, the planet's premiere Sr. Acquisitions Editor; Andy Cummings, Dummies Royalty; David Herman, technical editing wizard; Andy Hollandbeck, who made what we wrote sound better; and all the dedicated production staff at Wiley. Additionally, we would like to thank Stephen Shafer of Schaf Photo, Ventura, California, for supplying us with sample images; and Don Mason of Don Mason Photography, Bakersfield, California, for helping us out with some color correction and his expert advice on digital color correction. Additionally, we would like to personally thank our good friend and colleague Deke McClelland. Deke's expert knowledge and advice has helped us on many occasion.

Barbara Obermeier: A special thanks to Ted Padova, my coauthor and friend, who always reminds me that there is still a one in fifty-three million chance that we can win the lottery.

Ted Padova: My first choice always in coauthoring a book is to do the job with Barbara Obermeier. Barbara is my right arm on everything, including telling me to turn my TV on when some world event happens. Without her, I'd live in a vacuum.

Publisher's Acknowledgments

We're proud of this book; please send us your comments through our online registration form located at www.dummies.com/register/.

Some of the people who helped bring this book to market include the following:

Acquisitions, Editorial, and Media Development

Project Editor: Rebecca Huehls

Sr. Acquisitions Editor: Bob Woerner

Copy Editor: Andy Hollandbeck

Technical Editor: David Herman

Editorial Manager: Leah Cameron

Media Development Manager: Laura VanWinkle

Media Development Supervisor: Richard Graves

Editorial Assistant: Amanda Foxworth

Cartoons: Rich Tennant (www.the5thwave.com)

Composition Services

Project Coordinator: Adrienne Martinez

Layout and Graphics: Denny Hager, Lynsey Osborn, Melanee Prendergast, Heather Ryan, Julie Trippetti

Proofreaders: David Faust, Leeann Harney, Lisa Stiers

Indexer: Sherry Massey

Publishing and Editorial for Technology Dummies

    Richard Swadley, Vice President and Executive Group Publisher

    Andy Cummings, Vice President and Publisher

    Mary Bednarek, Executive Acquisitions Director

    Mary C. Corder, Editorial Director

Publishing for Consumer Dummies

    Diane Graves Steele, Vice President and Publisher

    Joyce Pepple, Acquisitions Director

Composition Services

    Gerry Fahey, Vice President of Production Services

    Debbie Stailey, Director of Composition Services

Contents at a Glance

Table of Contents

Introduction

*W*hat was once a consumer-grade, low-level program for beginning image editors and a junior cousin to the powerful Adobe Photoshop program has evolved and matured to stand on its own merits now in version 4.0. You won't find much comparison between Adobe Photoshop Elements and Adobe Photoshop in this book, nor will you see any suggestions that you should consider using Photoshop for one thing or another. We don't make suggestions simply because Photoshop Elements is a powerful tool that satisfies many needs of amateurs and professionals alike.

Who should buy Elements (and ultimately this book)? The range of people who can benefit from using Elements is wide and includes a vast audience. From beginning image editors to intermediate users to more advanced amateurs and professionals, Elements has something for everyone. We'll even stick our necks out a little and suggest that many Photoshop users can benefit greatly by adding Elements to their software tool cabinet. Why? Because Elements offers you some wonderful creation tools that Photoshop hasn't yet dreamed of supporting. For example, you can create postcards, greeting cards, calendars, and photo albums with just a few mouse clicks. You can place orders with online service centers that professionally print your photo creations. All these opportunities are available in Elements, and we cover these and many more creation ideas in Chapters 15 and 16.

We have to make one exception here and say that Elements is not for everyone. The down side to the program is that version 4 is supported only on Windows. Adobe is no longer releasing a Macintosh version, so the poor Mac users can't explore all the power available in this new release. Our suggestion to the Mac users: buy a second computer. None of the Mac programs gives you the power that you find in Elements when it comes to image editing and packaging creations.

To set your frame of mind to thinking in Photoshop Elements terms, don't think of Elements as a scaled down version of Adobe Photoshop. Those days are past. If you're a digital photographer and you shoot your pictures in JPEG and/or camera RAW, Elements has the tools for you to open, edit, and massage your pictures into professional images. If you worry about color-profile embedding, forget it; Elements can handle the task, as we explain in Chapter 4 (where we talk about Camera Raw format) and Chapter 14 (where we talk about color profiling and printing). For the professional, Photoshop Elements has just about everything you need to create final images for color printing and commercial printing.

For the beginning and intermediate users, you'll find some of Photoshop Elements' quick fix operations a breeze to use to help you enhance your images, as we explain in Chapters 9 and 10. And when it comes time to print some homemade greeting cards, calendars, and photo albums, Elements provides beginners, intermediate users, and professionals easy-to-follow steps to package your creations, as we cover in Chapters 15 and 16.

About This Book

Elements is a feature-rich program, and this book is an effort to provide a comprehensive introduction. So although we may skip over a few little things, all you need to know about using Photoshop Elements for designing images for print, sharing, Web hosting, packaging in many different ways, e-mailing, and more is covered in the pages ahead. If you're ready to go a bit further, we also included Bonus Chapters on this book's Web site at www.dummies.com/go/elements4.

As we said, Photoshop Elements has something for just about everyone. Hence, we know our audience is large, and not everyone will use every tool, command, or method described in this book. Therefore we added a lot of cross-references in the text in case you want to jump around. You can just about go to any chapter and start reading; if some concept is dependent on more explanation, we point you in the right direction to get some background when it's necessary.

Conventions Used in This Book

Throughout this book, we point you to menus where commands are accessed. A couple things to remember are the references for where to go when we detail steps in a procedure. For accessing a menu command, you might see something like this:

Choose File➪Get Photos➪From Files and Folders.

When you see commands like this, we're asking you to click the *File* menu to open the drop-down menu and then click the menu command labeled *Get Photos* to open a submenu. Then, in the submenu, select the command *From Files and Folders.*

Another convention we use refers to context menus. A context menu jumps up at your cursor position and shows you a menu similar to the menu you select at the top of the Elements workspace. To open a context menu, just click the right mouse button, or as we like to say, *right-click* the object in question.

Finally, a third item to remember relates to using keystrokes on your keyboard. When we mention that some keys need to be pressed on your keyboard, the text looks like this:

Alt+Shift+Ctrl+S

In this case, you hold down the Alt key, Shift key, and Ctrl key and then press the S key. Then release them all together.

How This Book Is Organized

This book is divided into logical parts in which related features are nested together in chapters within six different parts. The parts of the book are as follows:

Part 1: Getting Started

If you just bought a digital camera and you're new to image editing in a program like Photoshop Elements, you're probably tempted to jump into fixing and editing your pictures. The essentials are usually not the most exciting part on any program or book. That's true with this book. The more mundane issues related to understanding some basics are assembled together in the first three chapters. Although not as exciting as many other chapters, there are some bits of information that are critical to understand before you start editing images. Be sure to review the first three chapters before you dive into the other chapters.

In Part I, we talk about the tools, menus, commands, preferences, workspaces, and some features to help you move around easily in the program. The more you pick up in the preliminary chapters, the easier you will adapt to the Elements way of working.

Part 11: Getting Organized

In Part II, we talk about getting photos in Elements, organizing your files, searching for files, grouping your photos, and much more information related to the Photoshop Elements Organizer. The Organizer is your central workplace, and knowing a lot about using the Organizer window helps you move around much faster in the program.

Part III: Selecting and Correcting Photos

This part relates to creating and manipulating selections. There's a lot to making selections in photos, but after you've figured it out (by reading Chapter 7), you can cut out a figure in a picture and drop it into another picture, drop in different backgrounds, or isolate an area that needs some brightness and contrast adjustment. In Chapter 8, we talk about layers and how to create and manage them in Elements. In many other chapters, we refer you back to the layers chapter because so many of the things you do in Elements are done on layers.

In Chapter 9, we talk about fixing image flaws and problems. That picture you took with your digital camera may be underexposed, overexposed, or may need some work to remove dust and scratches, need a little sharpening, or have some other imperfection that requires editing. All the know-hows and how-tos are in this chapter.

In Chapter 10, we cover correcting color problems, brightness, and contrast. We show you ways to quickly fix photos as well as some methods for custom image corrections.

Part IV: Exploring Your Inner Artist

This part is designed to bring out the artist in you. With Elements' easy application of filter effects, you can turn a photo image into a drawing or apply a huge number of different effects to change the look of your image.

In Chapter 12, we talk about drawing and painting, so you can let your artistic expression run wild. We follow up in Chapter 13 by talking about adding text to photos so you can create your own layouts, posters, cards, and so on.

Part V: Printing, Creating, and Sharing

One of the most critical chapters in the book is Chapter 14, in which we talk about printing your pictures. If your prints don't look the way they do on your monitor, you need to read and reread this chapter.

If screen viewing is of interest to you, we cover a number of different options for viewing your pictures on-screen in Chapter 15. For slide shows, Web-hosted images, animated images, viewing your photos on your TV, and even creating movie files, this chapter shows you the many ways you can view your Elements images on-screen.

We wrap up this part with Chapter 16, in which we cover making creations and sharing files. You have a number of different options for making creations to share or print.

Part VI: The Part of Tens

We wrap up the book with the Part of Tens chapters. We offer ten tips for composing better images and ten other fun, interesting creations that you can make with Elements, but that didn't fit in elsewhere in the book.

Icons Used in This Book

In the margins throughout this book, you'll see icons that indicate that something important is stated in the respective text:

This icon informs you that the item discussed is a new feature in Photoshop Elements 4.

Tips tell you about an alternate method for a procedure, a shortcut, a workaround, or other helpful information related to working on tasks in the section being discussed.

Pay particular attention when you see the warning icon. This information informs about when you may experience a problem performing your work in Elements.

This icon is a heads-up for something you may want to commit to memory. Usually it tells you about a shortcut for a repetitive task, where remembering a procedure can save you time.

After all, Elements is a computer program. No matter how hard we try to simplify explaining features, we can't entirely avoid the technical. When we cover technical details that are interesting (to some) but not essential to know, we use this icon to alert you.

Where to Go from Here

As we said before, the first part of this book is like a foundation for all the other chapters. Try to spend a little time going through the first three chapters in Part I. After that, feel free to jump around based on what you want to accomplish, and pay special attention to the cross-referenced chapters if you get stuck on a concept.

When you need a little extra help, refer back to Chapter 1, where we talk about using the online help documents available in Elements.

If you have questions, comments, suggestions, or complaints, send your comments here:

```
customer@wiley.com
```

We wish you much success and enjoyment with Adobe Photoshop Elements 4, and it is our sincere wish that the pages ahead provide you with an informative and helpful view of the program.

Part I
Getting Started

The 5th Wave By Rich Tennant

@RICHTENNANT

NATIONAL TABLOID PHOTO IMAGING WORKSHOP

"Remember, your Elvis should appear bald and slightly hunched. Nice Big Foot, Brad. Keep your two-headed animals in the shadows and your alien spacecrafts crisp and defined."

In this part . . .

Here you have it . . . a computer book specifically designed to help you get the most out
of a computer software program — and not just
any software program, but a powerful one with
many complicated features. You probably want to
jump in and perform some spiffy editing operations to get that prize photo looking the best you
can. But there are a few basics that need to be
understood when editing your photos.

In this first part, we talk about some essentials to
help you fully understand all the parts ahead. We
first talk about your Photoshop Elements working
environment and describe the many tools and features you can use for all your Elements sessions.
We also cover the very important task of getting
color set for optimum viewing on your computer
monitor and describe some essentials you need to
know about color as it relates to photo images.
This first part of the book contains some important information that you should plan to carefully
review and understand before going too far into
all the Elements features. Don't pass it up. Turn
the page and start getting acquainted with Adobe
Photoshop Elements basics.

Getting to Know the Work Area

*1*n Elements' work areas, you find quite a collection of tools, palettes, buttons, and options. Just a quick glance at the Elements workspace when you enter the Standard Edit mode shows you some of the power that Elements offers with just a click of your mouse. With all the possibilities, the Elements workspace can be intimidating. To ease your introduction to the many options for editing your pictures, we break them down for you in this chapter.

Elements has several work areas, and we start off by introducing you to the one you'll likely use most often, Standard Edit mode. This is the mode in which you can be creative with all the tools and features Photoshop Elements is known for, such as filters, drawing tools, layers, and more. We then introduce other work areas and tools you may not be as familiar with — Quick Fix mode for making common corrections to photos, Creation Setup mode for collecting your photos into creations such as calendars, and the Photo Bin for navigating among all your open images.

Before you start working in Elements, you'll find it helpful to know how to undo edits so you can start over easily and where you can find additional sources of help within Elements. We also explain one of the handiest ways to select tools and enter common commands — keyboard shortcuts.

Elements also includes the Organizer, a powerful tool for acquiring your images and keeping them organized. The Organizer includes features that help you view and search for images, too. We introduce the Organizer in Part II.

Getting Around in Standard Edit Mode

Standard Edit mode offers bundles of tools for editing your images, from correction tools for fixing color and clarity to filters, layers, and more for creating entirely original images either from existing photos or from scratch. But all these tools also make Standard Edit mode complex.

Figure 1-1 shows Elements in Standard Edit mode, highlighting all the tools and features we discuss in the sections that follow.

Jumping to Standard Edit mode

You can move into Standard Edit mode in a couple of ways:

- **From the initial Welcome screen,** click Edit and Enhance Photos and open a photo. Your Elements window appears in Standard Edit mode, as shown in Figure 1-1.
- **From the Organizer,** click Edit in the Shortcuts Bar and select Go to Standard Edit from the drop-down menu.

Examining the Image window

Not surprisingly, the Image window's tools and features are most useful when an image is actually open in the window. To get an image into the image window (refer to Figure 1-1), follow these steps:

1. **Click the Open tool in the Shortcuts bar.**

   The standard Open dialog box appears. It works like any ordinary Open dialog box you find in other applications.

2. **Move around your hard drive by using methods you know to open folders and select a picture.**

   If you haven't yet downloaded digital camera images or acquired scanned photos and want an image to experiment with, you can use an image found in your My Pictures folder that was installed with Windows.

3. **After selecting a picture, click Open.**

   The photo opens in a new image window in Elements.

Maximize mode

Tile windows

Tools palette

Cascade windows

Shortcuts bar

Search Help topic

Menu bar

Options bar

Palettes

Toggle
between modes

Photo Bin

Figure 1-1: The Photoshop Elements workspace shown when you open a file in Standard Edit mode.

REMEMBER

You can open as many image windows in Elements as your computer memory can handle. As each new file is opened, a thumbnail image is added to the Photo Bin at the bottom of the screen, and the image windows are stacked, with the current active image on the topmost window. To bring another open file to the foreground and make it active, click the respective thumbnail in the Photo Bin.

Here's a quick look at important items in the image window, shown in Figure 1-2:

Image area   Title bar

Information box   Size box

Magnification box

Figure 1-2: The image window displays an open file within the Elements workspace.

✔ **Scroll bars** become active when you zoom in on an image. You can click the scroll arrows, move the Scroll bar, or grab the Hand tool in the Tools palette and drag within the window to move the image around.

✔ **The Magnification box** shows you at a glance how much you've zoomed in or out.

✔ **The Information box** shows you a read-out for a particular tidbit of information. You can choose what information you want to see in this area by choosing one of the options from the pop-up menu, which we discuss in more detail later in this section.

When working on an image in Elements, you always want to know the physical image size, the image's resolution, and the color mode (these terms are explained in more detail in Chapters 3 and 4). Regardless of which menu option you choose in the status bar, you can get a quick glimpse at these essential stats by clicking the Information box, which displays a pop-up menu like the one shown in Figure 1-3.

Width: 2560 pixels (17.778 inches)
Height: 1920 pixels (13.333 inches)
Channels: 3 (RGB Color, 8bpc)
Resolution: 144 pixels/inch

16.3%   Scratch: 70.9M/466.8M

Figure 1-3: Click the readout in the status bar and a pop-up menu shows you important information about your file.

✔ **The Size box** enables you to resize the window. Move the cursor to the box and a diagonal line with two opposing arrows appears. When the cursor changes, drag in or out to size the window smaller or larger.

You can also resize the window by dragging any of the other corners in or out.

✔ Click **the Minimize button** (the _ button in the upper-right corner of the image window) and the window hides from view. It's still open; you just click the image in the Photo Bin to maximize the window.

- ↙ If you click **the Maximize button** (the button with the box-shaped icon), the Title bar shown at the top of the window disappears and provides you a little more room for viewing images in the window.

- ↙ You can click **the Close button** (it's shaped like an X) to close the active image window and keep Elements open. Alternatively, you can use the keyboard shortcut Ctrl+W or menu command File⇨Close to close the active window.

Now that you're familiar with the image window overall, we want to introduce you to the Information box's pop-up menu, which enables you to choose the type of information you want to view in the Information box. Click the right-pointing arrow to open the menu, as shown in Figure 1-4. Here's the lowdown on the options you find in the pop-up menu:

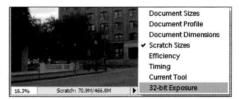

Figure 1-4: From the pop-up menu in the status bar, you select commands that provide information about your file.

- ↙ **Document Sizes:** Shows you the saved file size.

- ↙ **Document Profile:** Shows you the color profile used with the file.

- ↙ **Document Dimensions:** Shows you the physical size in your default unit of measure, such as inches.

- ↙ **Scratch Sizes:** As shown in Figure 1-4, displays the amount of memory on your hard drive that is consumed by all documents open in Elements. For example 20M/200M indicates that the open documents consume 20 megabytes, and a total of 200 megabytes are available for Elements to edit your images. As you add more content to a file — such as adding new layers, the first figure grows while the second figure remains static.

- ↙ **Efficiency:** This indicates how many operations you are performing in RAM as opposed to using your scratch disk. When the number is 100%, you are working in RAM. When the number drops below 100%, you are using the scratch disk. If you continually work below 100%, it's a good indication that you need to buy more RAM to increase your efficiency.

- ↙ **Timing:** Indicates the time it took to complete the last operation.

- ↙ **Current Tool:** Shows the name of the current tool selected from the Tools palette.

- ↙ **32-bit Exposure:** This menu command provides you an option for adjusting the preview image for viewing a High Dynamic Range (HDR) document on your monitor.

Don't worry about trying to understand all these terms. The important thing to know is that you can visit the pop-up menu and change the items at will during your editing sessions.

Moving through the Menu bar

Like just about every program you launch in Windows, Elements supports drop-down menus. The menus are logically constructed and identified to provide commands for working with your pictures (commands that you don't find supported in tools and palettes). A quick glimpse at the menu names gives you a hint of what might be contained in a given menu list.

The ten different menus are as follows:

- **File menu:** Just as you might suspect, the File menu contains commands for working with your picture as a file. You find commands for saving, opening, processing, importing, exporting, and printing in the menu list. We cover saving files in Chapter 3 and printing or exporting for other output in Part V.

- **Edit menu:** As you might guess, the old-fashioned Copy/Cut/Paste commands are located here. Additionally, you have some important file settings commands in the menu, including preferences, which we cover in more detail in Chapter 2.

- **Image menu:** You find yourself in the Image menu when you want to affect changes to the entire image, such as changing a color mode or cropping, rotating, and resizing images. For details about sizing and color modes, check out Chapter 3. For more about cropping and rotating images, flip to Chapter 9.

- **Enhance menu:** Just the name of this menu should tell you what commands to expect here. This is where you go to change image appearances, such as changing the brightness and contrast, adjusting color and lighting, and doing some smart fix-up work to improve image appearance. In Chapters 9 and 10, you find out how to use correction tools so your images look their best.

- **Layer menu:** As we describe in great detail in Chapter 8 (a whole chapter just about layers), most kinds of editing you do in Elements are best handled using layers. Elements neatly tucks away all the relevant commands associated with working in layers right here.

- **Select menu:** Of just about equal importance to layers is working with selections. Whereas the Image menu contains commands that are applied to the entire image, you can edit isolated areas of images by using the commands in the Select menu. In order to isolate an area, you need to create a selection, as we explain in Chapter 7. This menu contains commands to help you with all the essential tasks related to working with selections.

- **Filter menu:** The Filter menu is where you leave the world of photography and explore the world of a fine artist. With tons of different filter commands, you can create some extraordinary effects. Find out all about filters in Chapter 11.

- **View menu:** Zooming in and out of images, turning on a grid, exposing horizontal and vertical rulers, adding annotations, and checking out the print size of your pictures are handled in the View menu. Chapter 5 unearths secrets of the Zoom tool, rulers, and more.

- **Window menu:** Elements supports a number of different palettes, as we explain later in this chapter. Elements has so many palettes, keeping them all open at one time is impractical. Thanks to the Window menu, you can easily view and hide palettes, reopen the Welcome window, tile and cascade open windows, and bring an inactive window to the foreground.

- **Help menu:** Hopefully, you get all you need right here in this book; but just in case we miss something (or the neighbor has borrowed it, fine book that it is), you have some interactive Help right at your mouse-tip in the Help menu. The menu also offers links to Adobe's Web site for more information and a little assistance, courtesy of the tutorials accessible in this menu. (Find a little more detail about accessing help later in this chapter.)

Uncovering the context menus

Context menus are common to many programs, and Photoshop Elements is no exception. They're those little menus that appear when you right-click, offering commands and tools related to whatever area or tool you right-clicked.

The context menus are your solution when you may be in doubt about where to find a command in a menu. You just right-click an item, and a pop-up menu opens. As you become familiar with Photoshop Elements and you find yourself struggling to find a menu command, always try to first open a context menu and look for the command you want in the menu list.

Because context menus provide commands respective to the tool you're using, the menu commands change according to what tool or feature you are using at the moment you open a context menu. For example, in Figure 1-5, you can see the context menu that appears after we create a selection marquee and right-click that marquee in the Image window. Notice that the commands are all related to selections.

Deselect

Select Inverse

Feather...

Layer via Copy

Layer via Cut

New Layer...

Free Transform

Fill Selection...

Stroke (Outline) Selection...

Last Filter

Figure 1-5: A context menu for selections.

Using the Tools palette

Elements provides a good number of palettes for different purposes. The one you'll find you use most is the Tools palette. In palette hierarchy terms, you typically first click a tool in the Tools palette and then use another palette for additional tool options or use the Options bar for fine-tuning your tool instruments. More often than not, clicking a tool in the Tools palette is your first step in most editing sessions.

Tools can be easily accessed in Elements by pressing shortcut keys on your keyboard. For a quick glance at the Tools palette and the keystrokes needed to access the tools, look over Figure 1-6.

If you accidentally press the Tab key on your keyboard, the Tools palette hides from view. Press Tab again and the Tools palette reappears.

Notice in the Tools palette that several tools appear with a tiny arrow pointing right and downward on the lower-right corner of each tool. Whenever you see this arrowhead, remember that more tools are nested within that tool group. Click a tool with an arrowhead and hold the mouse button down. A pop-up toolbar opens, as shown in Figure 1-7, and offers you more tool selections within that group.

To select tools within a tool group by using keystrokes, press the Shift key and strike the respective key (shown in Figure 1-6) to access the tool. Keep the Shift key down and repeatedly press the shortcut key to scroll through all tools in a given group.

The shortcuts work for you at all times except when typing text. Be certain to click in the Tools palette to select a tool if your last edit was made with one of the Type tools.

The tools are varied, and you may find that you won't use all the tools in the Tools palette in your workflow. Rather than describe the tool functions here, we address the tools in the remaining chapters in this book as they pertain to the respective Elements tasks.

Figure 1-6: You access Tools by clicking the tool in the Tools palette or typing the respective character on your keyboard.

Figure 1-7: Click and hold the mouse button on a tool that has a tiny arrowhead, and a pop-up toolbar opens.

Playing with palettes

Elements provides you with a bunch of palettes that contain settings and options used to refine the tools you select in the Tools palette and tasks you perform to edit images. As an example of how a palette is used, assume for a moment that you want to let your creative juices loose and create a Picasso-esque painting — something that you can easily do in Photoshop Elements.

You first click the Brush tool and then click a color in the Color Swatches palette. On a new canvas, you begin to paint. When you want to change color, you click again in the Color Swatches palette on a different color. This kind of interactivity between the Tools palette and another palette is something you will frequently use in Elements.

Palettes are accessed from either the Palette Bin or from the Window menu. Many options in palettes are intuitive. To become familiar with various palette options, just poke around a little, and most of the options will become familiar to you.

Selecting tool options from the Options bar

When you click a tool in the Tools palette, the Options bar offers you choices specific to a selected tool. Figure 1-8 shows the options available when the Clone Stamp tool is selected.

Figure 1-8: The Options bar provides attribute choices for a tool selected in the Tools palette.

Juggling all your interface options

With all the settings you can use for any given tool, it can become downright frustrating trying to figure out exactly where to select an option for the edit you want to make. To help simplify the process of using tools and selecting options for the tools, here's what you might do in a normal workflow:

1. **Select a tool in the Tools palette.**

   Obviously, you need to know what task you want to perform, so selecting the proper tool to complete the task is important to know up-front.

2. **Take a quick look at the Options bar.**

   Before moving to other options choices, be certain you look over the choices in the Options bar. If you want to use a tool like the Brush tool or the Clone Stamp tool, perhaps you want to make a decision about what size brush tip you want to use. This choice is specific to the selected tool and therefore appears as an Options bar choice.

3. **Open a palette for more options.**

   If you, for example, want to use the Brush tool to apply some color to an image, after selecting the Brush tip in the Options bar, open the Color Swatches palette and select a color.

4. **Open the More menu.**

   Maybe the color you want to use doesn't appear in the Color Swatches palette. Your next stop is the More menu. From the menu choices, you can load different swatch libraries that provide more color options.

Try following the same sequence when you want to edit images in Elements by first selecting a tool, then checking out the Options bar, opening palettes related to providing choices for the task at hand, and finally clicking the More button for additional choices in the palettes.

Looking at the Shortcuts bar

You find the Shortcuts bar just above the Options bar and below the Menu bar. The Shortcuts bar, shown in Figure 1-9, serves two purposes. Tools in the Shortcuts bar are available for quick access to some of the most common tasks you perform in Elements. Secondly, buttons appear for quick access to Elements' other functions that involve organizing documents, browsing photos, or viewing a calendar.

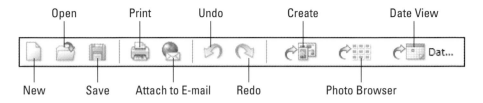

Figure 1-9: In Standard Edit mode, the Shortcuts bar provides tools and viewing options.

Depending on your editing mode, such as Standard Edit, Quick Fix, or one of the other viewing modes, the Shortcuts bar changes to provide different tools and buttons. Figure 1-9 shows how the Shortcuts bar appears when viewed in Standard Edit mode.

The Shortcuts bar contains tools and buttons grouped together as follows:

✓ The first group offers quick access to file management commands. You can create a new file, open a file, or save a file by clicking one of the first three tools in the Shortcuts bar.

✓ Click the Print tool to print a file or the Attach to E-mail tool to attach an open document to a new e-mail message in your default e-mail program.

✓ Click Undo to undo an edit and Redo to redo an undone edit.

✓ For a quick jump to all the wonderful organizing features provided in Elements, such as creating slide shows, calendars, and postcards or writing to video discs, click the Create button. Click Photo Browser to open the Photo Browser window, where you can easily manage your pictures. The Date View shows you a calendar, where you can add thumbnails of your pictures.

Changing Workspaces

When you're in Standard Edit mode, discussed in preceding sections, you can apply any kind of edits to a picture, improve the appearance, and apply all that Elements offers you. This mode is the richest editor in Elements in terms of accessing all features. Because Elements has so many different kinds of editing opportunities, the program offers you other workspace views, tailored to the kinds of tasks people typically want to perform.

Using Quick Fix mode

The Quick Fix mode is designed to provide you with just those tools that are needed to prepare a picture for its intended destination, whether it be printing, on-screen viewing, or one of the other organizing items. Use this mode to make your pictures look good. You won't find tools for adding text, painting with brushes, or applying gradients in Quick Fix mode. Rather, what you find is a completely different set of palettes for balancing contrast and brightness, lighting, sharpening, and so on. This mode is like having a digital darkroom on your desktop, where you take care of perfecting an image like you would in analog photography darkrooms.

To enter the Quick Fix mode while you are in Standard Edit mode, click the Quick Fix button adjacent to the Shortcuts bar; the view changes, as shown in Figure 1-10.

If you want to start up Elements in Quick Fix mode, click the Quick Fix button in the Welcome screen when you first launch the program.

There are several differences between Standard Edit mode and Quick Fix mode:

- **Completely different sets of palettes are docked in the Palette Bin.** All the palettes in Quick Fix mode are related to adjusting brightness controls and are designed to improve the overall appearance of your pictures. In addition, all the Window menu commands for accessing palettes are grayed out. While you work in Quick Fix mode, Elements is insistent on limiting your use of palettes to just those palettes docked in the Palette Bin. Moreover, you cannot undock palettes from the Palette Bin by dragging them out, as you can in other modes.

- **The Tools palette disappears.** Quick Fix mode offers you only the Zoom tool, Hand tool, Genie Brush tool, Crop tool, and Red Eye Removal tool in the Tools palette. None of the other Elements tools are accessible while you work in this mode.

- **Multiple viewing options are available.** Notice in Figure 1-10 that there are two views of the same image. One view displays the raw, unedited image. The After view shows you the results of changes you make with palette options and menu commands.

If you want to return to the Standard Edit mode, click the Standard Edit button.

Figure 1-10: Click Quick Fix in Standard Edit mode, and the workspace changes.

Using Creation Setup

To organize your pictures for display in a variety of different ways, you begin by accessing the Creation Setup window. While in either Standard Edit or Quick Fix mode, click the Create button on the Shortcuts bar. The Creation Setup window opens, as shown in Figure 1-11.

We cover each option available in the Creation Setup window in greater detail in Chapter 16.

Figure 1-11: Click Create in either Standard Edit or Quick Fix mode to open the Creation Setup window.

Using the Photo Bin

The Photo Bin displays thumbnail views of all your open images. Regardless of whether you work in Standard Edit or Quick Fix mode, you can immediately see a small image of all the pictures you have open at one time, as shown in Figure 1-12. You can also see thumbnail views of all the different views you create for a single picture. Find out all the details in the sections that follow.

Figure 1-12: All open pictures and new views are displayed as thumbnails in the Photo Bin.

If you want to rearrange the thumbnails in the Photo Bin, just click and drag horizontally to reorganize the order of the thumbnails.

Creating different views of an image

What? Different views of the same picture, you say? Yes indeed. You might create a new view when you want to zoom in on an area for some precise editing and then want to switch back to a wider view. Here's how you do it:

1. **Click an image's thumbnail in the Photo Bin.**

   The respective photo appears in the image window as the active document.

2. **Choose View⇨New Window for *<filename>*.**

   Note that *<filename>* is the name of the file in the image window.

3. **Zoom to the new view.**

   A new view appears for the active document, and you see another thumbnail image added to the Photo Bin.

   To zoom quickly, click the Zoom tool and click a few times on the picture in the image window to zoom into the photo.

4. **Toggle views of the same image.**

   Click one thumbnail and you see the opening view; click the other thumbnail and you see the zoomed view.

Hiding the Photo Bin

The Photo Bin takes up a lot of room at the bottom of the image window, and you're not likely to want it open all the time while editing some pictures. Fortunately, Elements provides you with two methods for hiding the Photo Bin when you want to create a little more editing real estate.

To temporarily hide the Photo Bin, do one of the following:

- Place the cursor over the separator bar between the Image window and the Photo Bin. When the cursor changes to two horizontal lines with vertical opposing arrowheads, drag down to collapse the Photo Bin. When the bin is collapsed, drag the separator bar up to open the bin.

- To auto-hide the Photo Bin, open a context menu (right-click inside the Photo Bin) and select Auto-hide from the menu choices. (Alternately, you can just click the separator bar where you see the tiny arrowhead to show/hide the bin.) When you use Auto-hide, the Photo Bin automatically hides when the cursor appears in the image window. The Photo Bin automatically opens when you move the cursor below the separator bar.

Retracing Your Steps

Ever since Apple Macintosh brought a windows interface to the masses, the Undo command has been one of the most frequently used menu commands in every program developed. You make a change to your document, and if you don't like it, you simply choose Edit➪Undo or press the keyboard shortcut, Ctrl+Z.

In Elements, your options to undo your work have expanded, as we explain in the following sections.

Using the Undo History palette

Elements takes the Undo command to new levels by offering you a palette in which all your changes (well, almost all) in an editing session are recorded and available for undoing at any step in an editing sequence.

Each edit you make is recorded in the Undo History palette. To open the palette, choose Window➪Undo History. Make changes to your document, and each step is recorded in the palette, as you see in Figure 1-13.

 If Elements slows down, and you're moving along at a snail's pace, open the More drop-down menu in the History palette and select Clear Undo History. Elements flushes all the recorded history and frees up some precious memory that often enables you to work faster.

Figure 1-13: The History palette records steps in an editing session.

We said *almost all* steps are recorded because the number of steps the History palette can record is controlled by a preference setting that tops out at 1,000 steps. If you choose Edit⇔Preferences and look at the General preferences, as we explain in more depth in Chapter 2, the number of history states defaults to 50. You can change the number to the maximum of 1,000 if you like. But realize that the more history states you record, the more memory Elements requires.

To undo the last edit, you can use the keyboard shortcut, Ctrl+Z. When you want to undo multiple edits, open the Undo History palette and click any item listed in the palette. Elements takes you to that last edit while scrubbing all the edits that follow the selected item. If you want to bring them back, just click again on any step appearing grayed out in the palette to Redo up to that level.

All your steps are listed in the Undo History palette as long as you remain in Elements and don't close the file. When the file is closed, all the history information is lost.

Reverting to the last save

As you work away in Elements, you should always plan on saving your work regularly. Each time you save in an editing session, the Undo History palette preserves the list of edits you made prior to the save and up to the maximum number of history states defined in the General preferences.

If you save, then perform more edits, and then want to return to the last saved version of your document, Elements provides you a quick, efficient way to do so. Choose Edit⇔Revert, and Elements eliminates your new edits and takes you back to the last time you saved your file.

When you choose Revert, the word *Revert* appears in the Undo History palette. You can eliminate the Revert command from the Undo History palette by right-clicking Revert in the Undo History palette and choosing Delete from a context menu. This returns you to the edits made subsequent to the last save.

Getting a Helping Hand

You can reach for this book when you want some details about accomplishing a task while working in Elements. However, for those little annoying moments, and just in case some coffee stains blot out a few pages in this book, you may want to look for an alternative feature description from another source.

Rather than accumulate a library of Elements books, all you need to do is look at Elements itself to find some valuable help information quickly and easily. If you're stuck on understanding some feature, you'll find ample help documents a mouse click away that can help you overcome some frustrating moments.

Using Help

Your first stop for exploring the helpful information Elements provides you is in the Help menu. Here, you find several menu commands that offer you information:

- **Photoshop Elements Help:** Choose Help➪Photoshop Elements Help or press the F1 key to open the Elements Help file. You can type in a search topic and press Enter to open a list of items that provide helpful information on the searched words.

  For quick access to the Help document, type the text you want to search into the text box on the right side of the menu bar in Standard Edit or Quick Fix mode.

- **Glossary of Terms:** As you read this book, if we use a term that you don't completely understand, open the Photoshop Elements glossary. Here, you find definitions of terms commonly used in photography and image editing, as well as terms related specifically to Elements.

- **Tutorials:** If you want to explore some advanced learning, check out the online tutorials provided by Adobe Systems.

- **Photoshop Elements Online:** This menu command launches your default Web browser and takes you to Adobe's Web site, where you can find information about Elements, problems reported by users, and some workarounds for getting a job done.

Using PDFs from the installation CD

A number of bonus files are stored in PDF form on your installation CD. PDF files require the free Adobe Reader program or one of the commercial Acrobat viewers. Adobe Reader can be installed from the CD during your installation process.

Depending on when you purchased your Elements installer CD, the version of Adobe Reader on the CD might be outdated. If you want to stay with the latest upgrade of Adobe Reader, open your Web browser and type this address in the Location bar:

```
www.adobe.com/products/acrobat/readermain.html
```

Adobe Systems provides easy, step-by-step instructions for downloading the most current, free Adobe Reader program and installing it on your computer.

Using ToolTips

As you move your cursor around tools and palettes, pause a moment before clicking the mouse. A slight delay in your actions produces a ToolTip, as shown in Figure 1-14. Elements provides you this sort of dynamic help as you move the cursor around the workspace and pause before moving to another location.

Figure 1-14: Place the cursor over a tool and pause a moment to open a ToolTip.

Using the How To palette

The default Palette Bin in Standard Edit mode contains the How To palette at the top of the bin. The How To palette lists some of the more common tasks you are likely to perform in Elements. Click the right-pointing arrowhead to expand a list and then click an item to open help information in the palette. You can scroll pages by clicking the arrows, return to the opening How To page by clicking the house icon, and print a topic by clicking the printer icon if you want to create hard copy of some help information.

Taking Charge with Shortcuts

As Emeril says, "It's time to kick it up a notch." Kicking it up a notch in Elements terms means leaving the pick and poke editing methods of the novice and graduating to techniques used by the swift keyboard master.

Using keyboard shortcuts greatly reduces your time in Elements and makes you much more proficient. The up side is that most of what you can do by moving the mouse and clicking a tool or menu command can be performed right from your keyboard by using combinations of keystrokes. The down side is that, because there are so many keyboard shortcuts to remember, learning all of them is nearly impossible.

The best way to remember keyboard shortcuts is to practice using them. After that, you might want to browse the resources where shortcuts are defined.

Here are some considerations to help you remember shortcuts and find more information about them:

- ✔ **For common tasks, always take special note of ToolTips and commands in a menu.** ToolTips provide a description of what a tool does, and they often display the keyboard shortcuts used to access the tools. Menu commands that support keyboard shortcuts list the shortcut keys to the right of command names.

- ✔ **Look over all the tips and alternate methods for performing an action that we describe throughout this book.** As you are introduced to more features in Elements, we try to offer you the keyboard shortcut options as well as tools and commands. Instead of giving you a list here, we provide keyboard shortcuts when explaining a feature.

- ✔ **Search the Help document.** Open the Elements Help document (Help➪ Photoshop Elements Help or press F1) and search for *keyboard shortcuts*. The Help document provides a comprehensive list of all the keyboard shortcuts you can use in Elements.

- ✔ **Stick with the essentials.** Try to commit to memory only those shortcuts that produce actions for your most common editing tasks.

The Cheat Sheet at the front of this book lists some common keyboard shortcuts so that you can reference them quickly and easily.

Memorizing keyboard shortcuts is not critical to your work in Photoshop Elements. You can do everything the program was designed for without ever using a shortcut. However, when you become familiar with keyboard shortcuts, you'll find yourself zooming through editing sessions with much more speed and efficiency. As a matter of fact, many advanced and professional users often forget where a menu command is contained because they rely so much on shortcut keys.

Getting Ready to Edit

*A*lthough not as exciting as firing up Elements and working on your precious pictures, customizing Elements for your personal work habits and properly setting up color management is critical to everything else you do in the program. This chapter explains how to take charge of Elements and customize your work environment by adjusting preference settings and setting up a color management system. If you're new to Elements or image editing in general, you might not know just how you want to set up certain features right away. However, you can always refer to this chapter and review and update settings and options later as you become familiar with other features in Elements.

Controlling the Editing Environment

Opening Elements for the first time is like moving into a new office. Before you begin work, you need to organize the office. At a minimum, you need to set up the desk and computer before you can do anything. In Elements terms, the office organization is specifying Preference settings. *Preferences* are settings that provide a means to customize your work in Elements and to fine tune the program according to your personal work habits.

What we offer here is a very brief description of what preference options are available to you. When you need some detail regarding one preference option or another, look at the help documents we discuss in Chapter 1. Use the help documents as a reference and you won't need to memorize the vast number of settings Elements provides you.

Launching and navigating Preferences

Preferences are all contained in a dialog box that's organized into ten panes. By default, when you open the Preferences dialog box, the opening pane is the General pane. To open the Preferences dialog box, do one of the following:

- ✔ **Choose Edit⇨Preferences.**
- ✔ **Press Ctrl+K.**

Using either method opens the dialog box to the General preferences pane, as shown in Figure 2-1.

Figure 2-1: The General preferences dialog box.

In Figure 2-1, you see a number of items that are common to all preference panes. Here's a quick introduction to what these items are and how they work:

- ✔ **Drop-down pane menu:** Click the topmost downward-pointing arrow and you see all the individual panes listed. You can select from the menu to jump to another pane.
- ✔ **OK:** Click OK to accept any changes made in any pane.

- **Cancel:** Click Cancel to return to the same settings as when you opened a pane. If you hold down the Alt key, the Cancel button changes to Reset and performs the same action as clicking the Reset button.

- **Reset:** If you change the settings options and click Reset, the action takes you back to the same settings as when you opened the Preferences dialog box.

- **Learn about Preferences:** Click the blue text and the Adobe Help Center opens where you find help information that's specific to this dialog box.

- **Prev:** Switches to the previous pane.

- **Next:** Switches to the next pane.

  You can also press Ctrl+(1 through 0 keys) to jump to another pane.

All these options are available regardless of the pane in view.

Checking out all the Preferences panes

The settings in the Preferences dialog box are organized into different panes, that reflect key categories of preferences. The following list briefly describes the types of settings you can adjust in each of the Preferences panes:

- As the name implies, **General** preferences apply to overall general settings you adjust for your editing environment.

- **Saving Files** preferences relate to options available for saving files. You can choose to add extensions to filenames, save files with layers or flatten layers when saving a file (as we explain in Chapter 8), save files with image previews that appear when viewing files as icons on your desktop, and save with some compatibility options.

- **Display and Cursor** preferences offer options for how certain tool cursors are displayed and how you view the Crop tool when cropping images.

- Working with the **Transparency** preferences requires an understanding of how Elements represents transparency. Imagine painting a portrait on a piece of clear acetate. The area you paint is opaque and the area surrounding the portrait is transparent. To display transparency in Elements, you need some method to represent transparent areas (Chapter 7 has more details). Open the Transparency preferences and you make choices for how transparency is viewed in your 2-D Elements environment.

- **Units and Rulers** preferences let you specify settings for ruler units, column guides, and document preset resolutions.

✔ The **Grid** preferences offer options for gridline color, divisions, and subdivisions. A *grid* shows you nonprinting horizontal and vertical lines. You use a grid to align objects, type, and other elements. You can snap items to the gridlines to make aligning objects much easier.

✔ The **Scratch Disks** preferences contains options for selecting *scratch disks.* Assume you have 100MB of free RAM (your internal computer memory), and you want to work on a picture that consumes 200MB of hard disk space. Elements needs to load all 200MB of the file into RAM. Therefore, an auxiliary source of RAM is needed in order for you to work on the image; Elements uses your hard drive. When a hard drive is used as an extension of RAM, we call this source a *scratch disk.*

If you have more than one hard drive connected to your computer, you can instruct Elements to use all hard drives, and you can select the order of the hard drives Elements uses for your extension of RAM. All disks and media sources appear in the drop-down menus you see for First, Second, Third, and Fourth.

Don't use USB external hard drives or other drives with connections slower than FireWire. Using slower drives will actually slow the performance of Elements.

✔ Memory — and the need to conserve and manage it well — is important to Elements. Yet another preference item for managing memory is the **Memory & Image Cache** settings.

Cache is a memory location on your hard drive that Elements uses to remember things like image levels, screen redraws, and histogram displays. (We explain more about using histograms in Chapters 4 and 10.) When one of these items is loaded in memory, it is stored in a cache location. The next time you use the same operation, Elements pulls the item from the cache. The result is much faster access to frequently used items.

You can set the cache level from 0 to 8 by typing a number in the text box. Setting the number to a lower value can help you free up memory so you can work on large images. If you have a lot of RAM and hard-drive memory to work with, caching is not a concern; you can set the cache to 8 for faster operations.

✔ **Type** preferences provide options for setting text attributes. You have options for using different quote marks, showing Asian characters, showing font names in English, and previewing font sizes.

✔ When you open the **Organize & Share** preferences pane, you lose the Preferences dialog box, and another Preferences dialog box opens, in which choices are made for the organizing environment itself. Because this set of preferences is handled in a completely different dialog box, we describe it in the next section.

Controlling the Organizing Environment

A whole different set of Preferences appears when you select Organize and Share in the Preferences dialog box. Initially, it may be confusing to you because the dialog box that opens when you select Organize and Share is also called Preferences. However, a quick glance at the dialog box shows you a different set of preference choices. In the following sections, you find a brief introduction to the Organizer and discover all the different organization preferences that Elements has to offer.

Understanding the Photoshop Elements 4.0 Organizer

We cover all you need to know about a wonderful tool called the Adobe Photoshop Elements 4.0 Organizer in Chapter 6. Rather than describe all that the Organizer offers you here in this chapter, we just want you to be aware that when setting the Organize & Share preferences, you're setting preference options for the Organizer.

To take a quick peek at the Organizer, click the Photo Browser button while in Standard Edit or Quick Fix mode.

Launching and navigating Organize & Share preferences

You can open the Organize & Share Preferences dialog box directly from the Edit menu while in either Standard Edit or Quick Fix mode. Choose Edit➪ Preferences➪Organize & Share. Doing so bypasses the Editing Preferences dialog box and takes you directly to the dialog box shown in Figure 2-2.

Figure 2-2: Choose Edit➪Preferences➪Organize & Share, and a new, different Preferences dialog box opens.

The Organize & Share Preferences dialog box uses the same metaphor to toggle through a number of panes that the main Preferences dialog box uses. However selecting the individual panes is handled by clicking the names in the list on the left side of the dialog box instead of selecting panes from a drop-down menu. Options common to all preference panes include:

- ✓ **Restore Default Settings:** Click Restore Default Settings to change all panes to the original defaults.

- ✓ **OK:** Click OK to accept new changes.

- ✓ **Cancel:** Click Cancel in any pane, and any changes made are not registered.

- ✓ **Help:** Click Help to open the Help window and find information about Organize & Share preferences.

Setting preferences in all the panes

With the Organize & Share Preferences dialog box open, here's a quick overview of what you find there:

- ✓ The items in the **General** preferences pane affect a miscellaneous group of settings applied to files when using the Create tool. Chapter 16 explains this tool in detail.

- ✓ **Files** preferences offer options for managing file data, connecting to missing files, prompting for backing up your data, saving catalogs, file and folder locations for saved files, and adjusting proxy file (a low-resolution display of a higher resolution image) sizes.

- ✓ **Folder Location View** preferences provide options for showing files and folders in groups and selected folders.

- ✓ With the **Editing** preferences, you can enable another application that provides some editing features not found in Elements to edit an image based on its file type. One good example for adding another editor is when editing video clips. If you have Adobe Premiere Elements, you can add Premiere as another editor. If you don't have Premiere installed, you can use another editor like Microsoft Media Maker.

- ✓ The **Camera or Card Reader** preferences handle acquiring images from digital cameras and media storage cards. Your computer may have built-in card readers in which you can insert a media card, such as Compact Flash or Smart Media, or a USB card reader that supports a media card. In other cases, you may have a cable that connects from your camera to a USB port on your computer. These preference options are used with media cards and camera connections.

> ⌐ If you scan images with a scanner connected to your computer (as opposed to downloading them from your camera), the **Scanner** preferences hold all the options you may want to set.

> ⌐ **Calendar** preferences relate to calendar creations. You have several options from which to choose for your calendar design. In Chapter 16, we cover creating calendars and explain a little more about these preference options.

> ⌐ **Tags and Collections** preferences help you find and sort your images, as we explain in much more detail in Chapters 5 and 6. Tag preferences offer options for sorting tags and icon views for tags.

> ⌐ If you have a mobile phone capable of taking pictures, you'll want to check out the **Mobile Phone** preferences. You can copy pictures from your phone to your computer, as we explain in Chapter 4. These preferences offer options for a folder location where mobile phone files are stored and an option for correcting red-eye automatically as files are opened. See Chapter 10 for more information on red-eye correction.

> ⌐ **Sharing** preferences relate to sharing files in e-mail and online. Options are available for setting e-mail and sharing settings.

> ⌐ **Services** preferences offer choices for handling program updates and online service orders. You can choose to check for program updates automatically or manually, choose options for printing and sharing images, and update creations, accounts, and more.

Customizing Presets

Part of the fun of image editing is choosing brush tips, swatch colors, gradient colors, and patterns to create the look you want. To get you started, Elements provides you with a number of different preset libraries that can be loaded and used at your will. So, for example, you can load a Brushes library to acquire different brush tips you use with the Brush tool. But you'll likely want to customize the preset libraries at least a little bit, too.

You can change libraries individually in respective palettes where the items are used. For example, you can change color swatch libraries in the Color Swatches palette, brush tips from Options bar choices, and so on. Another way you can change libraries is to use the Preset Manager, shown in Figure 2-3.

We cover using the presets in Chapter 12, which is where you can find out how to use the many different presets Elements provides you. The important thing to note here is that you can change the presets according to your editing needs.

To open the Preset Manager dialog box, choose Edit⇨Preset Manager. The options you have available include the following:

- **Preset Type:** Open the drop-down menu to choose from Brushes, Swatches, Gradients, and Patterns.

- **More:** The More drop-down menu lists different viewing options. You can view the library items as text lists or as thumbnail views.

- **Done:** Any changes you make in the Preset Manager are recorded and saved when you click Done.

- **Load:** Click this button to open another library. Elements provides you with several libraries from which to choose for each Preset Type.

- **Save Set:** Any changes you make in the Preset Manager can be saved as a new library. Use this option if you make a change so you don't disturb the original presets.

Figure 2-3: The Preset Manager dialog box provides a central area where libraries can be changed.

- **Rename:** Each item in a library has a unique name. If you want to rename an item, click the thumbnail in the Preview window, click Rename, and type a new name in the dialog box that appears.

- **Delete:** Click an item in the Preview window and click Delete to remove the item from the library.

- **Help:** Click Help to open the Help document and find out more about managing presets.

Getting Familiar with Color

We could spend a whole lot of time and many pages in this book delving into the complex world of color theory and definitions. You wouldn't likely read it, and we're not so inclined to reduce this book from a real page-turner to something that's likely to sedate you. Rather, in the following sections, we offer some fundamental principles to make your work in Elements easier when editing color images.

Introducing color channels

Your first level of understanding color is to understand what RGB is and how it comes about. *RGB* stands for *Red, Green, and Blue.* These are the primary colors in the computer world. Forget about what you know about primary colors in an analog world; computers see primary colors as RGB.

RGB color is divided into *color channels*. Although you can't see the individual channels in Elements, you still need to understand just a little about color channels.

When you see a color pixel (a tiny square dot), the color is represented as different levels of gray in each channel. This may sound confusing at first, but stay with us for just a minute. When you have a color channel, like the red channel, and you let all light pass through the channel, you end up with a bright red. If you screen that light a little with a gray filter, you let less light pass through, thereby diluting the red color. This is how channels work. Individually, they all use different levels of gray that permit up to 256 levels of light to pass through them. When you change the intensity of light in the different channels, you ultimately change the color.

Each channel can have up to 256 levels of gray that mask out light. The total number of possibilities for creating color in an RGB model is achieved by multiplying the values for each channel together (256 x 256 x 256). The result is more than 16.7 million; that's the total number of colors a computer monitor can display in RGB color.

This is all well and good as far as theory goes, but what does that mean in practicality? Actually, you see some of this information in tools and dialog boxes you work with in Elements. As an experiment, open a file in Elements and choose Enhance➪Adjust Lighting➪Levels; the dialog box shown in Figure 2-4 opens.

Notice that the Channel drop-down menu shows you Red, Green, and Blue as individual channels as well as a composite RGB selection. Furthermore, the Output Levels show you values ranging from 0 on the left to 255 on the right. Considering that 0 is a number, you have a total of 256 different levels of gray.

Figure 2-4: Select Enhance➪Adjust Lighting➪ Levels to open the Levels dialog box.

What's important is that you know that your work in color is related to RGB images that comprise three different channels. There are 256 levels of gray that can let through or hold back light and change brightness values and color. See Chapters 9 and 10 for more on using tools like Levels to adjust color in this way.

Understanding bit depth

Another important item to understand about channels is *bit depth*. A bit holds one of two values; one value is for black, the other for white. When you have

256 levels of gray, you're working with an 8-bit-per-channel image — 8 bits with 2 possible values each = 2^8 = 256 possible levels of gray. Multiply 8 bits per channel times your 3 channels and you get 24 bits, which is the common bit depth of images you print on your desktop printer.

Now, take a look at the Image⇨ Mode menu. You should see a menu selection that says 8 Bits/Channel, as shown in Figure 2-5. When you open an image in Elements, if this menu command is grayed out, you are working with a 24-bit image, or an image of 8-bits per channel.

But what does it mean when you can select the 8 Bit/Channel menu command? You can be certain that your image is not an 8-bit-per-channel image. This command may be selectable because some digital cameras and most low-end consumer-grade scanners can capture images at

Figure 2-5: When 8 Bits/Channel is selectable, you know your image bit depth is higher than 8 Bits/Channel.

higher bit depths. You can scan a photo on a scanner at 16 bits per channel. When you do, you end up with 4,096 levels of gray. When you take a picture with a quality digital camera, you can capture 32-bit-per-channel images, and you end up with a file containing 32,768 levels of gray. That's a lot!

Now here's the catch. All files need to be reduced to 8 bits per channel before you print them because that's all the information any printer uses. In addition, many tools, commands, and palette options work only with 8-bit-per-channel images. So you ask, "What's the benefit of acquiring images at higher bit depths than I can print them?"

If you attempt to adjust brightness and contrast or other image enhancements in an 8-bit-per-channel image, you often destroy some data. You can get some noticeable image degradation if moving adjustment sliders too far while working with 8-bit-per-channel images. When you edit your 16-bit and 32-bit images, you don't destroy data. You simply inform Elements which 256 of the total available levels of gray you want to use. The end result is an image with more continuous gray tones than you can achieve in 8-bit-per-channel images. (For more information on image bit-depth, see Chapter 3.)

Getting Color Right

In Elements, when it comes to color, the challenge isn't understanding color theory or definitions, but rather matching the RGB color you see on your computer monitor as closely as possible to your output. Output can be a printout from a color printer or a screen view on a Web page.

We say match "as closely as possible" because you can never expect to achieve a perfect match. There are far too many printer and monitor variables to deal with. The best you can hope for is a very close match.

In order to match color between your monitor and your output, you need to first calibrate your monitor and then choose a color profile. In the following sections, you find all the details.

Calibrating your monitor

Adobe Gamma is a Control Panel device installed with Photoshop Elements. You use Adobe Gamma to adjust your monitor brightness and correct for any colorcasts or tints. The idea behind using Adobe Gamma is that it makes your monitor reflect to a close approximation of the overall brightness of your output. If your monitor displays a dark image and your printer prints a lighter image, something is out of sync. To correct the problem, start with the Adobe Gamma Control Panel device.

Here's what you do to set up your monitor using Adobe Gamma:

1. **Choose Start⇨Settings⇨Control Panel.**

   The Control Panel folder opens on your desktop.

2. **Double-click the Adobe Gamma item in the folder.**

   The Adobe Gamma Control Panel opens.

3. **Click Wizard at the bottom of the control panel to open the Adobe Gamma Wizard.**

4. **Type a name in the Description text box to name your calibration. Click Next to advance to the next pane.**

   Two squares appear, which help you adjust brightness and contrast. The large outer square should appear rich black, and a smaller square inside the larger one should appear charcoal black.

5. **Squint your eyes and adjust the hardware controls on your monitor for brightness and contrast until you can see no difference in the colors. Click Next to advance to the next pane.**

6. **When the Select Phosphors pane appears, leave this pane alone unless you know that the default phosphors are incorrect.**

   In almost all cases, you see the correct selection in the drop-down menu.

7. **Click Next to show the Gamma settings.**

   The Gamma settings determine how your monitor defines how bright image midtones appear.

8. **Deselect the View Single Gamma Only check box.**

   You see three individual grid boxes representing the red, green, and blue colors in your monitor. A slider appears below each grid.

9. **Squint your eyes and move a slider until the outer horizontal lines look like the solid inner square. Move the sliders back and forth for each grid box.**

10. **Click Next to advance to the next pane in the wizard: Set the Hardware White Point.**

    Adjusting for proper hardware white point takes care of any colorcast on your monitor.

11. **Click the Measure button and click OK in the next dialog box until you see three squares. Then do one of the following, depending on what you see:**

    The center square represents the current setting. On the left and right, you see slight tonal differences in the color of the squares.

    - **If the center square looks like a neutral gray with no colorcast,** press Esc and click Next.

    - **If one of the other squares on the left or right side of the center square appears more neutral,** click it so that it moves to the center. Keep clicking additional squares until you feel you have a neutral gray with no colorcast. Press Enter when finished and click Next.

12. **Leave the Adjust White Point setting at the default option (Same as Hardware) and click Next.**

    The final pane provides you an option to compare your new settings with the settings in place before you opened the Adobe Gamma Control Panel device.

13. **Click the Before and After radio buttons back and forth several times to see the original default compared to the new setting reflected on your monitor. If everything looks OK, click Finish.**

14. **In the Save As dialog box that appears, click Save to save your monitor profile.**

    The target folder is the Color folder; the path is `Windows\system32\spool\drivers\color`. Be certain to save your profile to this folder. By default, Elements looks to this folder when you want to load a color profile. After you click Save, the name you provided in Step 4 appears as the profile name.

There's much more to getting color right than setting up your monitor. For more information on handling color, read through Chapter 3.

Choosing a color profile

When you work in Elements and print files to color printers, your colors are much truer when using color profiles. Color profiles contain information about the color reproduction capabilities of a device, such as a scanner, a digital camera, a monitor, or a printer. Using color profiles ensures that you get better color matches between these devices. So, for example, if you see green trees in a photo on your monitor, with the help of a color profile for your printer, the same green color values are output to the printer. Without the help of color profiles, you can experience tremendous shifts in color between devices.

You access your color profile settings by choosing Edit⇨Color Settings. The color settings dialog box opens, as shown in Figure 2-6.

The options you have in the Color Settings dialog box include the following:

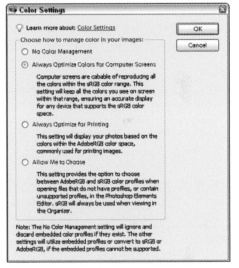

Figure 2-6: The Color Settings dialog box.

- ✔ **No Color Management:** If you find that the files you print to your desktop printer are true to the color you see on your monitor when No Color Management is selected, leave it alone and consider yourself lucky. If it ain't broke, don't fix it.

- ✔ **Always Optimize Colors for Computer Screens:** Check this radio button (new in Elements 4.0) when you work with images you intend to e-mail, to host on Web sites, or to use with one of the Organize options for producing creations like videodiscs and slideshows that are intended for screen viewing. The profile used for this setting is sRGB, which is a default color profile developed by Microsoft that assumes most monitors are likely to see the same color.

- ✔ **Always Optimize for Printing:** Choose this option (also new) when you intend to print your pictures to desktop color printers. The profile used is AdobeRGB, developed by Adobe Systems. Adobe developed this profile to optimize output to all kinds of printing devices.

- ✔ **Allow Me to Choose:** This is yet another new option. When you choose it, Elements prompts you for a profile assignment when you open images containing no profile. This setting is handy if you work back and forth between screen and print images.

When you select your color settings and use a profile, or when you are prompted to use a profile, you can embed the profile in the images you save. Embedding a profile occurs simply when you select a check box in the Save or Save As dialog box, as we explain in more detail in Chapters 4 and 15. This means that anyone else opening your image can honor the profile you used when you last edited your file.

Only some file formats support profile embedding. When you choose File➪Save or File➪Save As, look at the Color area in the dialog box. If you can check the box for *ICC Profile: AdobeRGB (1998),* then the format selected in the Format drop-down menu supports profile embedding. If the check box is grayed out, you need to select a different profile from the Format drop-down menu.

Working with Resolutions, Color Modes, and File Formats

*W*hen you open a picture in Photoshop Elements, you are looking at a huge mass of pixels. These *pixels* are tiny colored squares, and the number of pixels in a picture determines the picture's *resolution*. This relationship between pixels and resolution is important for you to understand in all your Elements work. It relates to creating selections (as we explain in Chapter 7), printing files (Chapter 14), and sharing files (Chapter 16).

Color modes are also represented as collections of pixels. Color modes are also important when using tools and when printing and sharing files.

This chapter explains some essential points about resolution, color modes, and the file formats you use to save your Elements images. We talk about changing resolution by resizing images, converting color modes, and saving the results in different file formats.

The Ubiquitous Pixels

Files you open in Elements comprise thousands or maybe millions of tiny square pixels. Each pixel has one and only one color value. The arrangement of the pixels of different shades and colors creates an illusion to your eyes when viewing an image on screen. For example, you may have black and white pixels arranged in an order that creates the impression that you're looking at something gray — not at tiny black and white squares.

Just about everything you do in Elements has to do with changing pixels. You surround them with selection tools to select what appear to be objects in your image, you make pixels darker or lighter to change contrast and brightness, you change shades and tints of pixels for color correction, and you perform a host of other editing possibilities.

We also have another term to throw at you when talking about pixels and Elements files. Your pictures are called *raster images.* When you have pixels, you have raster data. If you open a file in Elements that was not made up of pixels, Elements *rasterizes* the data. In other words, Elements converts other data to pixels if the document was not originally composed of pixels.

In addition to raster data, there's also vector data, which we talk more about in Chapter 13. But for this chapter, you just need to focus on raster data.

In order to use most of the tools and commands in Elements, you must be working on a raster image file. If your data is not rasterized, many tools and commands are unusable.

Understanding resolution

The number of pixels in a file determines your image resolution. If you have 72 pixels across a one-inch horizontal line, your image is 72 pixels per inch (ppi). If you have 300 pixels in one inch, your image resolution is 300 ppi.

Image resolution is critical to properly outputting files:

- ✔ **When you print images:** If the resolution is too low, the image prints poorly. If the image resolution is too high, you waste time processing all the data that needs to be sent to your printer.

- ✔ **When you show images on screen:** Just as images have resolution inherent in the files, your computer monitor displays everything you see on it in a fixed resolution. Computer monitors display images at 72 ppi. That's all you get. What's important to know is that your best viewing of your photos on your computer monitor is always when viewing images at a 72 ppi image size.

  As an example, take a look at Figure 3-1. You see an image reduced to 50% and then at different zoom sizes. As the sizes change, the resolution display on your monitor changes. At a 100% size, you see the image exactly as it will print. The 100% size represents the image displayed on your monitor at 72 ppi, regardless of the resolution of the file.

50% 100% 200%

400% 800%

Figure 3-1: The same image is viewed at different zoom levels.

This relationship between the image resolution and viewing at different zoom levels is an important concept to grasp. If you grab an image off the Web and zoom in on it, you may see a view like the 800% view in Figure 3-1. If you acquire a digital camera image, you may need to zoom out to a 16% view to fit the entire image in the Image window.

The reason these displays vary so much is all due to image resolution. That Web page image you grabbed off the Web might be a 2-inch-square image at 72 ppi, while that digital camera image might be a 10-x-15-inch image at 240 ppi. To fill the entire window with the Web image, you need to zoom in on the file. As you zoom in, the resolution is lowered. The more you zoom, the lower the resolution on your monitor.

As you zoom in or out of an image, you change the resolution as it appears on your monitor. No resolution changes are made to the file. The image resolution remains the same until you use one of Elements' tools to reduce or add to image resolution.

Understanding image dimensions

Image dimensions involve the physical size of your file. If the size is 4 x 5 inches, the file can be any number of different resolution values. After the file is opened in Elements, you can change the dimensions of an image, the resolution, or both.

When you change only the dimensions of an image (not the number of pixels it contains), there's an inverse relationship between the physical size of your image and the resolution. As image size is increased, resolution decreases. Conversely, as you raise resolution, you lower image size.

The Art of Resampling

In some cases, images are too large, and you need to reduce their resolution and physical size. In other cases, you may need higher resolution to output your images at larger sizes. This method of sizing — changing both the size as well as the number of pixels — is referred to as *resampling* an image.

Specifically, reducing resolution is called *downsampling*, and raising resolution is known as *upsampling*.

Use caution when you resample images; when you resample, you toss away pixels or manufacture new pixels. I discuss the details later in this section.

Changing image size and resolution

You can change an image's size and resolution in a couple of different ways. One method is cropping images. You can use the Crop tool with or without resampling images. For more information on using the Crop tool, see Chapter 9. Another method is to use the Image Size dialog box, which you'll find yourself using in many of your editing sessions in Elements.

To resize an image with the Image Size dialog box, follow these steps:

1. **Choose Image⇨Resize⇨ Image Size.**

   Alternatively, you can use the keyboard shortcut Ctrl+Alt+I. The Image Size dialog box opens, as shown in Figure 3-2.

Image Size

Pixel Dimensions: 46.8M

Width: 3504   pixels

Height: 2336   pixels

Document Size:

Width: 14.6   inches

Height: 9.733   inches

Resolution: 240   pixels/inch

Scale Styles

Constrain Proportions

Resample Image: Bicubic

OK   Cancel   Help

Figure 3-2: Choose Image⇨Resize⇨Image Size to open the Image Size dialog box.

The Pixel Dimensions area in the Image Size dialog box shows the file size (such as 46.8M). This number is the amount of space the image takes up on your hard drive. The width and height values are fixed unless you click the Resample Image check box at the bottom of the dialog box.

2. **In the Document Size area, you can redefine dimensions and resolution. The options include:**

    - **Width.** Type a value in the text box to resize the image's width and tab out of the field to implement the change. From the drop-down menu to the right of the text box, you can choose a unit of measure: percent, inches, centimeters, millimeters, points, picas, or columns.

    - **Height.** The Height options are the same as the Width options with the exception of no column setting. If you keep the sizing proportional, you typically edit either the Width or Height text box, but not both. As you size either Width or Height, the resolution sizes inversely.

    - **Resolution.** Edit the text box to change resolution and press the tab key to change the value. As resolution is edited, the Width and Height are changed inversely.

3. **If you're okay with resampling your image to get the desired size, select the Resample Image check box.**

    With this check box selected, you can change dimensions and pixels at the same time, which results in reducing or increasing the number of pixels. When the box is unchecked, the values for dimensions are linked together. Changing one value automatically changes the other values.

    Before you resample your image, however, be sure to check out the section, "Understanding the results of resampling," later in this chapter.

4. **If you select the Resample Image check box, you can choose a resampling method as well as other resample options.**

    In the drop-down list, you find choices for choosing a resampling method. See Table 3-1 for details. The two check boxes above the Resample Image check box become active when you check the Resample Image box. Here's what they do:

    - **Scale Styles.** Elements has a Styles palette from which you add a variety of different style effects to images (see Chapter 11 for details). When you apply a style, like a frame border, the border appears at a defined width. When you check the box for Scale Styles and then resize the image, the Styles effect is also resized. Leaving the check box unchecked keeps the style at the same size while the image is resized.

    - **Constrain Proportions.** By default, the box is checked, and you want to keep it that way unless you want to intentionally distort an image.

5. **When you're done selecting your options, click OK to resize your image.**

Table 3-1	Resampling Methods	
Method	*What It Does*	*Best Uses*
Nearest Neighbor	The method is faster and the results produce a smaller file size.	This method is best used when you have large areas of the same color.
Bilinear	This method produces a medium-quality image.	You might use this option with grayscale images and line art.
Bicubic	This method is the default and provides a good-quality image.	Unless you find better results in using any of the other methods, leave the default at Bicubic and be done with it.
Bicubic Smoother	This method improves on the Bicubic method, but you'll notice a little softening of edges.	If sharpness is not critical, and you find Bicubic not quite doing the job, try this method.
Bicubic Sharper	This method produces good-quality images and sharpens the results.	Downsampling high-resolution images that need to be output to screen resolutions and Web pages.

Understanding the results of resampling

As a general rule, reducing resolution is okay, but increasing resolution isn't. If you need a higher-resolution image and you can go back to the original source, like rescanning the image or reshooting a picture, then always favor creating a new file using the resolution you want over resampling in Elements. In many cases, images can be severely degraded when upsampling an image.

If you take a picture with a digital camera and you want to add the picture to a Web page, the image needs to be sampled at 72 ppi. In most cases, you'll visit the Image Size dialog box, check the box for Resample Image, add a width or height value, and type **72** in the Resolution text box. What you end up with is an image that looks great on your Web page. In Figure 3-3 you can see an image that was downsampled in Elements from over 14 inches horizontal width.

Figure 3-3: Downsampling images most often produces satisfactory results.

If you start out with an image that was originally sampled for a Web page and you want to print a large poster, you can forget about using Elements or any other image editor. Upsampling low-resolution images often turns them to mush, as you can see in Figure 3-4.

Can upsampling be used for any purpose, you may ask? In some cases, yes, you can upsample with some satisfactory results. You can experience better results with higher resolutions of 300 ppi and more if the resample size is not extraordinary. If all else fails, try applying a filter to a grainy, upsampled image to mask the problem. Chapter 11 has the details.

Figure 3-4: Upsampling low-resolution images often produces severely degraded results.

Choosing a Resolution for Print or On-Screen

The importance of resolution in your Elements work is paramount to printing files. Good ol' 72 ppi images can be forgiving, and you can get many of your large files scrunched down to 72 ppi for Web sites and slide shows. With output to printing devices, it's another matter. There are many different printing output devices, and their resolution requirements vary.

For your own desktop printer, plan to print a variety of test images at different resolutions. You can quickly determine the best file attributes by running tests. When you send files to service centers, ask the technicians what file attributes work best with their equipment.

For a starting point, look over the recommended resolutions for various output devices in Table 3-2.

Table 3-2	Resolutions and Printing	
Output Device	*Optimum Resolution*	*Acceptable Resolution*
Desktop color inkjets	300 ppi	180 ppi
Large-format inkjets	150 ppi	120 ppi
Professional photo lab printers	300 ppi	200 ppi
Desktop laser printers (black and white)	170 ppi	100 ppi
Magazine quality — offset press	300 ppi	225 ppi
Screen images (Web, slide shows, video)	72 ppi	72 ppi

Go Ahead . . . Make My Mode!

Regardless of what output you prepare your files for, you need to consider color mode and file format. In Chapter 2, we talk about RGB color mode. This color mode is what you use to prepare color files for print on your desktop color printer or when preparing files for photo service centers.

But you can also use color modes other than RGB. If you start with an RGB color image and you want to convert to a different color mode, you have menu options for converting color. Photoshop Elements uses an algorithm (a mathematical formula) to convert pixels from one mode to another. In some cases, the conversion via a menu command produces good results, and in other cases, you can use some different options for converting modes.

In the following sections, we introduce the modes that are available in Elements and explain how to convert from RGB to the mode of your choice: bitmap, grayscale, or indexed color.

Another mode you may have heard of is CMYK. Although the CMYK mode is not available in Photoshop Elements, you should be aware of what it is and the purposes of CMYK images. CMYK is commonly referred to as *process color* and contains percentages of Cyan, Magenta, Yellow, and Black colors. This mode is used for commercial printing. If you design a magazine cover in Elements and send the file off to a print shop, the file is ultimately converted to CMYK.

Converting to bitmap mode

The bitmap mode is most commonly used when printing line art, such as black-and-white logos, illustrations, or black-and-white effects you create from your RGB images. Also, you can scan your analog signature as a bitmap image and import it into other programs, such as the Microsoft Office programs. For the creative among us, you can combine bitmap images with RGB color to produce many interesting effects.

Elements' bitmap mode is not the same as the Windows .bmp file format. In Elements, bitmap mode is a color mode. A .bmp file can be an RGB color mode image, a grayscale color mode image, or a bitmap color mode image.

One important thing to keep in mind is that, when you combine images into single documents, as we explain in Chapter 8, you need to convert bitmap files to grayscale or color if you want to merge the images together with an RGB image. If you convert to grayscale, Elements takes care of converting grayscale to RGB mode.

As an example of an effect resulting from combining grayscale and color images, look over Figure 3-5. The original RGB image was converted to a bitmap and then saved as a different file. The bitmap was converted to grayscale and dropped on top of the RGB image. After adjusting the opacity, the result is a grainy effect with desaturated color.

You can acquire bitmap (.bmp) mode images directly in Elements when you scan images that are black and white. Illustrated art, logos, your signature, a copy of a fax, and so on might be the kind of files you scan directly in bitmap mode. Additionally, you can convert your images to bitmap mode.

Converting RGB color to bitmap is a two-step process. You need to first convert to grayscale, and then from grayscale, you convert to bitmap. If you select the bitmap menu command while in RGB color, Elements prompts you to convert to grayscale first.

Figure 3-5: You can create some interesting effects by combining the same image from a bitmap file and an RGB file.

To convert RGB mode to bitmap, do the following:

1. **Open an image that you want to convert to bitmap in either Standard Edit or Quick Fix mode.**

2. **Choose Image⇨Mode⇨Bitmap.**

    If you start in RGB mode, Elements prompts you to convert to grayscale.

3. **Click OK, and the Bitmap dialog box opens.**

    The Bitmap dialog box provides options for selecting the output resolution and a conversion method.

4. **Select a Resolution.**

    By default, the Output dialog box shown in Figure 3-6 displays the current resolution. You can edit the text box and type a new resolution value or accept the default.

Figure 3-6: Type a resolution for your output and select the conversion method from the Use drop-down menu.

5. **From the Method drop-down menu, you can choose from the following settings:**

   - **50% Threshold**
   - **Pattern Dither**
   - **Diffusion Dither**

   Look over Figure 3-7, and you can see a comparison of the different methods used in converting RGB images to bitmaps.

6. **Click OK to convert your image to Bitmap mode.**

RGB Image   50% Threshold

Pattern Dither   Diffusion Dither

Figure 3-7: An original RGB image converted to bitmap using 50% Threshold, Pattern Dither, and Diffusion Dither.

Converting to grayscale mode

Grayscale images have black and white pixels and any one of 256 levels of gray. By converting an RGB image to grayscale, you can make it look like a black-and-white photo.

You can convert an image to grayscale in one of two ways, but remember that one of these methods isn't as good as the other. We recommend that you *avoid* converting to grayscale by choosing Image⇨Mode⇨Grayscale. When Elements performs this conversion, it removes all the color from the pixels, so you loose some precious data during the conversion and can't regain the color after conversion. If you convert an image to grayscale, save the file, and delete the original from your hard drive or memory card, the color image is lost forever. You could save a secondary file, but this can add a little confusion and require some more space on your hard drive.

As an alternative to using the menu command for converting images to grayscale, try the following method:

1. **Open an RGB image in Elements.**

2. **Duplicate a layer.**

   The default Palette Bin contains the Layers palette. In this palette, you find a pop-up menu when you click More in the top-right corner. From the menu commands, select Duplicate Layer. (For more information on working with layers, see Chapter 8.)

3. **Choose Enhance⇨Adjust Color⇨Adjust Hue/Saturation (or press Ctrl+U) to open the Hue/Saturation dialog box.**

4. **Drag the Saturation slider to the far left, as shown in Figure 3-8, to desaturate the image.**

   All color disappears, but the brightness values of all the pixels remain unaffected. (For more information on using the Hue/Saturation dialog box and the other Adjust Color commands, see Chapter 10.)

Figure 3-8: Open the Hue/Saturation dialog box and move the Saturation slider to the far left to eliminate color.

5. **Turn off the color layer by clicking the eye icon.**

In the Layers palette, you see two layers, as shown in Figure 3-9. You don't need to turn the color layer off to print the file in grayscale, but turning it off can help you remember which color layer you used the last time you printed or exported the file.

Following the preceding steps provides you a file that contains both RGB and grayscale. If you want to print the color layer, you can turn off the grayscale layer. If you need to exchange files with graphic designers, you can send the layered file, and the design professional can use both the color image and the grayscale image.

Figure 3-9: The Layers palette shows the grayscale and color layer. You can turn layers on or off by clicking the eye icon.

The other advantage of converting RGB color to grayscale by using the Hue/Saturation dialog box is that you don't affect any changes in the brightness values of the pixels. Moving the Saturation slider to desaturate the image affects only the color. The luminance and lightness values remain the same.

In Figure 3-10, you can see an RGB image as it appears in an unedited RGB mode. In Figure 3-11, you can see the results of the RGB image converted to grayscale using the Image➪Mode➪Grayscale menu command, and the same image converted to grayscale using the Hue/Saturation dialog box. The image converted with the Hue/Saturation dialog box contains a little more detail in the highlights (light areas of the image) and in the shadow areas.

Figure 3-10: An RGB image used to convert to grayscale.

Grayscale menu command

Hue/Saturation dialog box

Figure 3-11: The top image was converted to grayscale with a menu command, and the bottom image was converted to grayscale using the Hue/Saturation dialog box.

Converting to indexed color mode

Indexed color is a mode you use occasionally with Web graphics. When saving indexed color images, you can, at times, create smaller file sizes than RGB that are ideal for using in Web site designs.

RGB images in 24-bit color (8-bits/channel) are capable of rendering colors from a palette of 16.7 million colors, as we explain in Chapter 2. An indexed color image is an 8-bit image with only a single channel. The total number of colors you get with indexed can be no more than 256. When you convert RGB images to indexed color, you can choose to dither the color, which displays the image with a dither effect much like we see with bitmapped images. This dithering effect makes the file appear as though it has more than 256 colors, and the transition between colors appears smoother than if no dithering were applied.

Upon occasion, index color images have an advantage over RGB images when hosting the images on Web servers: The fewer colors in a file, the smaller the file size. When you prepare images for Web hosting, you can choose to use indexed color or RGB color. Whether you choose one over the other really depends on how well the image appears on your monitor. If you have some photos that you want to show on Web pages, you're best off using RGB images and saving in a format appropriate for Web hosting, as we explain a little later in this chapter.

If you have files composed of artwork such as logos, illustrations, and drawings, you may find that the appearance of index colors is no different than viewing the same images as RGB. If that's the case, you can keep the index color image and use it for your Web pages.

To convert RGB images to indexed color, choose Image⇨Mode⇨Indexed Color; the Indexed Color dialog box opens. A number of different options are available to you, and, fortunately, you can preview the results as you make choices. Get in, poke around, and you can see the options applied in the image window.

Saving Files with Purpose

Photoshop Elements files are saved in a variety of different formats. Some of the format types require you to convert a color mode before the format can be used. Therefore, you have a relationship between formats and saving files. Additionally, bit depths in images also relate to the kinds of file formats you can use when saving files.

Before you go too far in Elements, you'll want to become familiar with file formats and the conversions that need to be made to save in one format or another. If you do nothing to an image in terms of converting modes or changing bit depth, you can save a file after editing in the same format that the file was opened. In many circumstances, you'll want to open an image and prepare it for some form of output, which requires more thought about the kind of file format you use when saving the file.

Using the Save/Save As dialog box

In most any program, the Save and Save As dialog boxes are familiar places where you make some choices about the file to be saved. Using Save As, you can save a duplicate copy of your image or a modified copy while retaining the original file.

To use the Save or Save As dialog box, choose File⇨Save, for files to be saved the first time, or File⇨Save As for any file, and a dialog box opens.

The standard navigational tools you find in any Save dialog box appear in the Elements Save/Save As dialog box. Some standard options you find in the Elements Save or Save As dialog box include:

- **File name:** This item is common to all Save dialog boxes. Type a name for your file in the text box.

- **Format:** From the drop-down menu, you select file formats. We explain the formats supported by Elements later in this chapter.

A few options make the Photoshop Elements Save/Save As dialog box different from other Save dialog boxes you may be accustomed to using. The Save Options area in the Save As dialog box provides the following choices:

- **Include in the Organizer:** If you want the file added to the Organizer, check this box. (For more information about using the Organizer, see Chapter 6.)

- **Save in Version Set with Original:** You can edit images and save a version of your image, but only in Quick Fix mode. When you save the file from the Quick Fix mode, this check box is active. Check the box and a version of the original is saved and appears in the Organizer.

- **Color:** Check the box for ICC (International Color Consortium) Profile. Depending on which profile you are using, the option appears for sRGB or Adobe RGB (1998). When the check box is checked, the profile is embedded in the image. See Chapter 2 for more information on profiles.

- **Thumbnail:** This option relates to your Saving Files preferences, which we discuss in Chapter 2. If you save a file with a thumbnail, you can see a mini representation of your image when viewing in folders or on the desktop. If you select Ask When Saving in the Saving Files preferences, the check box can be checked or disabled. If choosing an option for Never Save or Always Save in the Preferences dialog box, this box is checked or unchecked for you and is grayed out. You need to return to the Preferences dialog box in order to change the option.

- **Use Lower Case Extension:** File extensions give you a clue as to what file format was used when a file was saved. Elements automatically adds the extension to the filename for you. Your choices are to use uppercase or lowercase letters for the extension name. Check the box for Use Lower Case Extension for lowercase, or uncheck the box if you want to use uppercase characters in the filename.

Saving files for the Web

You save files for Web hosting in a different dialog box than when saving files for other output. Choose File➪Save for Web, and the Save for Web dialog box opens. We explain all you need to know about how to use the Save for Web dialog box in Chapter 15. If you're in a hurry to understand how Web images are saved, jump over to Chapter 15.

Understanding file formats

When you save files from Elements, you need to pick a file format in the Format drop-down menu found in both the Save and Save As dialog boxes.

As you choose from the different format options, keep the following in mind:

✏ File formats are especially important when you exchange files with other users. Each format has a purpose, and other programs can accept or reject files depending on the format you choose.

✏ Whether you can select one format or another when you save a file is dependent on the color mode, the bit depth, and whether layers are present. If a format is not present in the Format drop-down menu when you attempt to save a file, you need to return to one of the edit modes and perform some kind of edit, such as changing a color mode or flattening layers, in order to save the file in your chosen format.

For a glimpse at all the file formats available to you, open a standard RGB color image in Standard Edit mode, choose File➪Save As, and click the down arrow to open the Format drop-down menu. As you can see in Figure 3-12, you have many options for choosing a format.

We explain most file formats supported by Elements and the purpose for each format in the following sections.

JPEG (*.JPG;*.JPEG;*.JPE)
Photoshop (*.PSD;*.PDD)
BMP (*.BMP;*.RLE;*.DIB)
CompuServe GIF (*.GIF)
Photoshop EPS (*.EPS)
JPEG (*.JPG;*.JPEG;*.JPE)
JPEG 2000 (*.JPF;*.JPX;*.JP2;*.J2C;*.J2K;*.JPC)
PCX (*.PCX)
Photoshop PDF (*.PDF;*.PDP)
Photoshop Raw (*.RAW)
PICT File (*.PCT;*.PICT)
Pixar (*.PXR)
PNG (*.PNG)
Scitex CT (*.SCT)
Targa (*.TGA;*.VDA;*.ICB;*.VST)
TIFF (*.TIF;*.TIFF)

Figure 3-12: Open the Format drop-down menu in either the Save or Save As dialog box, and the formats supported by Elements appear.

Photoshop (*.PSD, *.PDD)

This format is the native file format for both Photoshop and Photoshop Elements. The format supports saving all color modes and bit depths, and you can preserve layers. Use this format when you want to save in a native format or when exchanging files with Photoshop users. Also use it when saving files that you need to return to for more editing. When you save layers, any text you add to layers is editable when you return to the file. (See Chapter 13 for more information on adding text to an image.)

BMP (*.BMP, *.RLE, *.DIB)

The term *bitmap* can be a little confusing. You have both a format type that is bitmap and a color mode that is also bitmap. Don't confuse the two. The bitmap *format* supports saving in all color modes and in all bit depths. The bitmap *color mode,* which we cover earlier in this chapter, is 1-bit black and white only.

Use the bitmap format when you want to add images to system resources, such as wallpaper for your desktop. Bitmap is also used with many different application programs. If you can't import images in other program documents, try to save as BMP.

CompuServe GIF (*.GIF)

Barb was a college coed and Ted had a moustache and wore a green leisure suit when CompuServe was the host for our e-mail accounts. We exchanged files and mail on 300-baud modems. Later, in 1987, CompuServe developed GIF (Graphics Interchange Format) to exchange files between mainframe computers and the ever-growing number of users working on Osbornes, Kaypros, Apples, and Radio Shack TRS 80s.

Today, GIF is a popular format for hosting Web graphics. GIF images can be indexed color or animated images and support the smallest file sizes. Use this format when you need fewer than 256 colors and when you want to create animation in your images. To find out how to create animated GIFs, see Bonus Chapter 1 on this book's Web site. (The Introduction has details about the Web site.)

Photoshop EPS (*.EPS)

Photoshop EPS (Encapsulated PostScript) files are sometimes used by graphic artists when designing jobs for commercial printing. The more popular format for creative professionals is TIFF, but Photoshop EPS has some advantages not found in other formats.

Depending on the color mode of your image, you have different options when using the Photoshop EPS file format. Select the format in the Save or Save As dialog box and click Save. If you're working on a bitmap image (1-bit), the EPS Options dialog box shown in Figure 3-13 opens.

Figure 3-13: When working on 1-bit bitmap images, the EPS options dialog box offers an option to save transparency where white appears in the document.

Notice the check box for Transparent Whites. You might have a circular logo for which you want the area around the circle to appear transparent. If you import the graphic in another program, you can see the black in the image while all the white area is transparent and shows any background through what was white in the original bitmap image. If you save a file in a higher bit depth, the EPS Options dialog box doesn't provide an option for making whites transparent.

JPEG (*.JPG, *.JPEG, *.JPE)

JPEG (Joint Photographic Experts Group) is perhaps the most common file format in use today. JPEG files are used with e-mail attachments, can be viewed in JPEG viewers and directly in Web browsers, and are used by many photo labs for printing files. Just about every program capable of importing images supports the JPEG format. Creative professionals wouldn't dream of using JPEG format in design layouts, but everyone else uses the format for all kinds of documents.

You need to exercise some caution when using the JPEG format. JPEG files are compressed to reduce file size. You can take an image of several megabytes and scrunch it down to a few hundred kilobytes. When you save a file with JPEG compression, you experience data loss. You may not see this on your monitor or have it appear noticeably on photo prints if you're using low compression while preserving higher quality. However, when you save with maximum compression, more pixels are tossed away, and you definitely will notice image degradation.

As you save, open, and resave images in JPEG format, each new save degrades an image more. If you need to submit JPEG images to photo labs for printing your pictures, keep saving in Photoshop PSD file format until you're ready to save the final image. Save as JPEG when you want to save the final file for printing and use a low compression with high quality.

When you select JPEG for the format and click Save, the JPEG Options dialog box shown in Figure 3-14 opens. You choose the amount of compression by typing a value in the Quality text box or by moving the slider below the Quality text box. The acceptable ranges are from 0 to 12, where 0 is the lowest quality and results in the highest compression, and 12 is the highest quality that results in the lowest amount of compression.

Notice that you also have choices in the Format area of the JPEG Options dialog box. The Progressive item creates a progressive JPEG file commonly used with Web browsers. This file type shows progressive quality as the file downloads from a Web site.

Figure 3-14: When saving in JPEG format, you make a choice for the amount of compression to apply to the saved image.

The image first appears in a low-quality view and shows higher resolution views until the image appears at full resolution when completely downloaded in your browser window.

For a peek at how the different compression levels appear in printed images, take a look at Figure 3-15.

Quality = 12

Quality = 8

Quality = 4

Quality = 0

Figure 3-15: Depending on the amount of compression applied to an image, the print results can show some file degradation.

JPEG 2000 (*.JPF, *.JPX, *.JP2, *. J2K, *.JPC)

JPEG 2000 is a newer JPEG file format. This format offers you the same quality modes as the JPEG format and an option to save the file with compression without tossing away pixels, in which case you get what is called a *lossless compression*. The JPEG 2000 dialog box shows you the results of the options choices you make in terms of the resulting file size right in the dialog box before you save the image.

If you need to save images in JPEG format for your commercial photo lab, check with the technicians and ask if they support JPEG 2000. If so, then save your files in this format with a lossless compression. When files are compressed with lossless compression, you can expect to lose about two-thirds of the original file size. For example, a 6MB file can be reduced to about 2MB when saved as JPEG 2000 in a lossless compression format. Note that if you save files with JPEG 2000 format for the Web, Web browsers need to have a plug-in to see the images.

PCX (*.PCX)

PCX is a native PC format first used with PC Paintbrush. Most programs today support newer file formats, and you're not likely to need to save in PCX format. If you have legacy files from years ago, you can open PCX files in Elements, edit them, and save them in a newer format.

Photoshop PDF (*.PDF, *.PDP)

Adobe PDF (Portable Document Format) was designed to maintain document integrity and exchange files between computers. PDF is one of the most popular formats used today and can be viewed in the free Adobe Reader program available for installation on your Elements CD installer or by downloading from Adobe's Web site.

PDF is all over the place in Elements. When you jump into the Organize mode and create slide presentations, cards, calendars, and so on, you can export your documents as PDF files. When you save in Photoshop PDF format, you can preserve layers and text. Text is recognizable in Adobe Reader (or other Acrobat viewers) and can be searched using Reader's Find and Search tools.

PDF files can be printed, hosted on Web sites, and exchanged with users of Windows, Macintosh, and Linux. All in all, this format is well suited for all the files you create in Elements that contain text, layers, and transparency, and when you want to exchange files with users who don't have Elements or Photoshop.

Photoshop Raw (*.RAW)

This format is used to exchange files between Windows and Mac users and mainframe computers. Unless you prepare files to be viewed on mainframes, don't bother saving in this format.

PICT File (*.PCT, *.PICT)

PICT (Picture) format is Apple's answer to PCX on Windows. This format originated with the 1984 introduction of the Macintosh and the MacPaint program. PICT files are great when creating slides and video files on the Macintosh and when printing your images on film recorders that don't use PostScript. You might use the format when requested by a Mac user or when sending files that need to be printed as slides on a non-PostScript film recorder.

PNG (*.PNG)

PNG (Portable Network Graphics) is another format used with Web pages. PNG supports all the color modes, 24-bit images, and transparency. Some browsers, however, may need a plug-in to see PNG files on Web pages. One disadvantage you have with PNG is that color profiles can't be embedded in the images, as they can with JPEG.

TIFF (*.TIF, *.TIFF)

TIFF (Tagged Image File Format) is the most common format used by graphic designers. TIFF is generally used when importing images in professional layout programs like Adobe InDesign and Adobe PageMaker and when commercial photo labs and print shops use equipment that supports downloading TIFF files directly to their devices. (**Note:** Direct downloads are used in lieu of opening a Print dialog box.)

Inasmuch as creative professionals have used TIFF for so long, a better choice for designers using a program like Adobe InDesign is saving in the native Photoshop PSD file format. This requires a creative professional to save only one file in native format without bothering to save both native and TIFF formats.

TIFF, along with Photoshop PSD and Photoshop PDF, supports saving layered files and works in all color modes. When you save in TIFF format, you can also compress files in several different compression schemes.

When you select TIFF for the format and click Save in the Save or Save As dialog box, the TIFF Options dialog box shown in Figure 3-16 opens.

Figure 3-16: Choose TIFF from the Format drop-down menu and click Save to open the TIFF Options dialog box.

In the Image Compression area, you have choices for:

- **NONE:** Selecting this option results in no compression. You use this option when sending files to creative professionals for creating layouts in programs like Adobe InDesign. None of the compression schemes below is recommended when printing files to commercial printing devices.

- **LZW:** This is a lossless compression scheme and results in much lower file sizes without destroying data.

- **ZIP:** ZIP is also a lossless compression scheme. You can favor ZIP compression over LZW when you have large areas of the same color in an image.

- **JPEG:** JPEG is lossy and results in the smallest file sizes. Use JPEG here the same as when you apply JPEG compression with files saved in the JPEG format.

Wireless BMP (*.WBM, *.WBMP)

This file format is used when saving files that will ultimately appear on cell phones, PDAs, and other small electronic devices. This format supports only 1-bit bitmap mode images.

File formats at a glance

We've been working with Photoshop, which saves in the same formats listed here, since 1989. At no time during the past 16 years have we used all the formats available to you in Photoshop Elements. At most, you'll use maybe three or four of these formats.

You don't need to remember all the formats and what they do. Just pick the ones you use in your workflow, mark Table 3-3 for reference, and refer to it from time to time until you have a complete understanding of how files need to be prepared to save in your desired formats. If you happen to receive a file from another user in one of the formats you don't use, come back to the description in this chapter when you need some detail on what the format is used for.

Table 3-3	File Format Attributes Supported by Photoshop Elements			
Format	**Color Modes Supported**	**Embed Profiles* Supported**	**Bit Depth Supported**	**Layers Supported**
Photoshop PSD, PDD	Bitmap, RGB, Index, Grayscale	Yes	1, 8, 24, H	Yes
BMP	Bitmap, RGB, Index, Grayscale	No	1, 8, 24, H	No
CompuServe GIF**	Bitmap, RGB, Index, Grayscale	No	1, 8, 24	No
Photoshop EPS	Bitmap, RGB, Index, Grayscale	Yes	1, 8, 24	No
JPEG	RGB, Grayscale	Yes	8, 24	No
JPEG 2000	RGB, Grayscale	Yes	8, 24, H	No
PCX	Bitmap, RGB, Index, Grayscale	No	1, 8, 24	No

Format	Color Modes Supported	Embed Profiles* Supported	Bit Depth Supported	Layers Supported
Photoshop PDF	Bitmap, RGB, Index, Grayscale	Yes	1, 8, 24, H	Yes
Photoshop RAW	RGB, Index, Grayscale	No	8, 24, H	No
PICT File	Bitmap, RGB, Index, Grayscale	Yes	1, 8, 24	No
Pixar	RGB, Grayscale	No	8, 24	No
PNG	Bitmap, RGB, Index, Grayscale	No	1, 8, 24, H	No
Scitex CT	RGB, Grayscale	No	8, 24	No
Targa	RGB, Index, Grayscale	No	8, 24	No
TIFF	Bitmap, RGB, Index, Grayscale	Yes	8, 24, H	Yes
Wireless BMP	Bitmap	No	1	No

H in the Bit Depth column represents higher bit modes, such as 16- and 32-bit images, which you might acquire from scanners and digital cameras. See Chapter 2 for more information on higher-bit images.
* Embedding profiles is limited to embedding either sRGB IEC61966-2.1 or AdobeRGB (1998).
** CompuServe GIF doesn't support saving layers, but it does support saving layers as frames. You use the frames when creating an animated GIF file used for Web pages.

Audio and video formats supported in Elements

In addition to the image formats listed in Table 3-3, Elements also supports audio and video files. The support is limited to adding and viewing audio and video files in the Organizer and printing the first frame in a video file. Other kinds of edits made to audio and video files require special software for audio/video editing.

Audio files can be imported in slide shows, as we explain in Chapter 15. The acceptable file formats for audio files include MP3, WAV, and WMA. If you have audio files in another format, you need to convert the file format. For these kinds of conversions, you can search the Internet for a shareware audio conversion program.

Video files can also be imported in slide shows, as we discuss in Chapter 15. Elements supports the WMV video format. Like audio files, if videos are saved in other formats, such as Apple's QuickTime, you need to convert the QT video format to WMV. For video conversion utilities, you can also find shareware programs to do the job. Search the Internet for a video converter. If you're interested in showing your photos on a TV, see Bonus Chapter 3 on this book's Web site for detailed steps.

Part II
Getting Organized

The 5th Wave   By Rich Tennant

Jeez—that's impressive! Let's see that airbrush effect again.

In this part . . .

*T*he first thing you'll want to do after opening the Photoshop Elements program is to access your pictures either from a digital camera, some photos you have on your hard drive, or by scanning photos with your scanner. In this part, we talk about how to access your pictures and get them into Elements for editing. We talk about organizing your pictures by using many impressive organizing features you have in the program as well as searching for photos, labeling them, and creating different versions of the same picture. When it comes to organizing pictures, Elements is one of the best tools you can find to keep your precious photos neatly cataloged and accessible.

Getting Your Images

*Y*ou have so many different sources to work with for getting a picture into Elements, where you can play with it, experiment on it, and edit it. If you have a digital camera, you're in the right place; we walk you through all kinds of different options for getting the shots you took with your camera into Elements.

If you have a digital scanner, you're in the right place, too! We talk about scanning photos as well. If you have some CDs, sources of files on the Internet, some massive collection of images written to a DVD, or even a picture or two you took with your cell phone, you're still in the right place!

In previous chapters, we flirt with opening files. If you followed some of the steps outlined for opening images up to this point, you should have a feel for using the Open tool and Open command. But there's more to acquiring images than just using the Open command, as you find out in this chapter.

This chapter covers all you need to know about getting images from all kinds of sources into Elements. This chapter answers all your questions about how to move around the workspaces to get your files into Elements.

Digital Cameras versus Scanners

If you don't have a digital camera, we encourage you to buy one as soon as you can. Digital cameras and Photoshop Elements were made to work together. If you've spent any time scanning images on a digital scanner, you'll appreciate the speed a camera offers you compared to a scanner when it comes time to get your images into Elements.

"But I can do more with my scanner than with a digital camera," you say? "Not really," we say. Just for starters, here are some of the benefits you have with digital cameras:

- **Faster access to files.** Copying images from a digital camera media card is much faster than scanning images from prints and film.

- **Higher-quality images.** Comparing costs of medium to higher-end scanners, you can shoot much better pictures with a good-quality SLR (Single Lens Reflex) camera with a quality lens than you can scan film or prints with a good-quality consumer-grade scanner.

- **OCR and text recognition.** Unless you have industrial-strength needs for scanning reams of text documents that need to be interpreted by optical character recognition (OCR) software, which converts images to editable text, you'll do just fine with a digital camera. If you scan individual pages on a scanner, shooting pages with a camera is much faster and can produce the same results when pages need to be converted to text.

- **3-D objects.** With digital cameras, you can shoot 3-D objects. Try scanning a pair of shoes on a scanner bed sometime — well, maybe some other three-dimensional object. The experiment isn't worth getting dirt all over your scanner.

- **Reduced costs.** With digital cameras, you eliminate film and film-processing costs. You can order photo prints in superstore outlets, at less than 10 cents apiece, that are printed on the same photo paper you get with prints from film. What's more, you can order prints of only the pictures that you want to keep instead of developing an entire roll to have just that one good photograph.

- **Organizing and archiving.** Digital images can be saved to DVD-ROMs, where you can add information for every image to keep them easily organized, as we explain in Chapter 5. Searching a DVD is much faster than searching through photo books of slides, film, or prints. Archiving digital images is fast and easy, and you don't need to worry about scratches, faded colors, or damaged originals.

- **Control over image processing.** With film, you're stuck with the processing time and temperature the photo lab uses to process your film. With some digital cameras, you can post-process images after shooting the image, as we explain in the last section of this chapter.

- **Video clips.** Many digital cameras provide you a video-shooting mode so you can shoot video.

These are some of the benefits you find with using a digital camera over using a scanner. Scanners do have their place, and some of the benefits you have with a scanner that you don't have with cameras involve

- **Auto document feeders.** You can buy scanners with automatic document feeders, where pages of documents can be scanned unattended. If you need to scan large volumes of pages to recognize text, this operation is much more practical than using a camera.

- **Legacy pictures.** You can shoot photo prints with digital cameras and, depending on the camera, you can produce images equal to or better than using a scanner. Filmstrips and slides, however, require using a scanner to acquire a digital image. You won't find a digital camera helping out here.

Digital SLRs: Should you give point-and-shoot the boot?

Digital cameras generally fall into one of two categories:

- **Point-and-shoot cameras** have fixed lenses, and the bulk of the cameras range in price from less than $200 to over $800. These cameras are suitable for shooting pictures for screen output and photo prints up to about 8 x 10 inches or more. (For details on taking pictures with point-and-shoot models, *Digital Photography For Dummies,* 5th Edition, by Julie Adair King, or *Digital Photography All-in-One Desk Reference For Dummies,* by David D. Busch, can help.)

- **Single lens reflex (SLR) cameras** use interchangeable lenses and have a whole bunch of options for how pictures are taken in terms of lighting, resolution, file formats, and more. These cameras cost from below $1,000 to several thousand dollars. (For an in-depth look at taking pictures with digital SLRs, check out *Digital SLR Cameras & Photography For Dummies,* by David D. Busch.)

As is the case in analog photography, after you get beyond the bells and whistles a camera body offers you, the quality of the lens often determines how good your images turn out. The lowest-priced single lens reflex cameras typically produce much better image quality than the highest-priced point-and-shoot cameras. Why? The quality of the lens on the SLR is much higher compared to the fixed lens on the point-and-shoot camera.

When choosing a digital camera, don't be fooled into thinking that more megapixels makes for a better camera. A good-quality SLR camera of 4 or 5 megapixels can produce images of much greater quality than an 8-megapixel point-and-shoot camera. The difference lies in lens quality and the camera's electronics. There are a number of other variables to consider, such as file formats, image sensors, options for lighting, film speed, and more.

If you're in the market for a digital camera, spend time studying camera attributes, reading reviews, and browsing manufacturer Web sites. As a general rule, if you're serious about your photography, a few more dollars spent on a single lens reflex camera provides you with much more camera power.

Grabbing Images from Your Camera

Copying photos from your digital camera to your computer so that you can work with them in Elements is simple if you're familiar with your camera and the tools at your disposal. In this section, you find some points to consider about choosing a resolution when you shoot your pictures as well as how to use the Microsoft Camera and Scanner Wizard and Adobe Photo Download Manager after you hook up your camera to your computer.

Choosing a file format

When you work with digital photos in Elements, the file format of your images is an important point to consider. You choose this format before you take your pictures, and the format is carried over to your computer when you pull images off your camera.

The most common file formats that digital cameras offer you are JPEG and Camera Raw. Some cameras offer you other options, but these two formats are the most common. Low-cost point-and-shoot cameras offer you only the JPEG format, while the more expensive cameras and the SLR types offer you both JPEG and Camera Raw.

- **JPEG:** Cameras that produce JPEG images process images with JPEG compression before saving them. It's as if your camera performs a darkroom method of film processing when the shot is taken.

  We describe the JPEG file format in Chapter 3.

- **Camera Raw:** This format provides you with an optimum image for editing in Elements. When a Camera Raw image is saved to a media source, all the information the sensor captured is saved with the file. These images are post-processed when you open them (see the "Everything You Want to Know about Camera Raw" section, later in this chapter, to find out about opening Camera Raw images). For example, you can open a Camera Raw image, and before the image opens in Elements, you can adjust temperature, exposure, and a bunch of other settings. You can return to the original Camera Raw file and change the temperature, exposure, and so on to open the file with different settings. Just like chemical temperature and development time affect analog film processing, similar options affect post-processing Camera Raw images. The difference between analog film and Camera Raw is that after your analog film is processed, you can't change the processing attributes. With Camera Raw, you can go back and post-process the image a hundred times, changing the processing attributes each time.

  Camera Raw also supports higher bit depth images than JPEG files do.

If you have a choice between just JPEG and both JPEG and Camera Raw, always choose the latter. You'll have much more editing control over your images, and ultimately you will get better results.

Using the Microsoft Scanner and Camera Wizard

Microsoft Scanner and Camera Wizard may automatically be launched when your computer is connected to a media source. You can use the wizard to download images from your media source to your computer.

To copy images from a media source or when your camera is connected to your computer, follow these steps:

1. **Hook up the media to your computer.**

   Connect your computer and your camera or external media reader, or insert a media source into a port or drive on your computer. The methods available to you should be detailed in the user's guide that shipped with your camera.

   When you connect your media to your computer, a dialog box opens, providing options for how to handle the media.

2. **Select Copy Pictures to a Folder on My Computer Using Microsoft Scanner and Camera Wizard and click OK.**

3. **Click Next in the opening pane in the wizard and you arrive at a pane in which you see thumbnail images of the pictures on your media source, as shown in Figure 4-1.**

Choosing camera media

When buying a digital camera, consider the media type supported and the connection ports. There are a number of different storage sources for digital cameras. You can purchase cameras with various types of cards, such as CompactFlash II, SmartMedia, memory sticks, and the like, or cameras with mini hard drives, CDs, and floppy disks. With storage media, everything relates to capacity and speed. How many images a source holds, how fast the storage source writes the saved files, and how fast you can pull the images off the card are some things to consider. With some cards, you have choices for buying the media in different speeds.

As you narrow down your options, read reviews, search the Internet, and look over the options provided by manufacturers.

Figure 4-1: Click Next to see thumbnails of your images in a scrollable window.

   4. **If you want to copy all images on the media source to your computer, click Next. If you want selected images copied to your hard drive, click the Clear All button to remove the check marks below each thumbnail. After the check marks are removed, check the pictures you want to copy and click Next.**

   5. **In the next pane in the Wizard, browse your hard drive to locate a folder where you want to copy your pictures. Then click OK.**

      The images are copied to the target folder.

Using Adobe Photo Download Manager

The Adobe Photo Download Manager (Photo Downloader) is installed with your Elements program. Photo Downloader acquires images from digital cameras connected to your computer, from card readers, and from card reader ports on your computer. Photo Downloader is an alternative application to Microsoft Scanner and Camera Wizard.

To use the Adobe Photo Download Manager:

   1. **Hook up the media to your computer.**

2. **Cancel out of the Microsoft Scanner and Camera Wizard.**

   Because the wizard auto-launches, the opening pane appears when you make a connection between your camera media source and your computer. To bail out of the wizard, click Cancel.

3. **Launch Adobe Photo Download Manager by choosing Start⇨ All Programs⇨Adobe⇨Adobe Download Manager⇨ Adobe Download Manager.**

   Alternately, you can launch Elements and click the View and Organize button in the Organizer or click the Photo Browser button when in either Quick Fix or Standard Edit mode.

4. **Select Photos to download.**

   The Photo Downloader program displays thumbnail images, much like Microsoft's wizard. The Photo Downloader offers a few more options for acquiring your images, though, as shown in Figure 4-2.

Rotate images   Auto-fix Red-eye

Figure 4-2: The Photo Downloader enables you to rotate images and fix red eye.

5. **Rotate when applicable by clicking the rotate images buttons.**

6. **On the right, follow the steps to identify the source, browse for a location folder, add a subfolder if you like, and then rename the files, if desired.**

7. **Click the Get Photos button to commence copying files from the source to your hard drive.**

   When the photos complete the downloading process, a dialog box opens and asks if you want to delete the original photos from your media source.

8. **Click Yes to delete or No to retain the originals.**

   Immediately after making your selection, the Organizer window opens. All the photos downloaded to your hard drive appear in a new Organizer window, as you see in Figure 4-3.

To simplify the process, stick with using one tool to acquire your digital camera images — either the Microsoft Wizard or the Adobe Photo Download Manager.

Figure 4-3: After downloading, thumbnail images of the copied files appear in a new Organizer window.

Resizing images from digital cameras

Depending on your camera and the camera settings you use, you may need to resize your images after you download them.

Camera image resolution, which is measured in megapixels (millions of pixels), is a factor in image size. If you have a 6-megapixel camera, the full-resolution images from your camera are about 3000 x 2000 pixels. The file size for a 6-megapixel image is about 5.7MB.

On screen, the resolution of all digital camera images is 72 ppi (pixels per inch). Using the 6-megapixel image as an example, the resolution at 72 ppi produces an image a little more than 41 x 27 inches. Regardless of whether your camera takes pictures at 3, 5, or 8 megapixels, the images are all captured at 72 ppi, but the dimensions vary according to the total number of pixels captured.

Invariably, you always visit the Image Size dialog box, deselect Resample Image, and edit the resolution text box when preparing images for print. (See Chapter 3 for more information on using the Image Size dialog box.) If your color printer requires 150 ppi, changing a 6-megapixel image from 72 ppi at 41 x 27 inches produces an image of a little more than 20 x 13 inches.

Using a Scanner

Scanners connect through the same ports as cameras and card readers. Unless you have a SCSI (Small Computer Systems Interface) device, which is yet another type of connection port, you'll be using either USB or FireWire. Most low-end scanners sold today are USB devices.

Even the lowest-end scanners provide 16-bit scans that help you get a little more data in the shadows and highlights. As with digital cameras, a scanner's price is normally in proportion with its quality.

Preparing before you scan

Just as you would clean a lens on a digital camera and set various menu selections before clicking the shutter button, you should prepare a few things ahead of time before scanning:

- **Connect the scanner properly.** Make sure you have all connections made to your computer according to the user manual that came with your scanner. If you just purchased a scanner, check for any lock bolts and remove them according to the user's manual instructions.

- **Clean the scanner platen.** Try to use a lint-free cloth and some glass cleaner and remove all dust and particles on the glass. The more dust particles you remove, the easier job you'll have editing your image in Elements.

✔ **Clean the source material.** Be certain the print or film you want to scan is free from dust and spots.

If you have old negatives that are dirty or that have water spots or debris that you can't remove with a cloth and film cleaner, soak the film in photo flo (a liquid you can purchase at a photo reseller). Be certain your hands are clean and then run the filmstrip between two fingers to remove the excess liquid. Turn on your shower full force with hot water only and hang film nearby to dry it. Remove when dry and you should see a surprisingly clean filmstrip compared to your soiled original.

✔ **Get to know your scanner software.** When you scan in Elements, the software supplied with your scanner takes charge, and you use the options choices in this software before it finally drops into an Elements Image window.

✔ **Prepare the artwork.** If you plan on scanning pages in a book or pamphlet, remove the pages or try to make photocopies so the piece you scan lays flat on the scanner platen. Make sure you observe copyright laws if you're scanning printed works. For faxes and photocopies, try to improve originals by recopying them on a photocopier with darker settings.

✔ **Find the scanner's *sweet spot*.** Every scanner has an area where you can acquire the best scans. This area is often called the *sweet spot*. To find the scanner's sweet spot, scan a blank piece of paper. The sweet spot is the brightest area on the resultant scan. Other areas should be darker. The sweet spot is most often in the top-left quadrant, the lower-right quadrant, or the middle of the page. Note the area and plan to place your source material within this area when scanning pictures.

Understanding image requirements

All scanning software provides you options for determining resolution and color mode before you start a new scan. You should decide what output you intend to use and scan originals at target resolutions designed to accommodate a given output. Some considerations include

✔ **Scan the artwork or photo at the size and resolution for the final output.** If you have a 3-x-5 photo that needs to be 1.5 x 2.5 inches on a Web page, scan the original with a 50% reduction in size at 72 ppi. (See Chapter 3 for information about resizing images.)

✔ **Size images with the scanner software.** If you have a 4-x-6 photo that needs to be output for prepress and commercial printing at 8 x 12 inches, scan the photo at 4 x 6 inches at 600 ppi (enough to size to 200% for a 300 dpi image).

✔ **Scan properly for line art.** *Line art* is 1-bit black and white only. When you print line art on laser printers or when preparing files for commercial printing, the line art resolution should match the device resolution. For example, printing to a 600 dpi (dots per inch) laser printer requires 600 ppi for a 1-bit line-art image. When printing to an image setter at a print shop or going direct to plate or press, the resolution should be 1200 dpi.

- ✔ **Scan grayscale images in color.** In some cases it won't matter, but with some images and scanners, you can get better results scanning in RGB color and converting to grayscale using the Hue/Saturation dialog box, as we explain in Chapter 3.

- ✔ **Scan in high bit depths.** If your scanner is capable of scanning in 16- or 32-bit, by all means scan at the higher bit depths to capture the most data. See Chapter 3 for more information about working with higher-bit images.

Using scanner plug-ins

Generally, when you install your scanner software, a stand-alone application and a plug-in are installed to control the scanning process. *Plug-ins* are designed to work inside other software programs like Photoshop Elements. When using the plug-in, you can stay right in Elements to do all your scanning. Here's how it works:

1. **The first thing to do after installing a new scanner and the accompanying software is to launch Elements and then open the Organizer by clicking View and Organize Photos in the Welcome Screen.**

2. **From the Organizer, open the Preferences dialog box by pressing Ctrl+K.**

3. **Click Scanner in the left column and adjust the Scanner preferences, as we describe in Chapter 2.**

When the Preferences dialog box sees your scanner, you know the connection is properly set up and you're ready to scan. Here's how to complete your scan:

1. **To open the scanner software from within Elements, choose File⇨ Get Photos⇨From Scanner (you must be in the Organizer window to access this menu command).**

   Elements may churn a bit, but eventually your scanner software appears atop the Organizer window, as you see in Figure 4-4. The window is the scanner software provided by your scanner manufacturer. (Your window will look different unless you use the same scanner I use.) Regardless of which software you use, you should have similar options for creating a preview; selecting resolution, color mode, and image size; scaling; and other options.

2. **Adjust the options according to your output requirements and recommendations made by your scanner manufacturer.**

3. **When everything is ready to go, click the Scan button, and the final image drops into an Elements Image window.**

Figure 4-4: When you scan from within Elements, your scanner software loads on top of the Elements workspace.

Scanning many photos at once

If you have several photos to scan, you can lay them out on the scanner platen and perform a single scan to acquire all images in one pass. Arrange the photos to scan on the glass and set up all the options in the scanner window for your intended output. When you scan multiple images, they form a single scan, as you can see in Figure 4-5.

After you scan multiple images, Elements makes it easy for you to separate each image into its own Image window, where they can be saved as separate files. Choose Image⇨Divide Scanned Pictures, and Elements magically takes each image and opens it in a separate window, while your original scan remains intact. The images are neatly tucked away in the Photo Bin, where you can select them for editing, as shown in Figure 4-6.

Figure 4-5: You can scan multiple images with one pass.

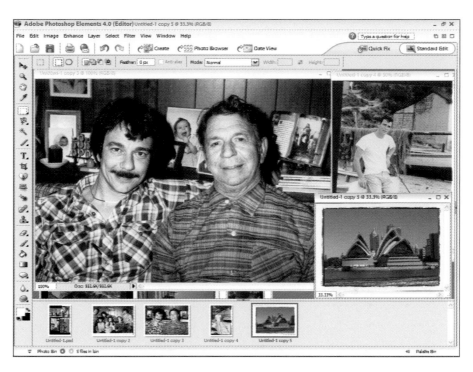

Figure 4-6: After choosing Image⇨Divide Scanned Pictures, the scan is split into separate image windows.

Getting Files from Storage Media

When you acquire images in Elements from media sources such as CD-ROMs, DVDs, external hard drives, and your internal hard drive, the process is very similar to opening files from digital cameras, which we explain earlier in this chapter. Insert a CD or DVD into the CD/DVD drive and the Windows Wizard opens just like when inserting a media cartridge or connecting a cable from your camera to your computer.

Likewise, you can also open these files in the Organizer. Just cancel out of the Wizard and follow these steps:

1. **Open the Organizer window from the Welcome screen or click Photo Browser from one of the editing modes.**

2. **When the Organizer window opens, choose File⇨Get Photos⇨From Files and Folders.**

   Alternately, you can click the Open tool or press Ctrl+O. The Get Photos from Files and Folders dialog box opens, as shown in Figure 4-7.

Figure 4-7: Use the Get Photos from Files and Folders dialog box to open images stored on CDs, DVDs, external drives, and your hard drive.

3. **Open the source drive from the listed drives and you see the photos stored on the media.**

4. **Select images and click the Get Photos button to open them in the Organizer, where they can be edited in Elements or saved to your hard drive.**

Using Online Services

Online printing and sharing services require you to set up an account with a service. You can access services provided by Adobe and Kodak from the Preferences dialog box. To use a service, you begin by setting up an account with the Organize and Share Preference settings in the Organizer, as we explain in Chapter 2.

You can create digital photo albums from your images and share them with friends, family, and coworkers. To initiate a sharing service, you send an e-mail invitation to others. Each member of your sharing group needs to set up an account individually. After everyone has an account, you and your friends can then order prints that are mailed from the online service center. All the kinds of prints you might order from a local superstore or photo lab are available from online services, including specialty items, like calendars.

After setting up an account and adjusting your preferences, open the Organizer and choose File➪Get Photos➪From Online Sharing Service. An Online Sharing Service Wizard opens, in which you step through an order process. (For more information about online sharing services, see Chapter 16.)

Phoning In Your Images

At first blush, you may get excited thinking you can just hook up your phone to your computer, like you can hook up a digital camera, and import your camera photos directly in the Organizer. Unfortunately, this technology is not available to Elements as of this writing. To get photos from your cell phone, you need to follow these steps:

1. **Copy photos from your phone to your computer either through a cable connection or via e-mail.**

   You use another utility, not Elements, to copy the pictures. Check your cell phone manual to find out how to transfer files from your phone to your computer.

   Where Elements comes in is simply identifying the folder where you copy your mobile phone images.

2. **In the Organizer, open the Specify Mobile Phone Folder by choosing File➪Get Photos➪From Mobile Phone.**

   The Specify Mobile Phone Folder dialog box opens, as shown in Figure 4-8.

Specify Mobile Phone Folder

Tip
Select the folder that Photoshop Elements will use to import photos from your mobile phone. Choose Watch Folders from the File menu to specify whether to automatically import, or notify you when new files are found.

Mobile Phone Folder
Look In: C:\Documents and Settings\Owner\My Documents\My Pictures   Browse...

☑ Automatically Fix Red Eyes

OK   Cancel

Figure 4-8: Choose File➪Get Photos➪From Mobile Phone in the Organizer.

3. **Click Browse and locate the folder where you copied your mobile phone images.**

   After locating the folder, Elements loads all photos in the folder in a new Organizer window.

4. **From the folder, you can select images to edit and print.**

Sometimes you can look at existing features in a program and get a clue for what may be coming in the next version or in a later release. As an example, look at the menu options for acquiring mobile phone images. There really isn't a reason for having this menu command in its current state because you can just as easily use many other methods for opening files. However, thinking ahead a little about the future of Photoshop Elements, this feature leads us to believe that, as mobile phones become more sophisticated in capturing images, you will eventually be able to capture images directly from your phone to the Photoshop Elements Organizer. Keep your eye on Elements and be certain to participate in regular upgrades to take advantage of new features as they are released.

Creating Images from Scratch

You may want to start from scratch by creating a new document in Elements. New blank pages have a number of uses. You can mix and merge images in a new document, as we explain in Chapter 8; create a canvas where you can draw and paint, as we explain in Chapter 12; or use the New dialog box to get some feedback on file sizes, dimensions, and resolution.

You can create new blank documents by using one of several options. On the Welcome screen, which appears when you first launch Elements, click Start from Scratch and the New dialog box opens, in which you choose the document size, resolution, and other attributes. Likewise, you can create new files while working in either editing mode or in the Organizer.

Here's how you create a new document while working in any editing mode:

1. **Open Elements and select an editing mode.**

   Click either Quick Fix Photos or Edit and Enhance Photos in the Welcome screen or select View and Organize Photos to open the Organizer.

2. **Open the New dialog box by choosing File⇨New⇨Blank File in any workspace. Alternately you can press Ctrl+N.**

   Either way, the New dialog box opens, as shown in Figure 4-9.

3. **Select file attributes.**

   Select the attributes for the new file. There are several options from which to choose:

   Figure 4-9: Regardless of the method used to create a new blank document, the New dialog box opens.

   - **Name.** Type a name for your file.

   - **Preset.** You can select a preset size from a long drop-down list. This is optional because you can change the file attributes in the other text boxes and drop-down menus.

- **Units.** Units come in handy when you want to examine dimensions in another unit of measure. If, for example, you have digital camera images at 3000 pixels by 2000 pixels, that number may not mean much. You can quickly select inches in either the Width or Height drop-down menu and the values in the text boxes convert to inches.

- **Dimensions.** Values in the Width and Height text boxes are independent. Either box can be edited without affecting the other.

- **Resolution.** Resolution here is similar to editing the resolution value in the Image Size dialog box when the Resample check box is checked. The resolution is an independent value and is not linked to the dimensions. If you want to know how resolution changes dimensions without resampling, create a new blank file at the known values and click OK. Then choose Image⇨Resize⇨ Image Size and change values in the Image Size dialog box, which we discuss in Chapter 3.

- **Color Mode.** Your choices are bitmap, grayscale, and RGB. (See Chapter 3 for more information about color modes.)

- **Background Contents.** You have three choices: White, Background Color, and Transparent. The selection you make results in the color of the blank image. If you choose Background Color, the current background color assigned in the Tools palette is applied to the background. See Chapter 12 for information on changing background color. If you choose Transparent, the image is created as a layer, as we explain in Chapter 8.

- **Image Size.** This value dynamically changes as you change Width, Height, and/or Resolution. The reported value is how much file size is required to save the uncompressed file.

 4. Click OK after setting the file attributes to create the new document.

In addition to creating new blank files, the New dialog box can be a helpful source of information for all your work in Elements. Suppose you want to know how many images you can copy to a 128MB USB storage device, or how large your digital camera files will print with a 150-ppi resolution. All you have to do is press Ctrl+N to open the New dialog box, plug in the values, and read the Image Size number or examine the file dimensions. If your files are going to be converted to grayscale, select Grayscale from the Color Mode drop-down menu to see how much your file size is reduced by checking out the Image Size number. This number is dynamic and changes with each change you make to the file attributes.

Everything You Want to Know about Camera Raw

We added this more elaborate description of Camera Raw in this part of the chapter after sharing with you all the other options you have for getting images in Elements. We recognize that not all of our readers have digital cameras capable of capturing Camera Raw images, so it may not be of much interest to you now.

If you don't have a camera capable of capturing Camera Raw images, you might want to look over this section to understand how this file format can benefit you. When you purchase a camera equipped with Camera Raw support, you'll have some understanding of the advantages of using the format.

Understanding Camera Raw

Camera Raw images enable you to post-process your pictures. When you take a picture with a digital camera in Camera Raw format, the camera's sensor records as much information as it can. When you open a Camera Raw file in Elements, you decide what part of that data is opened as a new image.

Suppose you have your camera set for exposure in tungsten lighting. Tungsten lighting would be used with tungsten flash photography in a studio. If you take this camera outside in daylight and shoot an image, all your images appear with a blue cast. This happens because tungsten lighting requires a cooler temperature than daylight. See Figure 4-10, later in this chapter, for an example of an image taken outdoors with settings for tungsten lighting.

If you acquire images that are saved in JPEG format, you need to do a lot of color correction after the image opens in Elements. If you shoot the image in Camera Raw, you just process the image with a warmer temperature (consistent with conditions when the shot was taken), and your color correction in Elements is a fraction of what it would be to fix a JPEG image.

Post-processing Camera Raw images requires a plug-in that is installed with Photoshop Elements. When you open a Camera Raw image, the Camera Raw plug-in takes over and provides you with a huge set of options for post-processing the image before you open it in one of the Elements editors.

Acquiring Camera Raw images

If you read through the first part of this chapter, you know how to acquire images from your camera and copy them to your hard drive. We won't bother going through those steps again; we'll just assume you have some Camera Raw images on your hard drive. That's where you want them, anyway. Opening files from your hard drive is much faster than working off media cards.

To open a Camera Raw image, follow these steps:

1. **Open the image by pressing Ctrl+O and selecting it in the Open dialog box.**

   If you want to select several images in a row, click the first image, hold down the Shift key, and then click the last image. If you want to select several nonadjacent images, Ctrl-click each image.

2. **Click Open in the Open dialog box, and all the selected images open in the Camera Raw window.**

   If selecting multiple images, only one image appears in the foreground (Figure 4-10) while the other images appear behind the foreground image.

   As you can see, you can use a vast number of options to post-process your image before you drop it into Elements. This window is like a digital darkroom where you can process the film and see what you're doing to the image before you accept the changes.

Figure 4-10: Open a Camera Raw image and the image opens in the Camera Raw plug-in window.

3. Choose from the options to post-process your images.

If you have your monitor properly calibrated, as we explain in Chapter 2, all the adjustments you make for Camera Raw are dynamically updated in the Image preview. Don't be shy. Poke around and adjust settings to see the results in the preview area. The more you play with the settings, the more you will learn about how to get the best out of Camera Raw.

You have a large number of settings in the Camera Raw window, as the following list shows. We suggest that you mark this section to refer back to when you work with Camera Raw images. The options you have are as follows:

- ✔ **Tools:** Five tools appear in the window:

  - Use the **Zoom tool** to zoom in and out of the image preview.

  - The **Hand tool** is used to move the image around like you do in the Elements image window.

  - The **Eyedropper tool** samples color in the image. We cover using Elements' Eyedropper tools in Chapter 12, and that information also applies to using the Eyedropper in the Camera Raw window.

    After the Eyedropper tool, you find two self-explanatory rotation tools.

  - **Rotate Left** appears first, and **Rotate Right** is the last tool you see below the Title bar.

- ✔ **Image Preview:** The Image Preview shows you all the changes you make before you eventually open the image in an Elements editor.

- ✔ **Preview:** Notice the Adjust and Details tabs. All adjustments you make in the tabs can be previewed when this box is checked. Unchecking the box shows you the image as you first opened it in the Camera Raw window.

- ✔ **Shadow/Highlight:** The Shadow and Highlight check boxes show clipping in the shadows (dark areas of the image) and highlights (light areas of the image). *Clipping* means that, in a certain area, data, and ultimately detail, has been lost in an image. Think of clipping as something you don't want to appear in your pictures. When you make adjustments with these two check boxes checked, shadow clipping is shown in blue and highlight clipping is shown in red in the image preview. Take a look at Figure 4-11, in which we exaggerated clipping to show how the clipping preview appears.

- ✔ **RGB values:** When you first open an image, you won't see any values in the RGB area. Click the Zoom tool, the Hand tool, or the Eyedropper tool and move the cursor over the image preview. As you move any of these tools around the image, the RGB values corresponding to the point below the cursor are reported in this area.

Figure 4-11: Shadow clipping appears in red and highlight clipping appears in blue.

✓ **Histogram:** The Histogram is a graph displaying all three channels (red, green, blue) in an image simultaneously. The Histogram changes as you change other options in the Camera Raw window.

The histogram graphs how pixels in an image are distributed. The distribution includes the number of pixels at each color intensity level (one of the 256 levels you find out about in Chapter 3).

If images have pixels concentrated in the shadows, you'll see the Histogram skewed to the left. Conversely, images with pixels concentrated in the highlights reveal a Histogram skewed to the right.

As you begin to understand histograms more, you can develop your skill to the point where a quick glance at the histogram will provide you a clue as to what adjustments you need to make to improve images.

✓ **Settings:** From this drop-down menu, you have choices for applying settings to the open image. If you change any setting, the menu option changes to *Custom*. If you previously made settings choices on a Camera Raw image and you want to return to the shot as it was taken by the camera, open the image and select Camera Raw Defaults. Another option you have is Previous Conversion. This selection is handy if you have a collection of images that all require the same settings. After adjusting the first image, open additional images and select Previous Conversion. The Camera Raw plug-in applies the last settings you made to a Camera Raw image to the current open file.

✔ **Adjust/Details tabs:** In Figure 4-12, you can see the options in the Adjust tab. Click the Details tab and the options change, as shown in Figure 4-12. Here you have three items to adjust by either dragging the sliders or typing values in the text boxes.

Figure 4-12: Click the Details tab to open the options for sharpness and noise reduction.

Sharpness sharpens images. You can choose to sharpen images in the Camera Raw window or in Elements. Try to avoid sharpening here and use the sharpening tools in Elements, as we explain in Chapter 9.

Luminance Smoothing is actually a noise reduction tool. You've probably seen images with a lot of noise. In extreme cases, they look like the pictures were printed on sandpaper. Noise in an image is okay if that's an effect you intentionally apply to a picture. However, if you want a smooth-looking image, you'll want to eliminate any noise introduced by the camera. Luminance Smoothing reduces grayscale noise. The next setting is Color Noise Reduction, which is used to reduce color noise.

✔ **White Balance:** White Balance settings are used to adjust the color balance of an image to reflect the lighting conditions under which the shot was originally taken. Think of the sensor in a digital camera capable of capturing the entire range of white balance the sensor can see. Here you make a choice not necessarily for what you see, but for the white balance for the shot you took. Therefore, if your camera is set for taking pictures under one set of lighting conditions, and you move to another set of lighting conditions and forget to change the settings, you can let the Camera Raw plug-in make a correction for the white balance because the sensor picked up the entire range and the necessary data are contained in the file.

In Figure 4-13, you can see a picture taken with the camera set for tungsten lighting, but the shot was taken outdoors in daylight. The white balance options selected in the Settings drop-down menu are listed in the figure.

✔ **Temperature:** If one of the preset White Balance options doesn't quite do the job, you can move the Temperature slider or edit the text box to settle on values between one White Balance choice and another. Use this item to fine-tune the White Balance.

✔ **Tint:** Tint is another fine-tuning adjustment affected by White Balance. This slider and text box are used to correct any green or magenta tints that may appear in a photo.

Figure 4-13: From the Settings drop-down menu, you have several choices for white balance.

✔ **Brightness adjustments.** You have several adjustment sliders and text boxes for controlling the image brightness and tonal range. Notice the Exposure setting. This item lets you correct photos taken at the wrong exposure. In analog darkrooms, you might ask technicians to push or pull film during processing, which results in longer and shorter processing times. Changing exposure times compensates for under- and over-exposing film. A nice advantage when using Camera Raw is that you can change exposure for one image and then later open the original Raw image and change to a different exposure value. Analog film can't be reprocessed, but with Camera Raw, you can reprocess over and over again.

Other options for the brightness and tonal controls are similar to the choices you have in the Elements Standard Editing mode. For more information on these adjustments, see Chapter 10.

✔ **Cancel/Reset:** When you open the Camera Raw window, the button you see by default is Cancel. Press the Alt key, and the button changes to Reset. If you want to scrub all the settings you made and start over, press Alt and click Reset.

✔ **Open/Update/Skip:** This one button has three different purposes.

- The default button is **Open**. Click Open after you choose all your settings to process the photo and open it in Elements.

- Press the Alt key, and the button changes to **Update**. If you click Update and then cancel out of the dialog box, the next time you open the file in the Camera Raw window, you'll see the changes you made before the Update button was clicked. This action lets you change a bunch of settings on several images that you intend to open and edit later in Elements.

- Press the Shift key and you see the **Skip** button. If you open several images at once, press Shift, and click Skip, the current active window is dismissed and you move to the next document.

✔ **Save:** Clicking Save merely saves your current settings. You can eliminate the settings saved with the file by selecting Camera Raw Defaults in the Settings drop-down menu.

✔ **Help:** Clicking this button opens a Help document to assist you in understanding more about Camera Raw.

✔ **Bit Depth:** If your camera is capable of shooting higher bit depths, they are listed here. If you want to convert to 8-bit images for printing, you can select the option from the drop-down menu.

✔ **Zoom:** From this drop-down menu, you can choose from several zoom presets. You can also edit the text box or click the minus (-) button to zoom out or the plus (+) button to zoom in. Using any option zooms the Image preview.

Viewing and Finding Your Images

*T*he Organizer is a powerful tool that helps you locate files and keeps your photos arranged and organized. You can easily access the Organizer by clicking the Photo Browser button in the Shortcuts bar while you're in one of the editing modes. Or, when you open the Welcome screen, click the View and Organize Photos button.

In this chapter, you discover how to view and organize your pictures in the Organizer and the Image window and how the many options help speed up your work in Photoshop Elements.

The Many Faces of the Organizer

The default Organizer view is like a slide sorter, and this view is one you're likely to use in all your Elements work sessions. The Organizer makes accessing photos an efficient means for opening a picture in one of the editors. Just double-click a photo in the Organizer, and you see the image zoom in size to fill an Organizer window. You can carefully examine the photo to be certain it's the one you want and then just select which editor you want to use from the Edit drop-down menu.

In addition to the default view in the Organizer, you have some other opportunities for examining your pictures. You can view pictures in a slide show, or you can view pictures side-by-side to compare them.

Adding files to the default Organizer view

Before you explore alternate viewing options in the Organizer, take a look at how you add photos to the thumbnail images you see in the Organizer window.

After copying the photos to your hard drive, as we explain in Chapter 4, here's how you go about adding those files to an existing group of images in the Organizer:

1. **View photos to add to the Organizer window.**

   Be certain you have photos in the Organizer window.

2. **In the Organizer, choose File⇨Get Photos⇨From Files and Folders.**

   The Get Photos from Files and Folders dialog box opens, as shown in Figure 5-1.

Figure 5-1: The Get Photos from Files and Folders dialog box.

3. **In the Get Photos from Files and Folders dialog box, choose Thumbnails from the View menu (the icon with the down arrow, to the far right of the Look In drop-down menu).**

   In Thumbnails view, thumbnail images of most of your files appear in a scrollable window. (Note: you may not see Camera Raw files and some files saved in different formats.) This view makes it easy to locate the files you want to add to the Organizer.

4. **Select files to add to the Organizer window.**

   Click a thumbnail and use either the Shift key or the Ctrl key to select additional photos. When you hold down Shift and click, all photos between the first thumbnail and the thumbnail you Shift-click are selected. When Ctrl-click, you can select a series of noncontiguous photos.

5. **Click Get Photos to add the selected photos to the Organizer window.**

 Back

6. **Add the new photos to the Organizer window you originally opened by clicking the Back button in the Shortcuts bar.**

   The photos you add to the Organizer may appear out of order when viewing the Organizer. Depending on the sort order we explain later in this chapter, the additional photos you added to the Organizer can appear before, after, or integrated within the original photos. Use the scroll bar in the Organizer to view the added photos.

Viewing photos in a slideshow (Full Screen View)

Are you ready for some exciting viewing in Photoshop Elements? As an alternative view of your Organizer files, you can see your pictures in a self-running slide show (Full Screen View), complete with transition effects and background music. Full Screen View takes you to a slide show view. For the purposes of clarity, think of Full Screen View and viewing a slide show as the same thing. Full-screen viewing temporarily hides the Elements tools and menus and gives you the most viewing area on your monitor to see your pictures.

Viewing files in a slide show mode can be helpful for taking a quick preview of the files you want to edit for all kinds of output as well as previewing photos that you might use for an exported slide show, which we explain in Chapter 15.

Setting up your images for viewing

To set up your slide show and/or enter Full Screen View, follow these steps:

1. **Click the Photo Browser button to open the Organizer and navigate to a folder of images you want to view.**

2. **Select individual images to see in a slide show or use all the images currently in the Organizer for your slide show.**

   If no images are selected when you enter Full Screen View, all photos in the Organizer window are shown in Full Screen View.

3. **Choose View⇨View Photos in Full Screen.**

   The Full Screen View Options dialog box shown in Figure 5-2 opens.

Figure 5-2: Choose View⇨View Photos in Full Screen to open the Full Screen View Options dialog box, where full-screen viewing options are selected.

4. **Choose the options for your slide show in the dialog box.**

   The Full Screen View Options dialog box offers a number of choices for viewing a slide show in Full Screen View. Table 5-1 explains each option.

5. **After you determine the attributes for full-screen viewing, click OK.**

   You enter a full-screen mode. For a moment the Full Screen View toolbar appears at the top of the window. This toolbar hides automatically after a few seconds. I explain in Table 5-1 how, if you check the box for Show Filmstrip, the full-screen view appears as shown in Figure 5-3.

Figure 5-3: When Show Filmstrip is checked, the full screen view shows thumbnail images of the files selected for viewing on the right side of the image window.

Table 5-1	Using the Full Screen View Options Dialog Box
Option	**What It Does**
Background music	You can choose a preinstalled sound file from the drop-down menu or click the Browse button to locate sound files stored on your computer. The sound file formats you can use with Elements are .mp3, .wav, and .wma. You can add sound files to the Organizer by choosing File⇨Get Photos⇨From Files and Folders and selecting sound files.
Play Audio Captions	You can add audio captions to images, as we explain in Bonus Chapter 1 on the Web. Check this box to play these captions.
Page Duration	You can specify the duration of each slide before it advances to the next slide. The text box accepts durations ranging from 1 to 3600 seconds.

(continued)

Table 5-1 *(continued)*

Option	What It Does
Include Captions	You can add text captions to images, as we explain in Chapter 6. If you want to see the text captions, check this box.
Allow Photos to Resize	Images appear at full-screen size when you check this box. Be certain you have sufficient resolution before resizing the images to fit the screen. Image resolution is optimal at 72 ppi at 100% size, as we point out in Chapter 3.
Allow Videos to Resize	Any video clips you add to the Organizer can be played in the slide show. If you check this box, the video frames are sized to full-screen size. You also need to be certain that the video supports sufficient resolution in order to clearly see the video frames. When in doubt, just test a movie clip in full-screen view and see if the quality is satisfactory.
Show Filmstrip	When this box is checked and you open the files in Full Screen View, a filmstrip appears along the right side of the full-screen window. Click the thumbnails in the filmstrip to jump to the selected slide.
Fade between Photos	This option adds a fade transition between slides.
Start Playing Automatically	Check this box and the slide show moves into a play mode automatically. If you don't check the box, you must click a tool in Full Screen View to start the play manually.
Repeat Slide Show	Check this box to create a continuous loop. You could use this option for a self-running kiosk.
Show This Dialog before Viewing in Full Screen	If you want dismiss the Full Screen View Options dialog box and keep it from appearing each time you enter full-screen views, deselect this box. To bring back this dialog box when you enter full-screen views, press Ctrl+K to open the General Preferences dialog box and click the Reset All Warning Dialogs button. If you want to keep the dialog box from opening but access it after entering Full Screen View, select Full Screen View Options from the Action drop-down menu in the Full Screen toolbar. See the next section for details on using the toolbar.

Working with the toolbar

While in Full Screen View, you can play the slide show and move back and forth between slides. These options and more are available to you in the toolbar that opens when you first enter full-screen viewing. After the toolbar disappears, you can bring it back simply by moving the mouse.

The toolbar shown in Figure 5-4 contains tools for the following:

Figure 5-4: The Full Screen View toolbar.

a Previous Photo (left-arrow key): Click this button to view the previous slide, or press the shortcut left-arrow key.

b Play/Pause (F5): Click this button to pause play. When play is paused, the icon changes, and you can click the new icon to resume play.

c Next Photo (right-arrow key): Click this button to view the next slide, or press the shortcut right-arrow key.

d Exit (Esc): Click this button or press Esc to exit Full Screen View.

e Rotate 90 Degrees Left (Ctrl+left-arrow key): Click this button to rotate the photo in the image window and in the Organizer default window.

f Rotate 90 Degrees Right (Ctrl+right-arrow key): Works the same as the previous button, but rotates to the right.

g Delete (Delete key): Deletes the photo in the image window from the slide show and the Organizer.

h Action Menu: The commands in this drop-down menu, as shown in Figure 5-5, provide options for editing images, printing, and organizing files. For more information on the editing options, see Chapter 9. For information on printing, see Chapter 14. For information on organizing, see Chapter 6

i Full Screen View: When you enter Full Screen View, this tool is selected.

j Side by Side/Above and Below: From this drop-down menu, you can choose to show two slides horizontally or vertically. The selected slide in the filmstrip is compared to the next slide in

Undo Rotate Right	Ctrl+Z
Redo	Ctrl+Y
Auto Smart Fix	Ctrl+Alt+M
Auto Red Eye Fix	Ctrl+R
Mark for Printing	
Attach Tag	▶
Remove Tag	▶
Add to Collection	▶
Remove from Collection	▶
Show Properties	Alt+Enter
✔ Show Filmstrip	Ctrl+F
Full Screen View Options...	

Figure 5-5: The Actions drop-down menu.

the filmstrip. Additionally, you can click a slide and Ctrl+click to compare two selected slides. To return to the default view, click the Full Screen View tool.

k **Fit in Window (Ctrl+0):** This tool zooms the views as large as needed to fill in the image window.

l **Actual Pixels (Ctrl+Alt+0):** Use this tool to see images at actual sizes.

m **Current zoom percentage:** Shows you the zoom level of the image in the image window. You can't edit this readout.

n **Zoom Out (Ctrl+–):** Click this tool to zoom out.

o **Zoom slider:** Move the slider left to zoom out and right to zoom in.

p **Zoom In (Ctrl++):** Click this tool to zoom in on the image.

q **Sync Pan and Zoom:** Panning and zooming are synchronized by default. When two slides are compared and appear side-by-side or one above the other, both images are sized together as you change the zoom level. Click the chain link icon to desynchronize the view.

r **Send Photos to Slide Show Editor:** The Full Screen View is a great way to preview a slide show, complete with transitions and sound. When everything looks good, click this tool to create a slide show file, as we explain in Chapter 15.

s **Show Only Navigation Controls:** You can collapse the toolbar to show only the first four tools (and this one). When the toolbar is collapsed, click the arrow again to expand to the default toolbar.

Moving around the Image Window

When you edit images in either Quick Fix or Standard Edit mode, you continually interact with the image window. Whether you're zooming in and out of a single window or viewing multiple windows, you need to comfortably work in this area for all your editing tasks. To help you move around the image window, Elements provides a rich set of tools. Try to become familiar with the many viewing options and keyboard shortcuts available in Elements, and all your editing jobs will be much easier. The following tools, menu commands, and palettes are essential tools for just about everything you do in Elements.

Zooming in and out of images

Zooming in and out of images is a task you perform routinely while editing images in the image window and also when working in other windows, such as the Camera Raw window and the Full Screen View window. Zooming in is necessary when you want to precisely edit a section of an image or examine detail in a small area. You then need to zoom out to see the edits as they compare to the entire image.

Zoom by clicking

The Zoom tool appears on the Tools palette. To use the tool for zooming in and out, take a look at how it all works:

1. **Click the Zoom tool in the Tools palette to select it (or simply press Z).**

2. **Move the cursor, now loaded with the Zoom tool, to the image window and click the place where you want to zoom.**

   To zoom in more, click again; keep clicking until you zoom far enough in.

3. **To zoom out of an image, keep the Zoom tool selected, hold down the Alt key, and click.**

   The cursor changes to a magnifying glass tool with a minus (-) symbol when you hold down the Alt key.

Zoom to a selection

Another way to change a view is to zoom to a target area in an image. Here's how:

1. **Click the Zoom tool in the Tools palette.**

2. **Drag a box around the area you want to zoom.**

   A dashed rectangle marquee appears as shown in Figure 5-6.

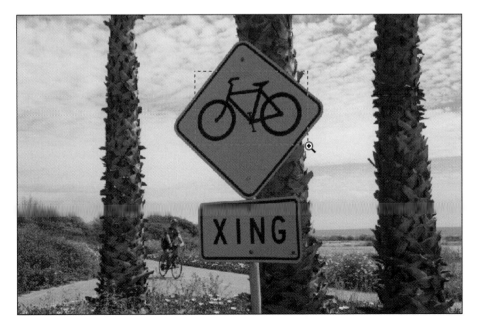

Figure 5-6: Click the Zoom tool in the Tools palette and drag around an area you want to zoom.

3. **Move the rectangle marquee if you need to adjust the selection.**

   Now it's time to get fancy. If you have a marquee drawn with the Zoom tool and the size appears just right, but you want to move just the rectangle, press the Spacebar while you keep the mouse button pressed. You can drag the marquee rectangle anywhere in the image to zoom to the area defined by the rectangle boundary.

4. **Release the mouse button.**

   The view zooms to fit the space defined by the marquee rectangle.

Using the Options bar

Above the image window and below the Shortcuts bar, you find the Options bar. The Options bar is ever-changing, offering different options as you select different tools in the Tools palette. When you click the Zoom tool, the Options bar changes, as shown in Figure 5-7. You have many similar choices for zooming in and out of images and a few options unique to the Options bar:

Figure 5-7: Click the Zoom tool in the Tools palette, and the Options bar changes to reflect choices for zooming in and out of images.

a Zoom In/Zoom Out tools: You can choose zoom in or zoom out as separate tools to avoid using the Alt key to toggle between the two.

b Zoom percentage: This figure shows you the current zoom level as a percentage. You can edit the text by typing values between 1 and 1600.

c Zoom slider: Click the right-pointing arrow and a slider bar opens. Drag the slider left to zoom out or right to zoom in.

d Resize Windows To Fit: Check this box to resize the window along with the image zoom. Uncheck the box to zoom in and out of an image while the Image window remains at a fixed size.

e Ignore Palettes: This check box is selected when you check the Resize Windows To Fit checkbox. Checking this box ignores palettes when using the Zoom tool so you can zoom to an area covered by the palettes. If you uncheck the box, you can't zoom to an area beneath the Palette Bin.

f Zoom All Windows: If you have multiple images open and check this box, zooming with the Zoom tool zooms all open documents simultaneously.

g Actual Pixels/Fit Screen/Print Size: The same options are available as discussed earlier, in the "Working with the toolbar" section.

Viewing multiple documents

When you need to view two or more images at once, choose Window➪Images to open a submenu of viewing options used for viewing multiple files. The Window menu also provides a list of all your open documents. Here's a list of options you find on the submenu:

- ✔ **Maximize Mode:** While in Maximize Mode, you see only one image window and lose the option for resizing the window by dragging the lower right corner in or out. If you want to bring back the title bar and the resizing options, return to the Window➪Images➪Maximize Mode command. Notice the check box next to Maximize Mode; click the check box to remove the check mark in the submenu and you minimize the Image window.

- ✔ **Tile:** Tiling images reduces Image window sizes to a size that accommodates viewing all images in scrollable windows within the Elements workspace. Choose Window➪Images➪Tile when multiple images are open to get a view similar to Figure 5-8.

- ✔ **Cascade:** Choose Window➪Images➪Cascade and the image windows overlap each other in a cascading view.

- ✔ **Match Zoom:** Set the zoom level for one of several images open in Elements and choose Window➪Images➪Match Zoom. All open documents are zoomed to the same level as the foreground image.

- ✔ **Match Location:** If you zoom into, for example, the top-right corner and then select Match Location, all open images zoom to the same location in the respective photos.

- ✔ **Bring image to foreground:** As you open photos, the open documents are listed by name in the Window menu. The current active document is the foreground image. If you want to edit another image, choose Window and select the image you want to edit, and that image comes to the foreground as the active image.

  Although you have a menu command to bring images to the foreground and make them active, you can perform the same action by clicking an image thumbnail in the Photo Bin.

Figure 5-8: Open several images in one of the editing modes and choose Window⟹Images⟹Tile to show all image windows.

Using Pan and Zoom

When you zoom in on a document larger than the image window can accommodate, scroll bars provide a means for moving the image inside the window. Moving the image around a window is *panning* the image.

 You can also use the Hand tool to pan the image. Zoom into an image and click the Hand tool. Click and drag the image around the window. If you want to zoom in or out while the Hand tool is selected, hold down the Ctrl key and the Hand tool temporarily changes to the Zoom In tool. Hold down Ctrl+Alt and the Hand tool temporarily changes to the Zoom Out tool.

Using the Navigator palette

The Navigator palette affords you several different options for both zooming and panning an image.

Figure 5-9: The Navigator palette.

To open the Navigator palette, choose Window⇨Navigator. The Navigator palette, shown in Figure 5-9, opens as a floating palette in the Elements workspace. (For more information on floating palettes, see Chapter 1).

While you select options for zooming in the Navigator palette, the image preview in the palette window stays fixed to show you the entire image. As you zoom in and out inside the palette, the corresponding zoom is applied to the active document.

Either use the zoom tools in the palette or drag the slider left and right to zoom in and out. If you place the cursor inside the image preview thumbnail, you can drag a rectangle and zoom into the image.

Using the Navigator palette can be particularly helpful if you use two monitors. Just drag the Navigator palette to your second monitor where you can change zoom levels without having the palette obscure the background image.

Sorting Your Photos

With all of Photoshop Elements' modes and workspaces, you need a consistent starting place to handle all your editing tasks. Think of the Organizer as Grand Central Station, and from this central location, you can take the Long Island Railroad to any destination you desire. In Elements terms, instead of heading out to Port Washington, you travel to an editing mode. Instead of going to the Hamptons, you journey through all the creation areas. In short, the Organizer is the central depot on the Photoshop Elements map.

In addition to being a tool to navigate to other workspaces, the Organizer is a management tool you can use to organize, sort, search, and describe photos with identity information. In terms of sorting and organizing files, Elements provides many different options, and we cover them all in the following sections.

Using sort commands

In the lower-left corner of the Organizer window is a pop-up menu that provides some sorting options, as shown in Figure 5-10. Alternatively, you can choose View⊅Arrangement, and a submenu providing the same commands opens.

Figure 5-10: The Organizer's sort options.

The sorting options available to you are

- **Date (Newest First):** Select this option to view images according to the date you took the photos, beginning with the most recent date.

- **Date (Oldest First):** This option displays photos in chronological order starting with the oldest file.

- **Import Batch:** You may import a batch of photos in one Photoshop Elements session and import another batch in the same session or in another session. When you select Import Batch, the images appear organized in groups, according to the date the batch was created. In Figure 5-11, you can see several batches imported and added as Collections, which we describe in Chapter 6.

- **Folder Location:** Click Folder Location and you see an Explorer pane on the left side of the Organizer window. You can browse your hard drive for folder locations and select a folder containing images you imported into the Organizer.

Sorting media types

Photos can also be sorted according to media type. Elements supports viewing photos, video files, audio files, creations, and PDF files. To select different media types, choose View⊅Media Types, and the Items Shown dialog box opens. Check the boxes for the media types you want to display in the Organizer window.

Figure 5-11: When importing photos in batches, you can sort files according to batch import dates.

Using Search Options

The Organizer's Find menu is devoted entirely to searching photos. From the Find menu, you can locate photos in collections, catalogs, and the Organizer window according to a variety of different search criteria.

In order to use the commands in the Find menu, you need to have photos loaded in the Organizer window or create Collections or Catalogs, which we explain in Chapter 6. The following categories can be searched in the Organizer

Searching by date

When you have a number of different files in an Organizer window from photos shot at different dates, you can narrow your search to find photos, and all other types of files supported by Elements, through a date search. To search files by date, do the following:

1. **Open files in the Organizer by choosing File⇨Get Photos and then choosing a submenu command for acquiring files.**

   To open files stored on your hard drive, choose the From Files and Folders submenu command.

2. **Select a date range by choosing Find⇨Set Date Range.**

   The Set Date Range dialog box, shown in Figure 5-12, opens.

3. **Specify the dates.**

   Type a year in the Start Date Year text box. Select the month and day from the Month and Day drop-down menus. Repeat the same selections for the End Date.

   Figure 5-12: Open the Set Date Range dialog box and specify the start and end dates.

4. **Click OK.**

   The thumbnails shown in the Organizer window include only files created within the specified date range.

Searching for untagged items

You can tag files with a number of different criteria, as we explain in Chapter 6. When tags are added to images, you can sort files according to tag labels. We cover sorting by tag labels in Chapter 6, too. For now, take a look at the Find menu and notice the Untagged Items command. If you haven't added tags to some items and you want to show only the untagged files so you can begin to add tags, choose Find⇨Untagged Items or press Ctrl+Shift+Q. Elements displays all files without tags in the Organizer window.

Searching collections

Collections are another item we address in Chapter 6. You can create collections and then select a collection in the Collections palette. Selecting a Collection is like having a first level of sorting. You can then search by date or other sort options discussed here to narrow down the choices.

Searching captions and notes

In Chapter 6, we talk about adding captions and notes to your files. When captions and/or notes are added to files, you can search on the caption name, contents of a note, or both. To search caption names and notes, do the following:

1. **Open files in the Organizer by choosing File➪Get Photos and then choosing a submenu command for acquiring files.**

   If you're opening files stored on your hard drive, choose the From Files and Folders submenu command.

2. **Choose Find➪By Caption or Note.**

   The Find by Caption or Note dialog box opens, as shown in Figure 5-13. Options in the dialog box are

   • **Find Items with Caption or Note:** In the text box, type the word(s) you want to search.

Figure 5-13: Choose Find➪By Caption or Note to open the dialog box in which search criteria for captions and notes are specified.

   • **Match Only the Beginning of Words in Captions and Notes.** Click this radio button when you know your caption or note begins with words you type in the text box.

   • **Match Any Part of Any Word in Captions or Notes.** Check this box if you're not sure if the text typed in the box is used at the beginning of a caption or note or if it is contained within the caption name or note text.

3. **Click OK.**

   The Results appear in the Organizer window.

Searching by history

Elements keeps track of what you do with your photos, such as printing, e-mailing, sharing, and a number of other tasks. You can search for files based on the file history by choosing Find➪By History. Selecting options in the By History submenu reports files found on date searches meeting the history criteria. The By History submenu options are as follows:

✔ **Imported on:** Select this option when you want to search files you imported in the Organizer.

✔ **Received from:** Select this option to find files e-mailed to you from other users.

✔ **E-mailed to:** Use this option when you want to search for files you e-mailed to other users.

- **Printed on:** Use this option when you want to search for files you printed.

- **Exported on:** Use this option for searching files exported to your computer or mobile phone.

- **Ordered Online:** Use this option to search for files that were ordered online.

- **Shared Online:** Use this option to find files you shared with other users online.

- **Used in Creations:** Use this option for searching files you used in Creations.

- **In HTML Photo Galleries:** Use this option to find files you used in Web galleries, which we explain in Chapter 15.

Searching metadata

Metadata includes both information about your images that is supplied by digital cameras and custom data you add to a file. Metadata contains descriptions of the image, such as the camera settings you used to take a picture, copyright information, and much more. We cover searching metadata in Bonus Chapter 3 on this book's Web site so that you can get a feel for how metadata is added to a file and how to view it.

Searching faces

If there is a magical method available to you for searching files in Elements, it has to be searching for faces. When you choose Find➪Find Faces for Tagging, Elements searches through files you select in the Organizer window and examines each image for a face — *Homo sapiens* faces to be exact.

Note that you must first select image thumbnails in the Organizer window and then choose Find➪Find Faces for Tagging. If you want to search through all files in the Organizer, press Ctrl+A or choose Edit➪Select All. Be aware that if you search through a large catalog, Elements will take some time to complete the search.

The results of the search magically include all photos containing faces in a new Organizer window. Although the command is intended to identify images you can tag, you can use the command for invoking a search and choose to view all files containing faces.

6

Organizing and Managing Your Photos

Downloading a bunch of media cards filled with photos and leaving them in folders distributed all over your hard drive is like having a messy office with papers stacked all over your desk. Trying to find a file, even with all the great search capabilities we cover in Chapter 5, can take you as much time as sorting through piles of papers. What you need is a good file-mangement system.

In this chapter, we talk about organizing and annotating files and the important task of backing up files. Be certain to take a little time to understand the organization methods that Elements provides and keep your files organized as you copy them to your hard drive and back up files to CD-ROMs or DVDs. Time you invest in organizing your pictures will help you quickly locate files when you need them.

Organizing Groups of Images with Collections

Elements provides you a great opportunity for organizing files in the form of collections. After you acquire your images in the Organizer, as we discuss in Chapter 4, you'll want to sort them out and add them to some permanent collections according to the dates you took the pictures, the subject matter, or some other categorical arrangement.

In the Organizer window, two palettes help you sort your pictures and keep them well organized. You use the Tags palette, which we talk about in the next section, to identify individual images by using a limitless number of options for categorizing your pictures. The second palette is the Collections palette. Here you can create collections and collection groups to neatly organize files.

Collections are handy when you want to use the many different creation options that we explain in Chapter 16. You create a collection from files stored in various folders on your hard drive and preview the images to be used in a creation. Select the images you want to use when creating slide shows, photo albums, and so on. When you finish with the creations, go back and delete the collection.

In the following sections, you find out how to create and manage collections.

Creating a new collection

To create a new collection and add photos to the collection, do the following:

1. **Open photos in the Organizer.**

   Open the Organizer window by clicking the Photo Browser button in an editing mode or selecting View and Organize Photos on the Welcome screen. Choose File⇨Get Photos⇨From Files and Folders. Note that you should have copied some photos to your hard drive, as we explain in Chapter 4.

2. **If you don't see the Collections tab and the Organize Bin open, choose Window⇨ Organize Bin.**

   By default, the Organize Bin should be open to the Collections tab.

3. **To create a new Collection, choose New⇨ New Collection on the Collections tab.**

   The Edit Collection dialog box opens, as shown in Figure 6-1.

Figure 6-1: The Edit Collection dialog box.

4. **Type a name for the Collection in the Name text box and add a note to describe the collection.**

   You might use the location where you took the photos, the subject matter, or other descriptive information.

5. **Click OK in the Edit Collection dialog box.**

   You return to the Organizer window.

6. **In the Organizer window, select the photos you want to add to your collection.**

   Click a photo and Shift-click another photo to select photos in a group. Click a photo and Ctrl-click different photos scattered around the Organizer window to select photos in a nonconsecutive order.

7. **To add the selected photos to the new collection, click one of the selected photos in the Organizer window and drag the photo thumbnail to the new collection icon in the Organize Bin.**

   When you release the mouse button, the photos are added to the new collection.

8. **Repeat Steps 3 through 7 to create collections for all the images you want to organize.**

9. **To view one or more collections, click the empty square(s) adjacent to a collection icon to show the photos within that collection in the Organizer window.**

   When you click the empty square, an icon in the shape of a pair of binoculars appears inside the square, as shown in Figure 6-2.

Figure 6-2: Click the empty square adjacent to the collection icon.

Working with collections

You can manage collections by using menu commands from the New drop-down menu and other commands from a context menu opened by right-clicking a collection in the Collections tab.

From the New drop-down menu, you have commands for

- ✔ **New Collection:** Create a new collection, as described in the steps earlier in this chapter.

- ✔ **New Collection Group:** You can group several collections in a collection group and share your files with a sharing service. Select multiple collections and select New Collection Group to open the Create Collection Group dialog box.

✓ **Save Collections to a File:** You can save collections to a file that can be retrieved using the From File command. This option is handy when you open a different catalog file and you want to import the same collection names created in one catalog file to another catalog file. (See "Cataloging Files," later in this chapter.)

✓ **From File:** Import a saved collection.

Right-click the mouse button on a collection name and the following menu commands appear:

✓ **Edit <collection name> Collection:** Select Edit <collection name> Collection and the Edit Collection dialog box opens, as shown in Figure 6-1. You can use this command to rename a collection or change the note. Alternatively, you can click the Pencil tool in the palette to open the same dialog box.

✓ **Delete <collection name> Collection:** Select a collection and click this menu option to delete a collection. Alternatively, click the Trash icon in the palette to delete a collection. Note that deleting a collection does not delete files.

✓ **Find Items in <collection name> Collection:** Opening a context menu on a collection not visible in the Organizer window and selecting this option is the same as when you click the empty square adjacent to a collection icon. All the photos in the collection appear in the Organizer window.

✓ **Add <number> Items to <collection name> Collection:** If you select one photo in the organizer, the number is one. Selecting more than one photo changes the number to the total number of selected images. When you open a context menu, the selected image(s) is added to the collection where the context menu is opened.

Collections are automatically saved with the Catalog you work with. By default, Elements creates a Catalog and auto-saves your work to the Catalog. If you happen to create another Catalog, as we explain next in this chapter, your collections disappear. You need to be aware of what Catalog is open when you create collections in order to return to them.

Cataloging Files

As you open files in the Organizer, all your files are automatically saved to a catalog. The files themselves are not really saved to the catalog, but rather links from the catalog to the individual files are saved. *Links* are like pointers that tell the catalog where to look for a file. As you add and delete files, the catalog is constantly updated.

As you open more files in the Organizer, the default catalog file grows, and the maximum size of the catalog file is limited only by your available hard drive space. Working with a single catalog file has some disadvantages. For example, if your catalog file becomes corrupted and unrecoverable, you lose all the work you've done organizing files into collections. If you work with many files, the Organizer performance slows down.

Rather than work with a single catalog file, you can fine-tune your file organization by creating several catalogs. You might want to organize files according to subject matter, dates, locations, or some other division of categories and create separate catalogs for each category. You find all the details in the sections that follow.

Splitting a big catalog into smaller catalogs

Here's how you go about breaking up a large catalog into a smaller one:

1. **Open files in the Organizer.**

   If you have a large collection of files, say 100 images or more, open in an Organizer window, you can start with your open files. If you don't yet have files open, use the File⇨Get Photos menu command and get photos from one of the submenu commands to load up the Organizer window.

2. **Open the Catalog dialog box, shown in Figure 6-3, by choosing File⇨Catalog.**

   Here's something to keep in mind when working with catalogs: You don't create or access catalogs by using menu commands. All the aspects of working with a catalog are handled in the Catalog dialog box.

Figure 6-3: Choose File⇨Catalog to open the Catalog dialog box.

3. **Duplicate the catalog file by clicking the Save As button in the Catalog dialog box.**

   The Save Catalog As dialog box opens. By using Save As, you are duplicating the current Organizer window and saving it as a new catalog file.

4. **Type a descriptive name for the catalog in the File Name text box and click OK.**

   When you're done, you return to the Organizer window.

5. **Add and delete files in the Organizer.**

   You can delete files that don't belong to your newly created catalog topic and add additional files by using the File⇨Get Photos menu command. Furthermore, you can add or delete collections, as described in the preceding section in this chapter. The view you create in the Organizer is automatically saved to your new catalog file.

When you delete a file from a catalog, Elements prompts you in a dialog box to confirm the deletion. Also in the dialog box is a check box for deleting files from your hard disk. If you check the box, the file is deleted from your hard disk. Be certain to exercise caution so you don't inadvertently delete your only copy of a photo.

Importing photos to a new catalog

To keep your photos organized and your catalog files smaller, you can start a completely new catalog before you import photos. Follow these steps:

1. **Choose File⇨Catalog and click New in the Catalog dialog box.**

2. **When the New Catalog dialog box opens, type a name for the new catalog in the File Name text box and click Save.**

3. **If you want to add free music files installed with Elements, check the box for Import Free Music into All New Catalogs.**

4. **You can use the File⇨Get Photos menu commands to add files to the new catalog.**

   When the Get Photos from Files and Folders dialog box opens, a list of media files appears in the dialog box when the Import Free Music into All New Catalogs checkbox is enabled. You can select the free music files to add to your collection; then navigate your hard drive and check the photos you want to add. After you've identified all files, click Open and the selected music files and photos are added to your new collection.

Switching to a different catalog

When you need to open a different catalog file, choose File⇨Catalog and click Open. All your catalogs appear in the default folder where the catalogs are saved. Click a catalog and click Open and the Organizer window changes to reflect files contained in the respective catalog.

Note in Figure 6-3 the Recover button. If you can't see thumbnail previews of images or open them in one of the editing modes, your catalog file may be corrupted. Click the Recover button to try to fix the problem.

Tag — You're It!

If you want to sort files into subcategories, Elements provides *tags* for identifying common files.

Think of a catalog as being a parent item and collections as its children. Within collections, you can sort files according to date by using sort options discussed in Chapter 5. If you still have a number of files in an Organizer window that are hard to manage, you can create tags that form subcategories within the collections. These tags can be

- Ratings you assign to files, such as five stars down to one star in the Favorites area of the Tags palette.

- Groups like family, friends, and places.

- Some other custom category you want to define by tagging files with these items.

After creating tags and applying the tags to files in a catalog, clicking the box adjacent to a tag name in the Tags palette in the Organize Bin shows you all files assigned to the given tag. You can further sort the tagged files according to date, as described in Chapter 5.

Tags are handled with menu commands from the Tags drop-down menu. Click the Tags tab in the Organize Bin and click the down arrow adjacent to the New button to open the menu. Menu options associated with tags are

- **New Tag:** Click this menu command to open the Create Tag dialog box, where new tags are added to the Tags palette.

- **New Subcategory:** Select this menu command to create a new subcategory.

- **New Category:** Select this menu command to create a new tag category.

- **From File.** Select this menu command to load tags that were saved using the Save Tags to File command.

- **Save Tags to File.** Select this menu command to save tags to an XML (eXtensible Markup Language) file. XML files can be exported and imported in various ways in Elements, such as when using Collections and Tags. You can then open a different catalog, use the From File command, and all the new tags created in another catalog are imported into the current open catalog. This feature can save you a lot of time organizing files.

As an example, suppose you're a wedding photographer and you create catalogs for each individual wedding you shoot (if you combine a few weddings in one catalog, you can create separate collections for each individual wedding). You can create tags for the pre-ceremony shots of the bride dressing, the groom dressing, another set of tags for the ceremony, and another set of tags for the reception. After you create your first catalog and identify the tags, export the file by using the Save Tags to File command. Each time you shoot a new wedding, you load the tags into a new catalog file by using the From File menu command.

Creating new tags

New tags can be added as subsets to existing tags. You can create new tags, add icons for the appearance of tags, and assign tags to selected files in a catalog file.

Here's how you go about creating tags:

1. **Choose File⇨Catalog and open a catalog you created for a particular category.**

   If you haven't created a catalog, use files you open in the Organizer window.

2. **On the Tags tab in the Organize Bin, choose New⇨New Tag.**

   The Create Tag dialog box opens.

3. **To add an icon appearance, click the Edit Icon button.**

   The icon you add appears in the Tags palette to help you easily identify tags. The Edit Tag Icon dialog box shown in Figure 6-4 opens.

4. **Click the Import button.**

   The Import Image for Tag Icon dialog box opens.

5. **Locate an image you want to use, select it, and click Open.**

   You can use any photo saved in .jpg, .bmp, .png, or .gif format. (See Chapter 3 for more information on file formats.) When the image is imported, an image preview is displayed in the dialog box, as shown in Figure 6-4.

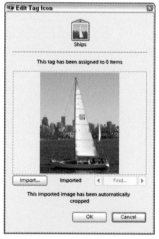

Figure 6-4: Click Edit Icon in the Create Tag dialog box to open the Edit Tag Icon dialog box.

6. **If the image preview is what you want, click OK in the Edit Tag Icon dialog box. If not, click the Import button and select another image.**

You return to the Create Tag dialog box, shown in Figure 6-5, after importing an icon.

7. The Category drop-down menu identifies all the categories currently in the Tags palette. Select the category where you want your new tag to appear as a child to the category.

8. Type a name for your tag in the Name text box.

9. Add a note to describe the tag.

10. Click OK when finished.

Your new tag is added to the Tags palette.

Figure 6-5: The Create Tag dialog box.

Creating new categories

In the Create Tag dialog box, the categories in the Category drop-down menu come from the category list in the Tags palette. If you want to use a category not available among the default tags, you can create your own new custom category by following these steps:.

1. Choose File⇨Catalog and open a catalog you created for a particular category.

If you haven't created a catalog, use files you open in the Organizer window.

2. On the Tags palette, choose New⇨ New Category.

The Create Category dialog box shown in Figure 6-6 opens.

3. Click the Choose Color button in the Create Category dialog box and select a color from the color palette that opens.

4. Type a name for the category in the Category Name text box.

5. Select an icon in the Category Icon list by clicking it.

Figure 6-6: The Create Category dialog box.

You can scroll the list of icons by dragging the slider bar back and forth or click the left and right arrows. All icons you can assign to a category are available from this list. Elements doesn't provide an option for creating custom icons for categories.

6. Click OK.

The category is added to the Tags palette.

Creating new subcategories

When you open the Organizer and click the Tags palette, you see several tag categories that Elements provides you by default. Categories such as Hidden, People, Places, Events, and Other are tags that always appear when you create any new collection. If you want to add custom subcategories to these default tags, Elements offers you a menu command to do so.

Do the following to create a subcategory:

1. **In the Organizer window, open a catalog in which you created a custom category.**

2. **On the Tags palette, choose New⇨ New Sub-Category.**

   The Create Sub-Category dialog box opens, as shown in Figure 6-7.

   Alternatively, you can right-click a tag in the Tags palette and select Create New Sub-Category in <category or subcategory name> Category.

3. **Type a name for the subcategory in the Sub-Category Name text box.**

Figure 6-7: The Create Sub-Category dialog box.

4. **Select a parent category from the Parent Category or Sub-Category drop-down list.**

   Subcategories appear as children below parent categories or below other subcategories. You can see all the categories and subcategories created in the open catalog.

5. **Click OK.**

   The subcategory is added below the category or subcategory in the Tags palette.

Assigning and managing tags

After creating categories and subcategories in the Tags palette, you'll want to assign tags to files. Once the tags are assigned, you can further manage the tags.

To assign tags to a file, do any of the following:

- ✔ **Drag and drop files to a tag.** You can drag one or more files shown in the Organizer window and drop the file(s) on top of a tag in the Tags palette. The file(s) is then tagged.

- ✔ **Drag and drop a tag to a file.** You can tag files by dragging and dropping a tag from the Tags palette to a file in the Organizer window or to a group of selected files.

- ✔ **Tag categories.** Drag a file to a category name or drag the category name in the Tags palette to the selected file(s). The tag appears at the root of a category and does not appear in any subcategories.

- ✔ **Tag subcategories.** Drag a file to a subcategory name or drag the sub-category name in the Tags palette to the selected file(s). The tag appears in the subcategory and does not appear in the root category.

- ✔ **Use a menu command.** Select a file or files in the Organizer and then right-click a category or subcategory name. From the context menu that appears, select Attach <category name> to <number> Selected Item(s).

Using a context menu opened by right-clicking a category or subcategory, you have menu options for managing files. The menu commands include the name of the category from which you open the context menu. The options in a context menu are

- ✔ **Create New Tag in <category name> Category:** Creates a new tag as if using the New Tag command from the New drop-down menu in the Tags palette.

- ✔ **Create New Sub-Category in <category name> Category:** Creates a new subcategory as if using the New Sub-Category command in the New drop-down menu in the Tags palette.

- ✔ **Edit <category name> Category:** Use this command when you want to edit a category name, icon appearance, or parent/subcategory.

- ✔ **Delete <category name> Category:** Select a category or subcategory and choose this menu command to delete it. Alternatively, you can click the Trash icon in the Tags palette.

- ✔ **Expand All Tags in <category name> Category:** Child subcategories can be either hidden or in view below a category name. Select this menu command to show the subcategories in the Tags palette.

- ✔ **Collapse All Tags in <category name> Category:** Select this command to hide subcategories in the Tags palette.

- ✔ **New Search Using <category name> Category:** Selecting this menu item results in the same view as when clicking the square in the Tags palette adjacent to a tag name. Only files with the selected tag are viewed in the Organizer.

- ✔ **Add Photos with <category name> Category to Search Results:** You can search for photos in the Organizer by using the search options discussed in Chapter 5. Use this menu item to add tagged files to the search results.

- ✔ **Exclude Photos with <category name> Category from Search Results:** Use this command to exclude tagged items from search results.

Note that if you open a context menu on a category name versus opening a context menu on a subcategory name, the menu items change. If you don't see an option that's listed here when opening a context menu on a category, open a context menu on a subcategory and you'll find the command.

Hiding Files That Get in the Way

Elements offers a few ways to hide files so you can keep your images organized and easy to find.

The hidden tag is in the Tags palette. This tag hides files in the Organizer window. You might use the hidden tag to hide similar images or one image with different variations while keeping only one image in view in the Organizer window. (You can tag files with the hidden tag by using any of the methods for tagging files that we discuss in the preceding section.) Files remain hidden when you check the box adjacent to the Hidden tag.

Other ways to hide images are to create *stacks* and *versions*. Again, thinking about an image with several different variations or versions, you can create a stack in which the best image is displayed in the Organizer window and all members of the stack group are hidden behind that foreground image. Additionally, you can create a version set, in which different versions of the same image are hidden while one version remains in view in the Organizer. In the following sections, we explain in more detail how you create stacks and versions.

Stack 'em up

Think of stacks like a stack of cards face-up. You see only the front card, and all the other cards are hidden behind that card. Stacks work the same way: You hide different images behind a foreground image. At any time, you can sort the images or display all images in the stack in the Organizer window.

To create a stack, follow these steps:

1. **In the Organizer, select several photos.**

   You can select any number of photos. You cannot stack audio or movie files.

2. **Choose Edit➪Stack➪Stack Selected Photos.**

   Elements stacks your photos. The first image you select remains in view in the Organizer window. In the upper right, an icon that looks like a stack of cards appears on the image thumbnail, as shown in the nearby figure. The thumbnail itself appears as though it sits atop a stack of other thumbnails.

After you stack a group of images, you can use the Stack submenu commands to manage the photos. Click a stack to select it and then choose Edit➪Stack. The submenu commands available include

- **Stack Selected Photos:** This command remains grayed out unless you have several photos selected to create a stack.

- **Unstack Photos:** Click a stack in the Organizer and select this command to return all images to the Organizer window and eliminate the stack.

- ✔ **Reveal Photos in Stack:** This command opens a new Organizer window and shows you all the individual images contained in a stack.

- ✔ **Flatten Stack:** After stacking some photos, this command becomes available.

  Be careful with this option. When you flatten a stack, all photos but the top photo are deleted from the catalog (not from your hard disk).

- ✔ **Remove Photo from Stack:** Selecting this command removes the selected photo(s) from the stack. The menu item is available only after you choose Reveal Photos in Stack. In the new Organizer window that appears, you can then select this menu command.

- ✔ **Set as Top Photo:** You also need to first Reveal Photos in Stack before accessing this command. If you don't like the topmost photo, select another and choose this menu command to move the selected photo to the top of the stack.

If you want to view all stacks in an Organizer window in an expanded form, choose View➪Expand All Stacks. Using this command does not require you to individually select stacks in the Organizer before expanding them.

Creating versions

Versions are similar to stacks, but you create versions from only one file. You can edit an image and save the edited version and the original as a version set. Additional edits can be made in either editing mode and saved to a version set.

To create a version set, do the following:

1. **Select an image by clicking it in the Organizer window.**

2. **Apply an edit.**

   For example, right in the Organizer, you can correct some brightness in your image. Choose Edit➪Auto Smart Fix to adjust contrast and brightness. See Chapter 10 for more details on adjusting contrast and brightness.

3. **View the items in the Version Set by clicking the image in the Organizer and choosing Edit➪Version Set➪Reveal Items in Version Set.**

   Elements automatically creates a version set for you when you apply the Auto Smart Fix to the file. A new Organizer window opens and shows two thumbnail images — one representing the original image and the other representing the edited version.

4. **To open the original in Standard Edit mode, select the original image and choose Edit➪Go to Standard Edit from the drop-down menu in the Organizer Shortcuts bar.**

5. **Edit the image in Standard Edit mode.**

   You can choose from many different menu commands to edit the image. As an example, change the color mode to Indexed Color by choosing Image⇨Mode⇨Indexed Color, as we explain in Chapter 3.

6. **Save a version by choosing File⇨Save As.**

7. **In the Save Options area of the Save As dialog box, check the boxes for Include in the Organizer and Save in Version Set with Original.**

8. **Click Save.**

   The edit made in Standard Edit mode is saved as another version in your version set.

When you have a version set, you can open the Edit⇨Version Set submenu and select menu commands that are similar to commands available with stacks (see the preceding section for details).

Sticking Digital Notes on Your Photos

A way to identify your files beyond the tagging capabilities discussed earlier in this chapter is to add *captions* and *notes.* When you add a caption and/or note, you can search captions and notes by choosing the Find⇨By Caption or Note menu command. Captions and notes are also helpful when creating different collections — like slide presentations and photo albums — by using the Create command, as we explain in Chapter 16.

Text captions are easy to create. Although you can select a thumbnail image in the Organizer window and select Edit⇨Add Caption, a better way is to use the Properties palette. Just follow these steps:

Figure 6-8: The Properties palette docked in the Organize Bin.

1. **To open the palette, select a thumbnail image in the Organizer, right-click it, and choose Show Properties from the context menu that appears.**

   Alternatively, you can select Window⇨ Properties. In either case the Properties palette opens, as shown in Figure 6-8.

2. **Type a caption by adding text to the Caption text box.**

3. **Type text in the Notes area in the palette to add a note.**

   That's all there is to it. You can also record audio notes about an image. Find out how in Bonus Chapter 1 on this book's Web site. (See the Introduction for details about the Web site.)

Automating Your Organization

If you have a number of common edits you want to make on a collection of photos, Elements lets you perform common changes to multiple files.

In earlier versions of Elements, you used the Process Multiple Files command for some of the features that have now been moved to the Export command in Photoshop Elements 4. Other features that were once in the Process Multiple Files dialog box, such as adding captions, have been moved to the Properties palette. File renaming can be part of the Export command, or you can use a menu option for renaming files in the Organizer.

Automating common tasks when you export

You may use the Export Selected Items dialog box frequently when acquiring images from digital cameras. What you may not know is that this dialog box can automate other common tasks, too:

- Add common base names for the filenames (for example, change names like DSC000001, DSC000002, and so on, to more descriptive filenames, like Budapest 001 and Budapest 002).
- Change file format.
- Change file size and quality.

Here's how you go about using options in the Export dialog box:

1. **Select files and open the Export Selected Items dialog box by choosing File➪Export➪To Computer.**

   The Export Selected Items dialog box opens, as shown in Figure 6-9.

   It's not critical to select files beforehand. You can identify files in another dialog box accessible from within the Export Selected Files dialog box. If you know ahead of time which files you want to export, go ahead and select them in the Organizer window.

2. **Select a file type.**

   From the File Type options, choose the format you want to use for the exported images. For more information on file formats, see Chapter 3.

3. **Select a size and quality.**

   If you select Original Format, resizing options are grayed out. You use this setting when you want to retain original size when you rename files. If you select JPEG, you can move the quality slider, as we explain in Chapter 3, for setting image quality of JPEG images. All other format options don't provide a quality option.

Figure 6-9: The Export Selected Items dialog box permits you to rename and change formats for batches of files.

For sizing images, select options from the Photo Size drop-down menu, where you find several fixed dimensions and an option for using a custom size.

4. **Select a target location for the new files by clicking the Browse button and selecting a folder.**

   If you want to create a new folder, you can click the Make New Folder button in the Browse for Folder dialog box that opens after you click the Browse button.

5. **If you want to keep the original filenames, select the Original Names radio button. If you want to rename files with a common base name, select Common Base Name and type a name in the text box.**

   The resultant files will be named <base name>001.extension, <base name>002.extension, <base name>003.extension, and so on.

6. **If you want to add files to the list for exporting, click the plus (+) symbol in the lower left.**

   This opens the Add Photos dialog box, shown in Figure 6-10, which offers a number of different options for selecting files to export. Among your choices are

   • **Photos Currently in Browser:** Use this button when you want to export all files shown in the Organizer window.

   • **Entire Catalog:** Use this button if you are viewing a catalog, tagged files, or a sorted group in which some files are temporarily hidden. When you select this option, all the hidden files are included in the export.

   • **Collection:** Click the Collection radio button and select from the drop-down menu a collection you want to export.

Figure 6-10: The Add Photos dialog box offers a number of options for exporting photos.

- **Tag:** Click the Tag radio button and select a tag from the drop-down menu. All files with the same tag are exported.

- **Photo Bin:** Click this radio button to select files in the Photo Bin. (See Chapter 4 for more information on using the Photo Bin.)

- **Show Favorites Only:** Favorites are those files you tagged with stars. Select Favorites and all files tagged with one or more stars are exported.

- **Show Hidden Photos:** Any file that may be hidden in the Organizer can be made visible in the file list and included in the export.

- **Select All:** As you add files to the list window, you can choose to export all files from the selected category. Click Select All and all the files are marked for export.

- **Deselect All:** If you want some files from the list window exported while others remain behind, click Deselect All and then individually check the boxes for all files you want to export.

- **Add Selected Photos:** When you add photos by using the options found under the Add Photos From area in the dialog box, the thumbnails for the images appear in a scrollable window inside the dialog box. You can choose individual photos by checking the boxes adjacent to each photo to be included in the export. After checking the photos you want to include, click this button. The button action does not dismiss the dialog box; it merely marks the files for inclusion.

- **Done:** Click this button to return to the Export Selected Items dialog box.

7. **Select any images you don't want included in the export by checking boxes adjacent to the thumbnails and clicking the minus (–) button.**

8. **Click Export, and Elements automatically exports the images to the selected folder.**

Renaming files

If you load up an Organizer window and you want to rename files, you don't need to use the Export command and wade through the options in the Export Selected Files dialog box. Just follow these steps:

1. **Select the files you want to rename.**

2. **Choose File⇨Rename.**

   The Rename dialog box opens.

3. **In the text box, type a base name for the files and click OK.**

   The selected files are renamed using a common base name. You'll find this a quick and easy way to rename those digital camera images.

Protecting Your Photos

The lesson most often learned *the hard way* by computer users is backing up a hard drive and the precious data you spent time creating and editing. We'll save you some aggravation right now before you spend any more time editing your photos in Elements.

Routine backup is critical for any kind of work you perform on computers.

We authors are so paranoid when writing a book that we back up our chapters on multiple drives, CDs, and DVDs as chapters are written. The standard rule is that if you spend sufficient time working on a project and it gets to the point at which redoing your work would be a major aggravation, it's time to back up files.

With files stored all over your hard drive, manually copying files to a second hard drive, CD-ROM, or DVD would take quite a bit of time. Fortunately, Elements makes the pains of finding files to back up a breeze.

Here's how you can use Elements to create a backup of your precious data:

1. **Choose File⇨Backup to open the Burn/Backup Wizard.**

   This wizard has three panes that Elements walks you through to painlessly create a backup of your files.

2. **Select the source to backup.**

   The first pane in the Burn/Backup Wizard offers two options:

   • *Copy/Move Files:* Use this option to copy files to the target media or hard disk location.

   • *Backup the Catalog:* Use this option to copy the catalog file.

3. **Click Next and select a backup method.**

   Depending on what you chose in the first pane, you have different options in the second pane. The options include

   Options for Copy/Move Files: If you select Copy/Move Files in the first pane, you can choose from the following:

   • *Move Files:* Check this box to move files to another media source and delete the files from your hard drive after moving them. Elements retains a file on your hard drive for identifying the source where files are copied. If you open the Organizer and attempt to edit a file, Elements prompts you to insert the media where the moved files are stored.

   • *Copy/Move All Files in the Stack:* Check this box to copy/move all files in Stacks.

   • *Copy/Move All Files in the Version Set:* Check this box to include all files in Version Sets.

Options for Backup the Catalog: If you select Backup the Catalog in the first pane, the options in Step 2 are

- *Full Backup:* Select this radio button to perform your first backup or when writing files to a new media source.

- *Incremental Backup:* Use this option if you have already performed at least one backup and you want to update the backed up files.

4. **Click Next and select the destination source.**

   Active drives, including CD/DVD drives attached to your computer, appear in the Select Destination Drive list, as shown in Figure 6-11. Select a drive, and Elements automatically assesses the write speed and identifies a previous backup file if one was created. The total size of the files to copy is reported in the wizard. This information is helpful so you know whether more than one CD or DVD are needed to complete the backup.

5. **If you intend to copy files to your hard drive or to another hard drive attached to your computer, click the Browse button and identify the path.**

   If you use a media source, such as a CD or DVD, Elements prompts you to insert a disc and readies the media for writing.

6. **Click the Back button if you need to revisit the first two steps and modify the options. When you're satisfied, click Done and the backup commences.**

   Be certain to not interrupt the backup. It may take some time, so just let Elements work away until you are notified that the backup is complete.

Figure 6-11: Step 3 in the wizard provides options for selecting the destination media for the backup.

Part III
Selecting and Correcting Photos

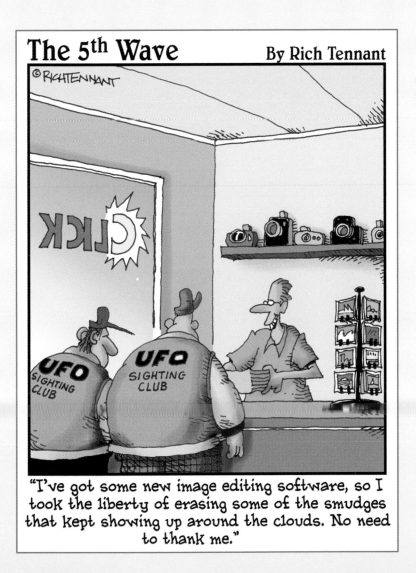

The 5th Wave By Rich Tennant

"I've got some new image editing software, so I took the liberty of erasing some of the smudges that kept showing up around the clouds. No need to thank me."

In this part . . .

*T*he wide array of editing features in Elements permit you to change, optimize, perfect, and combine images into composite designs. In this part, you find out how to select image content and later how to alter that content for a variety of purposes such as correcting color, changing the appearance, and extracting the content so you can introduce it in other photos. Because photos comprise many thousands of tiny pixels, you need to develop some skill in selecting just the pixels you want to use for any given editing task.

In addition to creating image selections, this part also covers correcting photos for image contrast and brightness, color correction, and color conversions from one color mode to another. Rarely will you ever encounter digital images that won't require some kind of correction. In the chapters ahead, you discover how to quickly master some powerful correction techniques.

Making and Modifying Selections

*I*f all you want to do is use your photos in all their unedited glory, then feel free to skip this chapter and move onto other topics. But if you want to occasionally pluck an element out of its environment and stick it in another, or apply an adjustment on just a portion of your image, then this chapter is for you.

Learning how to make accurate selections is one of those skills that is well worth the time invested. In this chapter, we cover all the various selection tools and techniques. We give you tips on which tools are better for which kinds of selections. But remember, you usually have several ways to achieve the same result. Which road you choose is ultimately up to you.

Defining Selections

Before you dig in and get serious about selecting, let us clarify for the record what we mean by *defining a selection*. By defining a selection, you specify which part of an image you want to work with. Everything within a selection is considered *selected*. Everything outside the selection is *unselected*. After you have a selection, you can then adjust just that portion, while the unselected portion remains unchanged. Or you can take the selected area and copy it into another image altogether. Want to transport yourself out of your background and onto a white sandy beach instead? Select yourself out of that backyard BBQ photo, get a stock photo of the tropical paradise of your choice, and drag and drop yourself onto your tropics photo with the Move tool. It's that easy.

When you make a selection, a dotted outline — variously called a *selection border,* an *outline,* or a *marquee* — appears around the selected area. Elements, being the sophisticated imaging program that it is, also allows you to partially select pixels, which allows for soft-edged selections. You create soft-edged selections by feathering or anti-aliasing the selection or by using a mask. Don't worry, we cover these techniques later in this chapter.

For all of the selection techniques described in this chapter, be sure that your image is in the Editor, in Standard Edit mode, and not in the Organizer.

Creating Rectangular and Elliptical Selections

If you can drag a mouse, you can master the Rectangular and Elliptical Marquee tools. These two tools are the easiest selection tools to use, so if your desired element is rectangular or elliptical, then by all means, grab one of these tools.

The Rectangular Marquee tool, as its moniker states, is designed to select rectangular or square selections. This is a great tool to use if you want to home in on the pertinent portion of your photo and eliminate unnecessary background.

Here's how to make a selection with this tool:

1. **Select the Rectangular Marquee tool from the Tools palette.**

   It looks like a dotted square. You can also press M to access the tool.

2. **Drag from one corner of the area you want to select to the opposite corner.**

   As you drag, the selection border appears. The marquee follows the movement of your mouse cursor.

3. **Release your mouse button.**

   You now have a completed rectangular selection, as shown in Figure 7-1.

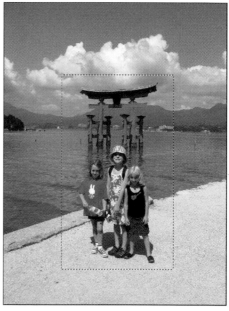

Figure 7-1: Use the Rectangular Marquee tool to create rectangular selections.

The Elliptical Marquee tool, which shares the same flyout menu as the Rectangular Marquee tool, is designed for elliptical or circular selections. This is the perfect tool for selecting balloons, clocks, and other rotund elements.

Here's how to use the Elliptical Marquee:

1. **Select the Elliptical Marquee tool from the Marquee flyout menu in the Tools palette.**

   Again, you can also use the keyboard short-cut. If the Rectangular Marquee is still visible, you need to press Shift+M. If the Elliptical Marquee tool is showing, press M.

2. **Position the crosshair near the area you want to select and then drag around your desired element.**

   With this tool, you don't drag from corner to corner. Instead, you drag from a given point on the ellipse. As you drag, the selection border appears.

3. **When you're satisfied with your selection, release your mouse button.**

   Your elliptical selection is done, as shown in Figure 7-2. If your selection isn't quite centered around your element, simply move the selection border by dragging inside the border.

Flat Earth

Figure 7-2: The Elliptical Marquee is perfect for selecting round objects.

TIP

You can move a selection while you're making it with either of the Marquee tools by pressing the spacebar while you're dragging.

Perfecting squares and circles with Shift and Alt

Sometimes you need to create a perfectly square or circular selection. To do so, simply press the Shift key after you begin dragging. When you have your desired selection, release the mouse button first and then release the Shift key.

When making an elliptical selection, making your selection from the center outward is often easier. To draw from the center, first click the mouse button and then, before you move the mouse, press Alt and drag. When you have your desired selection, release your mouse button first and then release the Alt key.

If you want to both draw from the center out and create a perfect circle or square, press the Shift key as well. After you have your desired selection, release your mouse button and then release the Shift+Alt keys.

Applying marquee options

The Marquee tools offer additional options when you need to make precise selections at specific measurements. You also find options for making your selections soft around the edges.

The only thing to remember is that you must select the options in the Options bar, shown in Figure 7-3, *before* you make your selection with the Marquee tools. They cannot be applied after the selection has already been made. The one exception is that you can feather a selection after the fact by choosing Select⇨Feather.

Figure 7-3: Apply marquee settings in the Options bar.

Here are the various marquee options available to you:

- **Feather:** Feathering creates soft edges around your selection. The amount of softness depends on the value, from 0 to 250 pixels, you enter. The higher the value, the softer the edges, as shown in Figure 7-4. Very small amounts of feathering can be used to create subtle transitions between selected elements in a collage. Larger amounts are often used when combining multiple layers so that one image gradually fades into another. If you just want a selected element to have a soft edge without the background, simply choose Select⇨Inverse and delete the background. See more on inversing selections in the "Modifying Your Selections" section, later in this chapter. For more on layers, see Chapter 8.

    Don't forget that those soft edges represent partially selected pixels.

- **Anti-alias:** Anti-aliasing barely softens the edge of an elliptical or irregularly shaped selection so that the jagged edges aren't quite so obvious. An anti-aliased edge is always only 1 pixel wide. We recommend leaving this option checked for your selections. It can help to create natural transitions between multiple selections when creating collages.

- **Mode:** The Mode drop-down list contains three settings:

    - **Normal** is the default setting, which allows you to freely drag a selection of any size.

    - **Fixed Aspect Ratio** lets you specify a fixed ratio of width to height. For example, if you enter **3** for width and **1** for height, you get a selection that's three times as wide as it is high, no matter what the size.

- **Fixed Size** lets you specify desired values for the Width and Height. This setting can be useful when you need to make several selections that must be the same size.

✓ **Width and Height:** When you select a Fixed Aspect Ratio or Fixed Size from the Mode drop-down list, you must also enter your desired values in the Width and Height text boxes. To swap the Width and Height values, click the double-headed arrow button between the two measurements.

The default unit of measurement in the Width and Height text boxes is pixels (px). But that doesn't mean you're stuck with it. You can actually enter any unit of measurement that Elements recognizes — pixels, inches, centimeters, millimeters, points, picas, or percents. Type your value and then type the word or abbreviation of your unit of measurement.

Feather 6 pixels   Feather 50 pixels

Corbis Digital Stock

Figure 7-4: Feathering creates soft-edged selections.

Making Freeform Selections with Lasso Tools

As we all know, you can't select everything with a rectangle or ellipse. Life is just way too freeform for that. Most animate, and many inanimate, objects have undulations of varying sorts. Luckily, Elements anticipated the need to capture these and provided the Lasso tools.

The Lasso tools enable you to make any freehand selection you can think of. Elements generously provides three types of lasso tools: the Lasso tool, the Polygonal Lasso tool, and the Magnetic Lasso tool. While all three tools are designed to make freeform selections, they differ slightly in their methodology, as we explain in the sections that follow.

To use these tools, all that's really required is a steady hand. You'll find that the more you use the Lasso tools, the better you become at your tracing technique. Don't worry if your initial lasso selection isn't super accurate. You can always go back and make corrections by adding and deleting from your selection. To find out how, see "Modifying Your Selections," later in this chapter.

If you find you really love the Lasso tools, you might want to consider investing in a digital drawing tablet and stylus. This makes tracing, and also drawing and painting, on the computer more comfortable. It better mimics pen and paper, and many users swear they will never go back to a mouse after trying it out.

Selecting with the Lasso tool

Using the Lasso tool is the digital version of tracing an outline around an object on a piece of paper. It's that easy. And you have only two choices on the Options bar — Feather and Anti-alias. To find out more about these options, see "Applying marquee options," earlier in this chapter.

Here's how to make a selection with the Lasso tool:

1. **Select the Lasso tool from the Tools palette.**

   It's the sixth tool from the top and looks like a rope. You can also just press the L key.

2. **Position the cursor anywhere along the edge of the object you want to select.**

   The leading point of the cursor is the protruding end of the rope, as shown in Figure 7-5. Don't be afraid to zoom into your object if you need to see the edge more distinctly. In my figure, I started at the top-left corner of the butterfly's wing.

3. **Hold down the mouse button and trace around your desired object. Try to include only what you want to select.**

As you trace around your object, an outline follows your mouse cursor.

Try not to release your mouse button until you return to your starting point. When you release your mouse button, Elements assumes you're done and closes the selection from wherever you released the mouse button to your starting point, creating a diagonal line across your image.

4. **Continue tracing around the object and return to your starting point; release the mouse button to close the selection.**

You see a selection border that matches your lasso line.

Lasso cursor

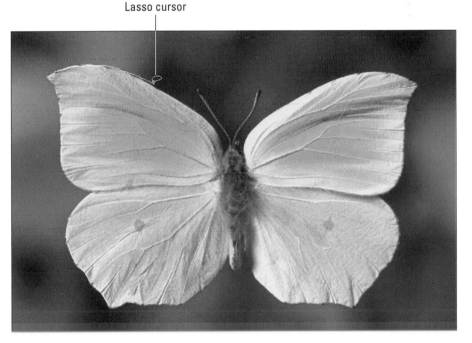

Corbis Digital Stock

Figure 7-5: The Lasso tool makes freeform selections.

Getting straight with the Polygonal Lasso tool

The Polygonal Lasso tool has a very specific mission in life: to select any element whose sides are straight. Think pyramids, stairways, skyscrapers, barns. You get the idea. It also works a tad differently than the Lasso tool. You don't drag around the element with the Polygonal Lasso. Instead, you click and release the mouse button at the corners of the element you're selecting. The Polygonal Lasso tool acts like a stretchy rubber band.

Follow these steps to select with the Polygonal Lasso tool:

1. **Select the Polygonal Lasso tool from the Tools palette.**

   You can also press the L key and then press Shift+L until you get the Polygonal Lasso tool.

2. **Click and release at any point to start the Polygonal Lasso selection line.**

   We usually start at a corner.

3. **Move (don't drag) the mouse and click at the next corner of the object. Continue clicking and moving to each corner of your element.**

   Notice how the line stretches out from each point you click.

4. **Return to your starting point** and click to close the selection.

   Be on the lookout for a small circle that appears next to your lasso cursor when you return to your starting point. This is an indication that you are indeed closing the selection at the right spot.

   Note that you can also double-click at any point and Elements will close the selection from that point to the starting point.

   Upon closing the polygonal lasso line, a selection border should appear, as in Figure 7-6.

Corbis Digital Stock

Figure 7-6: Upon closing the lasso line, Elements creates a selection border.

Snapping with the Magnetic Lasso tool

The third member of the Lasso team is the Magnetic Lasso. We aren't huge fans of this Lasso tool, which sometimes can be hard to work with. But we show you how it works so you can decide for yourself whether to use it. The Magnetic Lasso tool works by defining the areas of the most contrast in an image and then snapping to the edge between those areas, as if the edge had a magnetic pull.

You'll have the most success using the Magnetic Lasso tool on images that have a well-defined foreground object and high contrast between that element and the background — for example, a dark mountain range against a light sky.

The Magnetic Lasso tool also has some unique settings, which you can adjust on the Options bar before you start selecting:

- **Width:** Determines how close to the edge (between 1 and 256 pixels) you have to move your mouse before the Magnetic Lasso tool snaps to that edge. Use a lower value if the edge has lots of detail or if the contrast in the image is low. Use a higher value for high-contrast images or smoother edges.

- **Edge Contrast:** Specifies the amount of contrast (from 1 to 100) that is required before the Magnetic Lasso snaps to an edge. Use a higher percentage if your image has good contrast between your desired element and the background.

- **Frequency:** Specifies how many points (from 1% to 100%) to place on the selection line. The higher the percentage, the greater number of points. As a general rule, if the element you want to select has a smooth edge, keep the percentage low. If the edge has a lot of detail, try a higher percentage.

- **Tablet Pressure (pen icon):** If you are the proud owner of a pressure-sensitive drawing tablet, select this option to make an increase in stylus pressure cause the edge width to decrease.

Follow these steps to use the Magnetic Lasso tool:

1. **Select the Magnetic Lasso tool from the Tools palette.**

   You can also press the L key and then press Shift+L until you get the Magnetic Lasso tool. The tool looks like a straight-sided lasso with a little magnet on it.

2. **Click the edge of the object you want to select to place the first *fastening point.***

Fastening points anchor down the selection line, as shown in Figure 7-7. You can start anywhere; just be sure to click the edge between the element you want and the background you don't want.

3. **Continue to move your cursor around the object, without clicking.**

As the selection line gets pinned down with fastening points, only the newest portion of the selection line remains active.

If the Magnetic Lasso tool starts veering off the desired edge of your object, back up your mouse and click to force down a fastening point. And, conversely, if the Magnetic Lasso tool adds a fastening point where you don't want one, press your Backspace key to delete it.

If the Magnetic Lasso isn't cooperating, you can temporarily switch to the other Lasso tools. To get the Lasso tool, press Alt and press the mouse button and then drag. To get the Polygonal Lasso tool, press Alt and click.

4. **Return to your starting point and click the mouse button to close the selection.**

You will see a small circle next to your cursor indicating that you're at the right spot to close the selection. You can also double-click, whereby Elements closes the selection from where you double-clicked to your starting point. The selection border appears when the selection is closed.

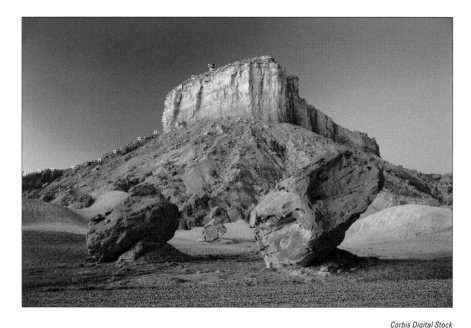

Corbis Digital Stock

Figure 7-7: The Magnetic Lasso tool snaps to the edge of your element and places fastening points to anchor the selection.

Working Wizardry with the Magic Wand

The Magic Wand tool is one of the oldest tools in the world of digital imaging. This beloved tool has been around since both Photoshop and Elements were in their infancies. It's extremely easy to use, but a little harder to predict what selection results it will present to you.

Here's how it works: You click inside the image, and the Magic Wand tool makes a selection. This selection is based on the color of the pixel you clicked. If there are other pixels that are similar in color to your target pixel, Elements includes them in the selection. What's sometimes hard to predict, however, is how to determine how *similar* the color has to be to get the Magic Wand tool to select it. Fortunately, that's where the *tolerance* setting comes in. In the sections that follow, we first introduce you to this setting and then explain how to put the Magic Wand to work.

Talking about tolerance

The tolerance setting determines the range of color that the Magic Wand tool selects. It's based on brightness levels that range from 0 to 255. That being said:

- Setting the Tolerance to 0 selects one color only.
- Setting the Tolerance to 255 selects all colors, or the whole image.

The default setting is 32. This means that when you click a pixel, Elements analyzes the value of that base color and then selects all pixels whose brightness levels are between 16 levels lighter and 16 levels darker.

What if an image contains a few shades of the same color? Not a huge problem. You can make multiple clicks of the Magic Wand to pick up additional pixels you want to include in the selection. You can find out how in the section, "Modifying Your Selections," later in this chapter. Or you can try a higher tolerance setting. Conversely, if your wand selects too much, you can also lower your tolerance setting.

So you can see by our talk on tolerance that the Magic Wand tool works best when you have high contrast images or images with a limited number of colors. For example, the optimum image for the Wand would be a solid black object on a white background. Skip the wand if the image has a ton of colors and no real definitive contrast between your desired element and the background.

Wielding the Wand to select

To use the Magic Wand tool and adjust tolerance settings, follow these steps:

1. **Select the Magic Wand tool from the Tools palette.**

   You can't miss it. It looks like a wand, or maybe a fuzzy lollipop. You can also just press W.

2. **Click anywhere on your desired element, using the default tolerance setting of 32.**

   Remember, the pixel that you click determines the base color.

   If the pixel gods are with you, and you selected everything you wanted on the first click, you're done. If your selection needs further tweaking, like the top image in Figure 7-8, continue to the next step.

3. **Specify a new Tolerance setting in the Options bar.**

Tolerance 32

Tolerance 80

Corbis Digital Stock

Figure 7-8: The Magic Wand selects pixels based on a specified Tolerance setting.

If the Magic Wand selected more than you wanted, lower the tolerance setting. If it didn't select enough, increase the value. While you're poking around the Options bar, here's a couple more options to get familiar with:

- **Contiguous:** Forces the Magic Wand to select *only* pixels that are adjacent to each other. Without this option, the tool selects all pixels within the range of tolerance, whether or not they're adjacent to each other.

- **Sample All Layers:** If you have multiple layers and enable this option, the Magic Want selects pixels from all visible layers. Without this option, the tool selects pixels from the active layer only. For more on layers, see Chapter 8.

4. **Click again on your desired element.**

   Unfortunately, the Magic Wand tool isn't magical enough to modify your first selection automatically. Instead, it deselects the current selection and makes a new selection based on your new Tolerance setting. If it still isn't right, you can adjust the Tolerance setting again. Try, try again.

Modifying Your Selections

It's time for a seventh-inning stretch in this chapter on selection tools. In this section, you find out how to refine that Marquee, Lasso, or Magic Wand selection to perfection. Although these tools do an okay job of capturing the bulk of your selection, if you take the time to add or subtract from your selection border a bit, you can ensure that you get only what you really want.

You're not limited to the manual methods described below, or even to keyboard shortcuts. You can also use the four selection option buttons on the right side of the Options bar to create a new selection (the default), add to a selection, subtract from a selection, or intersect one selection with another. Just choose your desired selection tool, click the selection option button you want, and drag (or click if you're using the Magic Wand or Polygonal Lasso tool). The add and select button are also available when using the Selection Brush. When adding to a selection, a small plus sign appears next to your cursor. When subtracting from a selection, a small minus sign appears. When intersecting two selections, a small multiplication sign appears.

Adding to a selection

If your selection doesn't quite contain all of the elements you wish to capture, you need to add those portions to your current selection border. To add to a current selection, simply press the Shift key and drag around the area you want to include. If you are using the Polygonal Lasso, click around the area. And if you're wielding the Magic Wand, just press the Shift key and click the area you want.

You don't have to use the same tool to add to your selection that you used to create the original selection. Feel free to use whatever selection tool you think can get the job done. For example it is very common to start off with the Magic Wand and fine-tune with the Lasso tool.

Subtracting from a selection

Got too much? To subtract from a current selection, press the Alt key and drag around the pixels you want to subtract. With the Alt key, use the same method for the Magic Wand and Polygonal Lasso as you do for adding to a selection.

Intersecting two selections

Get your fingers in shape. To intersect your existing selection with a second selection, press the Shift and Alt keys together and drag with the Lasso tool. Or if you're using the Magic Wand or Polygonal Lasso, press and click instead of dragging.

Avoiding key collisions

If you read the beginning of this chapter, you found out that by pressing the Shift key, you get a perfectly square or circular selection. We just told you that if you want to add to a selection, you press the Shift key. What if you want to create a perfect square while adding to the selection? Or what if you want to delete part of a selection while also drawing from the center out? Both require the use of the Alt key. How in the heck does Elements know what you want? Here are a few tips to avoid keyboard collisions. Grab your desired Marquee tool.

✔ **To add a square or circular selection, press Shift and drag.** As you drag, keep your mouse button pressed, release the Shift key for just a second, and then press it down again. Your added selection area will suddenly snap into a square or circle. You must then release the mouse button first, then release Shift key last.

✔ **To delete from an existing selection while drawing from the center outward, press Alt and drag.** As you drag, keep your mouse button pressed, release the Alt key for just a second, and then press it down again. You will now be drawing from the center outward. Again, release the mouse button first, then release the Alt key last.

Painting with the Selection Brush

If you like the more organic feel of painting on a canvas, you'll appreciate the Selection Brush. Using two different modes, you can either paint over areas of an image that you want to select or paint over areas you don't want to select. This great tool also lets you make a basic, rudimentary selection with another tool, such as the Lasso, and then fine-tune the selection by brushing additional pixels into or out of the selection.

Here is the step-by-step process of selecting with the Selection Brush:

1. **Select the Selection Brush from the Tools palette, or simply press the A key.**

   This tool works in either Standard Edit or Quick Fix mode.

2. **Specify your Selection Brush options in the Options bar.** Here's the run down on each:

   • **Brush Presets:** Choose a brush from the presets drop-down palette. To load additional brushes, click the downward-pointing arrow to the left of Default Brushes and choose the preset library of your choice. You can select the Load Brushes command from the palette pop-up menu.

- **Brush Size:** Specify your desired brush size, from 1 to 2500 pixels. Enter the value or drag the slider.

- **Mode:** Choose between *Selection* and *Mask*. Choose Selection to add to your selection, and choose Mask to subtract from your selection. If you choose Mask mode, you must choose some additional Overlay options. An *overlay* is a layer of color (that shows onscreen only) that hovers over your image, indicating protected or unselected areas. You must also choose an Overlay Opacity between 1 and 100% (described in a Tip, later in this section). You can also choose to change the Overlay Color from the default red to another color. This can be helpful if your image contains a lot of red.

- **Hardness:** Set the hardness of the brush tip, from 1 to 100%.

3. **If your mode is set to Selection, paint over the areas you wish to select.**

   You see a selection border. Each stroke adds to the selection. If you inadvertently add something you don't want, simply press the Alt key and paint over the undesired area. After you finish painting what you want, your selection is ready to go.

4. **If your mode is set to Mask, paint over the areas you *do not* want to select.**

   This mode does the opposite of the Selection mode. When you're done painting your Mask, choose Selection from the Mode drop-down menu, or simply choose another tool from the Tools palette, in order to convert your mask into a selection border.

   As you paint, you see the color of your overlay. Each stroke adds more to the overlay area, as shown in Figure 7-9. When working in Mask mode, you are essentially covering up, or masking, the areas you wish to protect from manipulation. That manipulation can be selecting, adjusting color, or any other Elements command. Again, if you want to remove parts of the masked area, press Alt and paint.

   Don't forget: If you painted your selection in Mask mode, your selection border is around what you *don't* want. To switch to what you do want, choose Select⇨Inverse.

   Which mode should you choose? Well, it's up to you. But one advantage to working in Mask mode is that you can partially select areas. By painting with soft brushes, you create soft edged selections. These soft edges result in partially selected pixels. If you set your Overlay Opacity to a lower percentage, your pixels will be even less opaque, or "less selected." If this partially selected business sounds vaguely familiar, it's because this is also what happens when you feather selections, as we discuss earlier in this chapter.

Corbis Digital Stock

Figure 7-9: The Selection Brush allows you to make a selection (right) by creating a mask (left).

Painting with the Magic Selection Brush

The word "Magic" in front of any noun usually makes us think we are in for an especially beneficial payoff. So when you see the *Magic* Selection Brush, you're probably thinking, "Whoa, Nelly, it's new, it's magic . . . this has gotta be good." Theoretically speaking, this new tool makes a selection when you simply draw, scribble, add a brush dot, or otherwise casually mar the area you wish to select. And what's more, theoretically speaking, you don't even have to precisely trace the object. Elements selects the object you want based on your brush stroke!

Okay, we'll cut the sarcasm and get to the point. While this tool has some potential, it really works the best when you provide it with as much data as possible. This means that rather than just adding a dot or scribble on your desired element, if you take a few seconds longer to paint at least a rudimentary outline around the element, you'll end up with a more accurate selection. By making a decent outline, you provide data for the tool's algorithm to figure out what it is you want to select. Similarly, if you further refine that initial selection by deleting and adding areas, you provide even more data, and the tool rewards you with an even more accurate selection. Unlike the Magic Wand, which allows you to add and delete incrementally to an existing selection, the Magic Selection Brush redraws your selection from scratch each time you modify it. It also differs from the Magic Wand in that it doesn't only analyze color to make the selection, but relies even more on texture.

By the way, this tool works in either Standard Edit or Quick Fix mode.

Now that you understand the mechanical reasoning behind the Magic Selection Brush, here's how to select with this new tool:

1. **Select the Magic Selection Brush tool from the Tools palette.**

   You can also press the F key.

2. **Specify the options in the Options bar.** Here is a description of the options:

   - **New Selection:** The default option enables you to create a new selection.

   - **Indicate Foreground (+ icon):** Allows you to add to an existing selection.

   - **Indicate Background (– icon):** Enables you to subtract from an existing selection.

   - **Overlay Color:** As with the Selection brush, you can change the color of your overlay from the default red to the color of your choice.

   - **Brush Size:** Choose a brush size, from 1 to 100 pixels, from the Size menu. If you want to try to make a more precise outline, we suggest using a smaller brush.

3. **Select an area by clicking your mouse on it, dragging a brush stroke around it, or painting over it. When you're done, release your mouse button.**

   Upon releasing the mouse, your selection border should appear. If the Magic Selection Brush gave you what you wanted, you're done. If your selection needs refinement, go to Step 4. (Most likely, we'll be seeing you at Step 4.)

4. **To add to your existing selection, activate the Indicate Foreground option in the Options bar. Click, drag, or paint over the areas you want to add. To delete from your existing selection, activate the Indicate Background option in the Options bar. Click, drag, or paint over the areas you want to remove from your existing selection.**

   Note that if your object is fairly detailed, like my Lacy Seahorse, you may even need to break out the Lasso or another selection tool to make some final clean-ups. Eventually, you should arrive at a selection you're happy with, as shown in Figure 7-10.

Corbis Digital Stock

Figure 7-10: The Magic Selection Brush analyzes color and texture to determine your desired selection.

Using the Cookie Cutter Tool

The Cookie Cutter tool is a cute name for a pretty powerful tool. You can think of it as a Custom Shape tool for images. But while the Custom Shape tool creates a mask and just hides everything outside the shape, the Cookie Cutter actually crops away everything outside the shape. The preset libraries offer you a large variety of interesting shapes, from talk bubbles to Swiss cheese. (I'm not being funny here, check out the food library.)

Here's the lowdown on using the Cookie Cutter:

1. **Choose the Cookie Cutter tool from the Tools palette.**

   There's no missing it; it looks like a heart. You can also press the Q key.

2. **Specify your options in the Options bar.** Here's the list:

   - **Shape:** Choose your desired shape from the preset library. To load other libraries, click the palette pop-up menu and choose one from the submenu.

   - **Shape Options:** These options let you draw your shape with certain parameters, as follows. **Unconstrained,** the default, enables you to draw freely. **Defined Proportions** enables you to keep the height and width proportional. **Defined Size** crops the image to the original, fixed size of the shape you choose. You can't make it bigger or smaller. **Fixed Size** allows you to enter your desired width and height. And **From Center** allows you to draw the shape from the center out.

- **Feather:** This creates a soft-edged selection. See "Applying marquee options," earlier in this chapter, for more details.

- **Crop:** Click this option to crop the image into the shape. Figure 7-11 shows an image cropped to the shape of an elephant.

3. **Drag your mouse on the image to create your desired shape. Size your shape by dragging one of the handles of the bounding box. Position your shape by placing your mouse cursor inside the box and dragging.**

   You can also perform other types of transformations, such as rotating and skewing. For more on transformations, see Chapter 9.

4. **Click the Commit button in the Options bar or press Enter to finish the cropping.**

   If you want to bail out of the bounding box and not crop, you can always press the Cancel button in the Options bar or press Esc.

Corbis Digital Stock

Figure 7-11: Crop your photo into interesting shapes with the Cookie Cutter.

Eliminating with the Eraser Tools

The eraser tools let you erase areas of your image. There are three eraser tools — the regular Eraser, the Magic Eraser, and the Background Eraser. The eraser tools look like those pink erasers you used in grade school, so you can't miss them. If you can't locate them, you can always press E and then Shift+E to toggle through the three tools.

When you erase pixels, those pixels are history, meaning they're gone. So before using the eraser tools, you should probably have a backup of your image stored somewhere. Think of it as a cheap insurance policy in case things go awry.

The Eraser tool

The Eraser tool enables you to erase areas on your image to either your background color or, if you're working on a layer, to a transparent background, as shown in Figure 7-12. For more on layers, check out Chapter 8.

To use this tool, simply select it, drag through the desired area on your image, and you're done. Because it isn't the most accurate tool on the planet, remember to really zoom in and use smaller brush tips to do some accurate erasing.

Corbis Digital Stock

Figure 7-12: Erase either to your background color (left) or to transparency (right).

There are several Eraser options to specify on the Options bar:

- **Brush Presets:** Click the drop-down palette to access the Brush presets. Choose the brush of your choice. Again, additional brush libraries are available from the Brushes pop-up menu.

- **Mode:** Select from Brush, Pencil, and Block. When you select Block, you're stuck with one size (a 16-x-16-pixel tip) and are not able to select other preset brushes.

- **Opacity:** Specify a percentage of transparency for your erased areas. The lower the Opacity setting, the less it erases. Opacity isn't available for the Block mode.

The Background Eraser tool

The Background Eraser tool is more savvy than the Eraser tool. It erases the background from an image while being mindful of leaving the foreground untouched. The Background Eraser tool erases to transparency on a layer. If you drag an image with only a background, Elements converts the background into a layer.

The key to using the Background Eraser is to carefully keep the *hot spot,* the crosshair at the center of the brush, on the background pixels as you drag. The hot spot samples the color of the pixels and deletes that color whenever it falls inside the brush circumference. But, if you accidentally touch a foreground pixel with the hot spot, it's erased as well. And the tool won't even be sorry about it! This tool works better with images that have good contrast in color between the background and foreground object, as shown in Figure 7-13. Also, if your image has very detailed or wispy edges (such as hair or fur), you're better off using the Magic Extractor command, described in the next section.

Corbis Digital Stock

Figure 7-13: The Background Eraser erases similarly colored pixels sampled by the hot spot of your brush cursor.

Here's the rundown on the Background Eraser options:

- ✔ **Brush Preset picker:** Provides settings to customize the size and appearance of your brush tip. The size and tolerance settings at the bottom are for pressure-sensitive drawing tablets.

- ✔ **Limits:** *Discontiguous* erases all similarly colored pixels wherever they appear in the image. *Contiguous* erases all similarly colored pixels that are adjacent to those under the hot spot.

- ✔ **Tolerance:** Like the Magic Wand and the Magic Eraser, the Background Eraser uses a tolerance setting. The value determines how similar the colors have to be to that of the color under the hot spot before Elements erases them. A higher value picks up more colors, whereas a lower value picks up fewer colors. See "Talking about tolerance," earlier in this chapter, for more details.

The Magic Eraser tool

You can think of the Magic Eraser tool as a combo Eraser and Magic Wand tool. It both selects and erases similarly colored pixels simultaneously. Unless you are working on a layer with the transparency locked (see Chapter 9 for more on locking), the pixels are erased to transparency. If you are working on an image with just a background, Elements converts the background into a layer.

The Magic Eraser shares most of the same options with the other erasers. Here are the unique options:

- ✒ **Anti-alias:** Creates a slightly soft edge around the transparent area.
- ✒ **Sample All Layers:** Samples colors using data from all visible layers, but erases pixels on the *active* layer only.

Using the Magic Extractor Command

The last selection tool in the Elements repertoire is the new Magic Extractor command. This command enables you to make selections based on your identification of the foreground and background portions of your image. This command is similar in methodology to the Magic Selection Brush tool. You specify your foreground and background by simply clicking these areas with the brush tool and "marking" them. Click the magic OK button, and your object or objects are neatly and painlessly extracted.

Though it isn't mandatory, you can make a rough selection first before selecting the Magic Extractor command. This obviously restricts what is extracted and could result in a more accurate selection.

Follow these steps to magically extract your element:

1. **Choose Image⇨Magic Extractor.**

   The huge Magic Extractor dialog box appears.

2. **Grab the Foreground Brush tool and click or drag to mark your foreground areas — or the areas you want to select.**

   The default color of the Foreground Brush is red.

   Again, like the Selection brush, the more accurate the data you provide to the command's algorithm, the more accurate your extraction will be. Be sure and use the Zoom and Hand tools to help magnify and move around your image as needed. For more on these tools, see Chapter 5.

You can also change the size of your Brush tip (from 1 to 100 pixels) under the Tool Options on the right side of the dialog box. If necessary, change the color of your foreground and background colors by clicking the swatch and choosing a new color from the Color Picker.

3. **Select the Background Brush tool and click or drag to mark the background area or the portions you don't want to select.**

The default color of the Background Brush is blue, as shown in Figure 7-14.

4. **Click Preview to view your extraction.**

Elements churns for a few seconds before presenting you with a look at your extraction. You can change the Preview by choosing either Selection Area or Original Photo from the Display pop-up menu.

If you want to see your selection against a different background, choose one, such as black matte for a black background, from the Background pop-up menu.

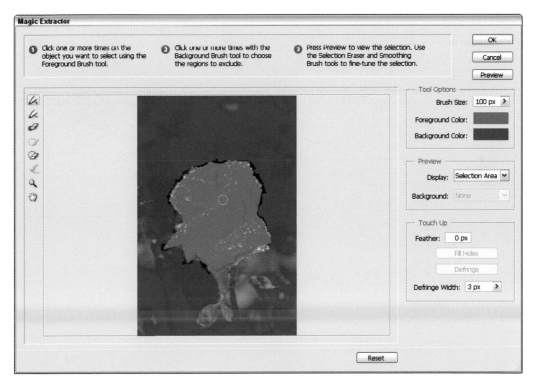

PhotoDisc/Getty Images

Figure 7-14: The Magic Extractor allows you to identify foreground and background areas.

5. **If you aren't happy with the preview of your selection, you can refine the selection by doing the following:**

   • To erase any markings, select the Point Eraser tool and click or drag over the offending areas.

   • To add areas to the selection, click or drag over your desired areas with the Add to Selection tool.

   • To delete areas from the selection, drag with the Remove from Selection Tool.

   • Drag over the edges with the Smoothing Brush tool to smooth the edges of your foreground selection.

   • To soften the edges of your selection, enter a value in the Feather option. Remember, the higher the value, the softer the edge.

   • Click the Fill Holes button to do just that.

   • Click Defringe to remove that halo of pixels between the foreground and background areas. Enter a value in the Defringe Width option.

   If things start to get messy, you can always start over by clicking Reset at the bottom of the dialog box.

6. **When you're pleased with the results, click OK to finish the selection process, as shown in Figure 7-15, and close the Magic Extractor dialog box.**

   Your newly extracted image appears as a new file.

Figure 7-15: A rose selected with the Magic Extractor.

Using the Select Menu

In this section, we breeze through the Select menu. Along with the methods we describe in the "Modifying Your Selections" section, you can use this menu to further modify selections by expanding, contracting, smoothing, softening, inversing, growing, and grabbing similarly colored pixels. And if that won't satisfy your selection needs, nothing will.

Selecting all or nothing

The Select All and Deselect commands are no-brainers. To select everything in your image, choose Select➪All or press Ctrl+A. To deselect everything, choose Select➪Deselect or press Ctrl+D. Remember, you usually don't have to Select All. If you don't have a selection border in your image, Elements assumes the whole image is fair game for any manipulation.

Reselecting a selection

If you have sacrificed that second cup of coffee to steady your hand and taken the time to carefully lasso around your desired object, you don't want to lose your selection before you've had a chance to perform your next move. But all it takes is a mere inadvertent click of your mouse while you have an active selection border to completely obliterate your selection. Fortunately, Elements anticipated such a circumstance and offers a solution. If you choose Select➪Reselect, Elements retrieves your last selection.

One caveat: The Reselect command works only for the *last* selection you made, so don't plan to reselect a selection you made last Tuesday, or even just 5 minutes ago if you selected something else after that selection. If you want to reuse a selection for the long term, you need to save it, as we explain in "Saving and loading selections," later in this chapter.

Inversing a selection

You know the old adage: If you can't be with the one you love, love the one you're with. Well, Elements is kind of like that. Sometimes it's just easier to select what you don't want rather than what you do want. For example, if you're trying to select your beloved in his or her senior photo, it's probably easier to just click the studio backdrop with the Magic Wand and then inverse the selection by choosing Select➪Inverse.

Feathering a selection

In the "Applying marquee options" section, we describe how to feather a selection when using the Lasso and Marquee tools by entering a value in the Feather box on the Options bar. Remember that this method of feathering requires that you set your Feather value *before* you create your selection. What we didn't tell you is that there is a way to apply a feather *after* you've made a selection.

Choose Select⇨Feather and enter your desired amount from .2 to 250 pixels. Your selection will be subsequently softened around the edges.

TIP

This method is actually a better way to go. Make your selection and fine-tune it by using the methods described earlier in this chapter. Then apply your feather. The problem with applying the feather *before* you make a selection is when you want to modify your initial selection. When you make a selection with a feather, the marquee outline of the selection adjusts to take into account the amount of the feather. That means that the resulting marquee outline doesn't resemble your precise mouse movement, making it harder to modify that selection.

Using the Modify commands

Although they definitely won't win any popularity contests, the commands under the Modify submenu may occasionally come in handy. Here is the scoop on each command:

✔ **Border:** Selects the area, from 1 to 200 pixels, around the edge of the selection border. By choosing Edit⇨Fill Selection, you can fill the border with color, as shown in Figure 7-16.

Corbis Digital Stock

Figure 7-16: Fill a border with color to create a stroke around your object.

✔ **Smooth:** Select this command to try to round off any jagged, raggedy edges. Enter a value from 1 to 100 pixels, and Elements looks at each selected pixel and then includes or deselects the pixels in your selection based on your value. Start with a low number, like 1–3 pixels. Otherwise, it may make your selection worse.

✔ **Expand:** Enables you to increase the size of your selection by a given number of pixels, from 1 to 100. This command is especially useful if you just barely missed getting the edge of an elliptical selection and need it a little larger.

✔ **Contract:** Decreases your selection border by 1 to 100 pixels. When compositing multiple images, it's often beneficial to slightly contract your selection if you plan on applying a feather. That way, you avoid picking up a fringe of background pixels around your selection.

Applying the Grow and Similar commands

The Grow and Similar commands are often used in tandem with the Magic Wand tool. If you've made an initial selection with the Magic Wand but didn't quite get everything you wanted, try choosing Select➪Grow. The Grow command increases the size of the selection by including adjacent pixels that fall within the range of tolerance value. The Similar command is like Grow, except that the pixels don't have to be adjacent to be selected. The command searches throughout the image and picks up pixels within the tolerance range.

These commands don't have their own tolerance options. They use whatever tolerance value is displayed on the Options bar when the Magic Wand tool is selected. You can adjust that tolerance setting to include more or fewer colors.

Saving and loading selections

Finally, there may be times when you toiled so long over a complex selection that you really want to save it for future use. This is not only possible, but highly recommended. And it's also a piece a cake. Here's how:

1. **After you've perfected your selection, choose Select➪Save Selection.**

2. **In the Save Selection dialog box, leave the Selection option at New and enter a desired name for your selection, as shown in Figure 7-17.**

   The Operation is automatically set to New Selection.

3. **Click OK.**

4. **When you want to access the selection again, choose Select➪ Load Selection and choose your desired selection from the Selection pop-up menu.**

Figure 7-17: Save your selection for later use to save time and effort.

To inverse your selection, click the Invert box. You'll notice that you now have available options to add to, subtract from, or intersect with your selection. These can come in handy if you want to modify your existing selection. For example, say you selected the center and petals of a flower but not the stem and leaves. You later decide you really need the whole flower. Rather than making a whole new selection, you can select just the stem and leaves and then choose Add to Selection, and you've got your whole flower. If you want, you can then save the flower as a new selection for later use.

Working with Layers

*U*sing Elements without ever using layers would be like typing a book on an old IBM Selectric typewriter. Sure, you could do it, but it wouldn't be fun. But an ever bigger issue would be when it came time to edit that book and make changes. Correction tape, white out, and erasers would make that task downright tedious, not to mention messy. The benefit of using layers is that you have tremendous flexibility. You can quickly make as many edits as you want for as long as you want, provided you keep your composite image in layers. Layers make working in Elements a lot more productive. Don't give a darn about productivity? Well, let's just say layers also make it a breeze for you to dabble in your more artsy side. This chapter gives you everything you need to know about layers. After you try them out, you'll wonder how you ever lived without them.

Getting to Know Layers

Think of layers as sheets of acetate or clear transparency film. You have drawings or photographs on individual sheets. What you place on each sheet doesn't affect any of the other sheets. Any area on the sheet that doesn't have an image on it is transparent. You can stack these sheets one on top of the other to create a combined image, or *composite* (or collage if you prefer). You can reshuffle the order of the sheets, add new sheets, and delete old sheets.

In Elements, layers are essentially a digital version of these clear acetate sheets. You can place elements such as images, type, or shapes on separate layers and create a composite, as shown in Figure 8-1. You can hide, add, delete, or rearrange layers. Being digital, layers of course have some added functionality. You can adjust how opaque or transparent the element on the layer is. You can also add special effects and change how the colors interact between layers.

When you create a new file with background contents of white or a background color, scan an image into Elements, or open a file from a CD or your digital camera, you basically have a file with just a *background.* There are no layers yet.

An image contains only one background, and you can't do much to it besides paint on it and make basic adjustments. You can't move the background or change its transparency or blend mode. How do you get around all of these limitations? Convert your background into a layer by following these easy steps:

Corbis, PhotoDisc/Getty Images

Figure 8-1: Layers enable you to easily create composite images.

1. **Choose Window⇨Layers to display the Layers palette.**

   The Layers palette is explained in detail in the next section.

2. **Double-click Background in the Layers palette.**

   Or you can choose Layer⇨New⇨Layer from Background.

3. **Name the layer or leave it at the default name of Layer 0.**

   You can also adjust the Blend Mode and Opacity of the layer in this dialog box if you need to. You can also do it via the Layer palette commands later.

4. **Click OK.**

   Elements converts your background into a layer, known also as an *image layer*.

When you create a new image with transparent background contents, the image doesn't contain a background but instead is created with a single layer.

Anatomy of a Layers palette

Elements keeps layers controlled in their own palette called, not surprisingly, a *Layers palette*. To display the Layers palette, shown in Figure 8-2, choose Window⇨Layers in the Editor in Standard Edit mode.

The order of the layers in the Layers palette represents the order in the image. We refer to this in the computer graphics world as the *stacking order*. The top layer in the palette is the top layer in your image, and so on. Depending on what you are doing, you can either work on a single layer or on multiple layers at once. Here are some tips on working with the Layers palette:

- ✔ **Select a layer:** Click its name or thumbnail. Elements highlights the *active layer* in the palette.

- ✔ **Select multiple contiguous layers:** Click your first layer and then Shift+click your last layer.

- ✔ **Select multiple noncontiguous layers:** Ctrl+click your desired layers.

- ✔ **View and hide layers:** To hide the layer, click the eye icon for that layer so that the eye disappears. To redisplay the layer, click the blank space in the eye column. You can also hide all the layers but one by selecting your desired layer and Alt+clicking the eye icon for that layer. Redisplay all the layers by Alt+clicking the eye icon again. Hiding all the layers except the one you want to edit can be helpful in allowing you to focus without the distraction of all the other imagery.

Only layers that are visible will print. This can be useful if you want to have several versions of an image (each on a separate layer) for a project within the same file.

✔ **Select the actual element (the nontransparent pixels) on the layer:** Ctrl+click the layer's thumbnail (not the name) in the palette.

✔ **Create a new blank layer:** Click the Create a New Layer icon at the top of the palette.

✔ **Create an adjustment layer:** Click the Create Adjustment Layer icon at the top of the palette. Adjustment layers are special layers that correct contrast and color in your image. You can also add fill layers — layers containing color, gradients, or patterns — via this command. We give you more details on adjustment and fill layers in upcoming sections.

✔ **Duplicate an existing layer:** Drag the layer to the Create a New Layer icon at the top of the palette.

✔ **Rearrange layers:** To move a layer to another position in the stacking order, drag the layer up or down in the Layers palette. As you drag, you see a fist icon. Release your mouse button when a highlighted line appears where you want to insert the layer.

Create a new layer   Create adjustment layer   Lock transparent pixels

Delete layer   Lock all

Link layers

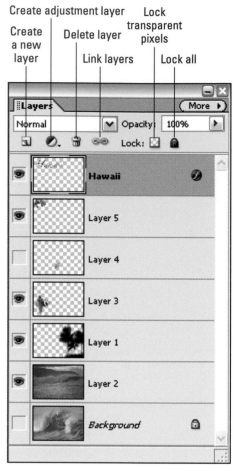

Figure 8-2: The Layers palette controls layers in your image.

If your image has a background, it always remains the bottommost layer. If you need to move the background, convert it to a layer by double-clicking the name in the Layers palette. Enter a name for the layer and click OK.

✔ **Rename a layer:** When you create a new layer, Elements provides default layer names (Layer 1, Layer 2, and so on). If you want to rename a layer, double-click the layer name in the Layers palette and enter the name directly in the Layers palette.

✔ **Determine what layer holds the element you want to edit:** Right-click the element. A context menu informs you what layer the element resides on and enables you to select that layer.

▸ **Adjust the interaction between colors on layers and adjust the transparency of layers:** You can use the blend modes and the opacity options at the top of the palette to mix the colors between layers and adjust the transparency of the layers, as shown in Figure 8-3.

▸ **Link layers:** Sometimes you want your layers to stay grouped as a unit to make your editing tasks easier. If so, link your layers by selecting the layers in the palette and then clicking the Link Layers icon at the top of the palette. A link icon appears to the right of the layer name. To remove the link, click the Link Layers icon again.

Corbis Digital Stock

Figure 8-3: We created this effect by using blend modes and opacity options.

▸ **Lock layers:** Select your desired layer and then click one of the two lock icons at the top of the palette. The checkerboard square icon locks all transparent areas of your layers. This prevents you from painting or editing any transparent areas on the layers. The lock icon locks your entire layer and prevents it from being changed in any way, including moving or transforming the elements on the layer. You can, however, still make selections on the layer. To unlock the layer, simply click the icon again to toggle off the lock.

By default, the background is locked and cannot be unlocked until you convert the background into a layer by choosing Layer⇨New⇨Layer from Background.

▸ **Delete a layer:** Drag it to the trash can icon.

Using the Layer and Select Menus

As with many features in Elements, there is usually more than one way to do something. This is especially true when it comes to working with layers. Besides the commands in the Layers palette, you also have two layer menus — the Layers menu and the Select menu, both of which you can find in the main menu bar at the top of the application window.

The Layers menu

Much of what you can do with the Layers palette icons, you can also do by using the Layers menu in the Menu bar and the Layers pop-up menu connected to the Layers palette (click the More button in the top-right corner). Commands such as New, Duplicate, Delete, and Rename are omnipresent throughout. But you will find commands that are exclusive to the palette, the main Layers menu, and the Layers pop-up menu. So if you can't find what you're looking for in one area, just go to another. Some of the commands require an expanded explanation and are described in sections that follow. But here's a quick description of most of the commands:

- ✔ **Delete Linked and Delete Hidden:** These commands delete only those layers that have been linked or hidden from display in the Layers palette.

- ✔ **Layer Style:** These commands manage the styles, or special effects, you apply to your layers. Find more on layer styles in an upcoming section.

- ✔ **Change Layer Content:** Depending on the type of layer you have selected, this command enables you to change or adjust the contents of your layer. For example, you can change the contents of a shape layer from a solid color into a pattern.

- ✔ **Arrange:** Enables you to shuffle your layer stacking order with commands like Bring to Front and Send to Back. Reverse, a new command, switches the order of your layers if you have two or more layers selected.

- ✔ **Group with Previous and Ungroup:** The Group command creates what is called a *clipping group,* in which a group of layers is constrained to the boundaries of a base layer. Find more details in an upcoming section.

- ✔ **Type:** The commands under the Type menu control the display of type layers. For more on type, see Chapter 13.

- ✔ **Simplify:** This command converts a type layer, shape layer, or fill layer into a regular image layer. Briefly, a *shape layer* is a layer that contains a vector object, whereas a *fill layer* is a layer containing a solid color, a gradient, or a pattern.

- ✔ **Merge and Flatten:** The various merge and flatten commands combine multiple layers into a single layer or, in the case of flattening, all of your layers into a single background.

- ✔ **Palette Options:** You can choose display options and choose to use a layer mask on your adjustment layers. Leave this option checked and read more about it in the upcoming section.

The Select menu

While the Select menu's main duties are to assist you in making and refining your selections, it does offer a few handy layer commands, all of which are new additions to the menu. Here's a quick introduction to each command:

- ✔ **Select all layers:** Want to quickly get everything in your file? Choose Select➪All Layers.

- ✔ **Select layers of similar type:** This command is helpful if you have different types of layers in your document, such as regular layers, type layers, shape layers, and adjustment layers, and you want to select just one type. Select one of your desired layers and then choose Select➪Similar Layers. For details on different types of layers, see the upcoming section.

- ✔ **Deselect all layers:** Choose Select➪Deselect Layers.

Working with Different Layer Types

There is layer life beyond just converting an existing background into a layer, which we describe earlier. In fact, Elements offers five kinds of layers. You'll probably spend most of your time creating image layers, but just so you're familiar with all types, the following sections describe each one.

Image layers

The image layer, usually just referred to as a layer, is the type of layer we were referring to when we gave the analogy of acetate sheets earlier in this chapter. You can create blank layers and add images to them, or you can create layers from images themselves. You can have as many image layers as your computer's memory will allow. Just keep in mind that the more layers you have, the larger your file size and the slower your computer will behave.

Each layer in an image can be edited without affecting the other layers. You can move, paint, size, apply a filter, and so on without disturbing a single pixel on any other layer, or the background for that matter. And when an element is on a layer, you no longer have to make a selection to select it (see Chapter 7 for selection info). Just drag the element with the Move tool.

We work more with image layers later in this chapter.

Adjustment layers

An adjustment layer is a special kind of layer used for correcting color and contrast. The advantage of using adjustment layers for your corrections, rather than applying them directly on the image layer, is that you can apply the corrections without permanently affecting the pixels. They are totally non-destructive. And because the correction is on a layer, you can edit, or even delete, the adjustment at any time. Adjustment layers, shown in Figure 8-4, apply the correction only to all the layers below them, without affecting any of the layers above them.

Corbis, PhotoDisc/Getty Images

Figure 8-4: Adjustment layers correct color and contrast in your image.

Another unique element to adjustment layers is that when you create one, you also create a *layer mask* on that layer at the same time. A layer mask is like a second sheet of acetate that hovers over the underlying layers. The layer mask allows you to selectively apply the adjustment to the layers below it by applying shades of gray — from white to black — on the mask. For example, by default, the mask is completely white. This allows the adjustment to be fully applied to the layers. If you paint on a layer mask with black, the areas under those black areas will not show the adjustment. If you paint with a shade of gray, those areas will partially show the adjustment. The darker the shade of gray, the less it will show the adjustment, as shown in Figure 8-5. Note that if you have an active selection border in your image before you add an adjustment layer, the adjustment is applied only to that area within the selection border. Your resulting layer mask also reflects that selection: The selected areas are white, while the unselected areas are black.

You can also use just the layer mask to creatively blend two layers together. Create an adjustment layer and just don't make any adjustment settings. Then use the layer mask to blend two layers. Be sure to sandwich the layer mask between your two layers. Then, select the topmost layer and choose Layer➪Group with Previous. Paint on your layer mask, as described earlier in this chapter, to selectively hide and show portions of your topmost layer.

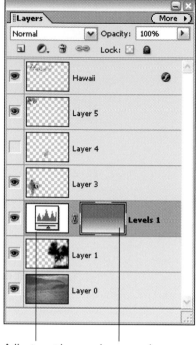

Adjustment layer   Layer mask

Corbis, PhotoDisc/Getty Images

Figure 8-5: Layer masks control the amount of adjustment applied to your layers.

Elements has eight kinds of adjustment layers, and you can use as many as you want. These adjustments are the same adjustments you find on the Enhance➪Adjust Lighting and Adjust Color and Filter➪Adjustments sub-menus. For specifics on each adjustment, see Chapters 9 and 10. Here's how to create an adjustment layer:

1. **Open an image that needs a little contrast or color correction.**

   Note that you don't need to convert your background into a layer to apply an adjustment layer.

2. **Click the Create Adjustment Layer icon in the Layers palette.**

3. **From the drop-down list at the top of the Layers palette, choose your desired adjustment.**

   The dialog box specific to your adjustment appears.

4. **Make your necessary corrections and click OK.**

After you close the dialog box, the adjustment layer appears in the Layers palette. The adjustment layer icon and a thumbnail appear on the adjustment layer. The thumbnail represents the layer mask described above.

You can paint on the layer mask to selectively allow only portions of your image to receive the adjustment. Use the Brush or Pencil tool to paint. Or you can also make a selection and fill that selection with any shade of gray, from white to black. And finally, you can use the Gradient tool on the mask to create a gradual application of the adjustment.

Like image layers, you can adjust the opacity and blend modes of an adjustment layer. Reducing the opacity of an adjustment layer reduces the effect of the adjustment on the underlying layers.

Here are a few last tips on using adjustment layers:

- **If you want to view your image without the adjustment,** click the eye icon in the left column of the Layers palette to hide the adjustment layer.

- **To delete the adjustment layer,** drag it to the trash can icon in the Layers palette.

- **To edit an adjustment layer,** simply double-click the adjustment layer in the Layers palette. You can also choose Layer⇔Layer Content Options. In the dialog box that appears, make any edits and then click OK. The only adjustment layer that you cannot edit is the Invert adjustment. It is either on or off.

- **To switch to a different adjustment layer,** choose Layer⇔Change Layer Content and select a different adjustment layer from the submenu.

Fill layers

A *fill layer* lets you add a layer of solid color, a gradient, or a pattern. Like adjustment layers, fill layers also include layer masks. You can edit, rearrange, duplicate, delete, and merge fill layers similarly to adjustment layers. You can blend fill layers with other layers by using the opacity and blend mode options in the Layers palette. Finally, you can restrict the fill layer to just a portion of your image by either making a selection first or by painting on the mask later.

Follow the steps below to create a fill layer:

1. **Open an image.**

Use an image that will look good with a frame or border of some kind. Remember that if you don't have a selection, the fill layer covers your whole image.

2. **Click the Create adjustment layer icon in the Layers palette. From the drop-down list, choose a fill of a solid color, gradient, or pattern.**

The dialog box specific to your type of fill appears.

3. **Specify your options, depending on the fill type you chose in Step 2:**

   • **Solid Color:** Choose your desired color from the Color Picker. See Chapter 12 for details on choosing colors and also on gradients and patterns.

   • **Gradient:** Click the down-pointing arrow to choose a preset gradient from the drop-down palette or click the gradient preview to display the Gradient Editor and create your own gradient.

   • **Pattern:** Select a pattern from the drop-down palette. Enter a value to scale your pattern if desired. Click Snap to Origin to make the origin of the pattern the same as the origin of the document. Select the Link with Layer option to specify that the pattern moves with the fill layer if you move it.

4. **Click OK.**

The fill layer appears in the Layers palette, as shown in Figure 8-6. Notice the layer mask that was created on the fill layer.

Corbis, PhotoDisc/Getty Images

Figure 8-6: Add a frame or border with a fill layer.

Shape layers

If you haven't made your way to Chapter 12 yet, you may be surprised to discover that Elements also lets you draw shapes with six different drawing tools. These shapes also have the added bonus of being *vector*-based. This means the shapes are defined by mathematical equations, which create points and paths, rather than by pixels. The advantage of vector-based objects is that you can freely size these objects without degradation. In addition, they will always print with smooth edges, not with the jaggies you're familiar with seeing in pixel-based elements.

To create a shape layer, grab a shape tool from the Tools palette and drag on your canvas. When you create a shape, it resides on its own unique shape layer, as shown in Figure 8-7. As with other types of layers, you can adjust the blend modes and opacity of a shape layer. You can edit, move, and transform the actual shapes. However, to apply filters, you must first *simplify* the shape layer. This converts the vector paths to pixels.

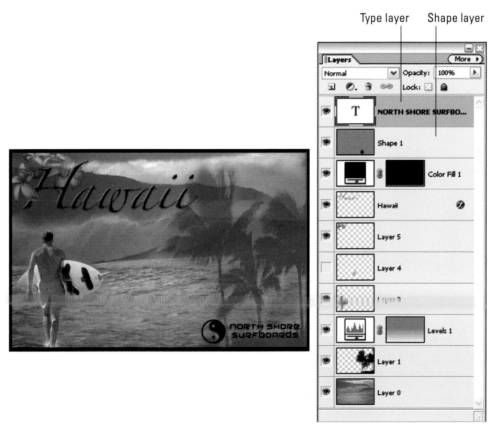

Corbis, PhotoDisc/Getty Images

Figure 8-7: Shape layers are vector-based, allowing for smooth edges and optimum print quality.

Type layers

To add words to your images, as shown in Figure 8-7, click your canvas with the Type tool and just type. It's really as easy as that. Well, you can specify options, such as a font family and size, in the Options bar, but when you click the Commit button on the Options bar, you create a type layer. In the Layers palette, you'll see a layer with a T icon. For details on working with type, check out Chapter 13.

Tackling Layer Basics

Image layers are the heart and soul of the layering world. You can create multiple image layers within a single image. Even more fun is taking several different images and creating a composite. Add people you like; take out people you don't. Pluck people out of boring photo studios and put them in exotic locales. The creative possibilities are endless. So in this section, we cover all the various ways to create image layers. We've already covered how to convert a background into a layer earlier in the chapter (see "Getting to Know Layers"). These next few sections describe how to create an image layer by using various other methods.

Creating a new layer from scratch

If you are creating a new blank file, you can select the Transparent option for your Background contents. Your new file is created with a transparent layer and is ready to go. If you have an existing file and want to create a new blank layer, here are the ways to do so:

- **Click the Create a New Layer icon at the top of the Layers palette.**

- **Choose New Layer from the Layers palette pop-up menu.**

- **Choose Layer⇨New⇨Layer.** Note that if you create a layer by using either of the menu commands, you are presented with a dialog box with options. Here you can name your layer and specify options for grouping, blending, and adjusting opacity. Provide a name for your layer and click OK. You can always adjust the other options directly in the Layers palette at a later time.

You can also use the Copy and Paste commands without even creating a blank layer first. When you copy and paste a selection without a blank layer, Elements automatically creates a new layer from the pasted selection. A better method of copying and pasting between multiple images, however, is to use the drag-and-drop method described later in this section.

The Copy Merged command on the Edit menu creates a merged copy of _all_ the visible layers within the selection.

After you create your layer, you can put selections or other elements on that layer by doing one or more of the following:

- ✔ Grab a painting tool, such as the Brush or Pencil, and paint on the layer.

- ✔ Make a selection on another layer or on the background within the same document or from another image entirely and then choose Edit➪Copy. Select your new blank layer in the Layers palette and then choose Edit➪Paste. You can also choose Select➪All and then copy and paste to transfer an entire image to the new layer.

- ✔ Make a selection on another layer or on the background within the same document or from another image and then choose Edit➪Cut. Select your new blank layer and then choose Edit➪Paste. Be aware that this action removes that selection from its original location and leaves a transparent hole, as shown in Figure 8-8.

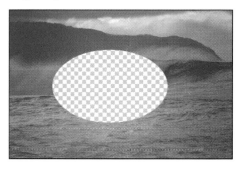

Corbis Digital Stock

Figure 8-8: When cutting a selection from a layer, take note of the resulting hole left in the original location.

Using Layer via Copy and Layer via Cut

Another way to create a layer is to use the Layer via Copy and Layer via Cut commands under the Layer menu. Make a selection on a layer or background and choose Layer➪New➪Layer via Copy or Layer via Cut. Elements automatically creates a new layer and puts the copied or cut selection on the layer. Again, remember that if you use the Layer via Cut command, your selection is deleted from its original location layer, and you are left with a transparent hole. If you use the background for the source, your background color fills the space. One final reminder: You can use these two commands only within the same image. You cannot use them between multiple images.

Duplicating layers

Duplicating layers can be helpful if you want to protect your original image while experimenting with a technique. If you don't like the results, you can always delete the duplicated layer. No harm, no foul.

To duplicate an existing layer, select it in the Layers palette and do one of three things:

- **Drag the layer to the Create a New Layer icon at the top of the palette.** Elements creates a duplicate layer with *Copy* appended to the name of the layer.
- **Choose Duplicate Layer from the Layers palette pop-up menu.**
- **Choose Layer➪Duplicate Layer.** If you use the menu methods, a dialog box appears, asking you to name your layer and specify other options. Provide a name for your layer and click OK. You can specify the other options later if desired.

Dragging and dropping layers

The most efficient way to copy and paste layers between multiple images is to use the drag-and-drop method. Why? Because it bypasses your clipboard, which is the temporary storage area on your computer for copied data. Storing data, especially large files, can bog down your system. By keeping your clipboard clear of data, your system operates more efficiently. If you've already copied data and it is lounging on your clipboard, choose Edit➪Purge➪Clipboard to empty your clipboard.

Here's how to drag and drop layers from one file to another:

1. **Select your desired layer in the Layers palette.**
2. **Grab the Move tool (four headed arrow) from the Tools palette.**
3. **Drag and drop the layer onto your destination file.**

   The dropped layer pops in as a new layer above the active layer in the image. You don't need to have a selection border to copy the entire layer. But, if you want to copy just a portion of the layer, make your selection before you drag and drop with the Move tool. If you want the selected element to be centered on the destination file, press the Shift key as you drag and drop.

Here's a handy tip. If you have several elements (but not touching one another) on one layer and want to select only one of the elements to drag and drop, use the Lasso tool to make a crude selection around the object without touching any of the other elements. Then press the Ctrl key and press the up-arrow key once. The element then becomes perfectly selected. Drag and drop with the Move tool as described in Step 3 above.

Using the Paste Into Selection command

The Paste Into Selection command lets you put an image on a separate layer while also inserting that image into a selection border. For example, in Figure 8-9, we used this command to make it appear as if our surfer is in the water.

Figure 8-9: Use the Paste Into Selection command to make one element appear as though it is coming out of another element.

You can do the same by following these steps:

1. **Make your desired selection on the layer in your destination image.**

   In our figure, we selected the area in the water where the surfer would be positioned.

2. **Select the image that will fill that selection.**

   The image can be within the same file or from another file. Our surfer was in another file.

3. **Choose Edit⇨Copy.**

4. **Return to the destination image layer and choose Edit⇨Paste Into Selection.**

   Elements converts the selection border on the layer into a layer mask. The pasted selection is visible only inside the selection border. In our example, the surfer only shows inside the selected area. His ankles and feet are outside the border and therefore are hidden.

Moving a Layer's Content

Moving the content of a layer is a piece of cake. Grab the Move tool from the Tools palette, select your layer in the Layers palette, and drag the element on the canvas to your desired location. You can also move the layer in 1-pixel increments with the keyboard arrow keys. Press Shift with the arrows to move in 10-pixel increments.

The Auto-Select Layer option in the Options bar enables you to switch to a layer when you click any part of that layer with the Move tool. But be careful if you have a lot of overlapping layers because this can sometimes be more trouble than it's worth.

Transforming Layers

When working with layers, you may find the need to scale or rotate some of your images. You can do so easily by applying the Transform and Free Transform commands. The methods to transform layers and transform selections are identical.

Here's how to transform a layer:

1. **Select your desired layer.**

   You can also apply a transformation to multiple layers simultaneously by linking the layers first.

2. **Choose Image⇨Free Transform.**

   A bounding box surrounds the contents of your layer. Drag a corner handle to size the contents. Press Shift while dragging to constrain the proportions. To rotate your contents, move your mouse cursor just outside a corner handle until it turns into a curved arrow and then drag. To distort, skew, or apply perspective to the contents, right-click and choose the desired command from the context menu. If you would rather enter your transform values numerically, you can do so in the fields in the Options bar.

   If you want to apply just a single transformation, you can also choose the individual Distort, Skew, and Perspective commands from the Image⇨Transform menu. Or to rotate, you can choose Image⇨Rotate.

3. **When your layer is transformed to your liking, double-click inside the bounding box or click the Commit button in the options bar.**

Try to perform all your transformations in one execution. Each time you transform pixels, you put your image through the interpolation process (see Chapter 3 for more on interpolation). If done to the extreme, it can degrade the quality of your image. This is why it is prudent to use the

Free Transform command rather than individual commands, so that all transformations can be executed in one fell swoop.

When the Move tool is active, you can transform a layer without choosing a command. Select the Show Bounding Box option on the Options bar. This option surrounds the layer, or selection, with a box with handles. Drag the handles to transform the layer or selection.

Flattening and Merging Layers

Layers are fun and fantastic, but they can quickly chew up your RAM and bloat your file size. And sometimes, to be honest, having too many layers can start to make your file tedious to manage, thereby making you less productive. Whenever possible, you can merge your layers to save memory and space. *Merging* combines visible, linked, or adjacent layers into a single layer (not a background). The intersection of all transparent areas is retained.

In addition, if you need to import your file into another program, certain programs do not support files with layers. Therefore you may need to flatten your file before importing it. *Flattening* an image combines all the visible layers into a background. Hidden layers are discarded, and any transparent areas are filled with white. We recommend, however, that before you flatten your image, you make a copy of the file with all its layers intact and save it as a native Photoshop file. That way, if you ever need to make any edits, you have that added flexibility of having your layers.

By the way, the only file formats that support layers are native Photoshop (.psd); Tagged Image File Format, or TIFF (.tif); and Portable Document Format, or PDF (.pdf). If you save your file in any other format, Elements automatically flattens your layers down into a background.

Merging layers

You can merge your layers in a couple of ways. Here's how:

- ⤳ Display only those layers you want to merge. Click the eye icon in the Layers palette to hide those layers you don't want to merge. Choose Merge Visible from the Layers palette pop-up menu or Layer menu.

- ⤳ Arrange the layers you want to merge adjacent to each other in the Layers palette. Select the topmost layer of that group and choose Merge Down from the Layers palette pop-up menu or Layer menu. Note that Merge Down merges your active layer with the layer directly below it.

Flattening layers

To flatten an image, follow these steps:

1. **Make certain that all layers you want to retain are visible because any hidden layers will be discarded.**

2. **Choose Flatten Image from the Layers palette pop-up menu or Layer menu.**

   All your layers are combined into a single background. Any transparent areas are filled with the background color, as shown in Figure 8-10.

   If you mistakenly flatten your image, choose Edit➪Undo or use your Undo History palette. (If you're not familiar with the History palette, see Chapter 1 for details.)

Corbis, PhotoDisc/Getty Images

Figure 8-10: Flattening combines all your layers into a single background.

9

Simple Image Makeovers

In This Chapter
▶ Cropping and straightening images
▶ Employing one-step auto fixes
▶ Editing with Quick Fix mode
▶ Fixing small imperfections

*F*ixing images quickly without pain or hassle is probably one of the most desirable features you'll find in Elements and one we're sure you'll want to embrace frequently. Whether you're an experienced photographer or an amateur shutterbug, cropping away unwanted background, tweaking the lighting or color of an image, or erasing away the minor blemishes of a loved one's face are all editing tasks you'll most likely tackle. With these simple image makeover tools in Elements, these tasks are as easy as clicking a single button or as difficult as a few swipes with a brush.

Cropping and Straightening Images

Cropping a photo is probably one of the easiest things you can do to improve the composition of your photo. Getting rid of the unnecessary background around your subject creates a better focal point. Another dead giveaway of amateurish photography is crooked horizon lines. Not a problem. Elements gives you several ways to straighten those images after the fact. So after your next photo shoot, launch the Elements Editor and get in there and crop and straighten your images before you show them off. No one will be the wiser that the images were digitally doctored.

Cutting away with the Crop tool

The most common way to crop a photo is by using the Crop tool. Simple, quick, and easy, this tool gets the job done. Here's how to use it:

1. **Select the Crop tool from the Tools palette in either Standard Edit or Quick Fix modes.**

   You can also press the C key. For details on the different workspaces, see Chapter 1. For full details on Quick Fix mode, see the upcoming section.

2. **Specify your Aspect Ratio options in the Options bar. Here are your choices:**

   • **No Restriction:** Allows you to freely crop the image at any size.

   • **Use Photo Ratio:** Retains the original aspect ratio of the image when you crop.

   • **Preset sizes:** Offers a variety of common photographic sizes. When you crop, your image then becomes that specific dimension.

   When cropping an image, Elements retains the original resolution of the file. What this means is, in order to keep your image at the same resolution while simultaneously eliminating portions of your image, Elements must resample the file. Therefore, it is important that you have sufficient resolution so that the effects of the resampling aren't as noticeable. This is especially true if you are choosing a larger preset size. If all this talk on resolution and resampling is fuzzy, be sure to check out Chapter 3.

   • **Width and Height:** Enables you to specify a desired width and height to crop your image.

3. **Drag around the portion of the image you want to retain and release your mouse button.**

   As you drag, a crop marquee bounding box appears. Don't worry if your cropping marquee isn't exactly correct. You can adjust it in the next step.

   The area outside the cropping marquee appears darker (called a *shield*) than the inside in order to better frame your image, as shown in Figure 9-1. If you want to change the color and opacity of the shield, or if you don't want it at all, change your Crop preferences (Edit➪Preferences➪Display & Cursors).

4. **Adjust the cropping marquee by dragging the handles of the crop marquee bounding box.**

   To move the entire marquee, position your mouse inside the marquee until you see a black arrowhead cursor and then drag.

   If you move your mouse outside the marquee, your cursor changes to a curved arrow. Drag with this cursor to rotate the marquee. This allows you to both rotate and crop your image simultaneously — handy for straightening a crooked image. Just be aware that rotation, unless it's in 90-degree increments, also resamples your image.

5. **Double-click inside the cropping marquee.**

   You can also just press Enter or click the green Commit button next to the marquee. Elements then discards the area outside the marquee. To cancel your crop, click the red Cancel button.

Cropping marquee   Handle

Shield   Cancel button

Commit button

Corbis Digital Stock

Figure 9-1: The area outside the crop marquee appears darker to allow for easier framing of your image.

Cropping with a selection border

You can also crop an image by using the Image➪Crop command in either Standard Edit or Quick Fix mode. First, make a selection with any of the selection tools and then choose the command. You can use this technique with any selection border shape. That is, your selection doesn't have to be rectangular. It can be round or even freeform. Your cropped image won't take on that shape, but Elements will crop as close to the boundaries of the selection border that it can, as shown in Figure 9-2. For details about making selections, see Chapter 7.

Straightening images

There may be times when you just didn't quite get that horizon straight when taking a photo of the beach. Or maybe you scanned a photo and it wasn't quite centered in the middle of the scanning bed. Not a big deal. Elements gives you several ways to straighten an image.

Corbis Digital Stock

Figure 9-2: Elements can crop to any selection border shape.

Using the Straighten tool

This new tool enables you to specify a new straight edge and then rotates the image accordingly. Here's how to use the Straighten tool:

1. **Select the Straighten tool from the Tools palette (or press the P key) in Standard Edit mode only.**

2. **Specify your desired setting from the Canvas Options in the Options bar. Here are your choices:**

- **Grow Canvas to Fit:** Rotates the image and increases the size of the canvas to fit the image area.

- **Crop to Remove Background:** Trims off background canvas outside the image area. This is helpful if you have scanned an image and have white areas around your photo that you want removed.

- **Crop to Original Size:** Rotates your image without trimming off any background canvas.

3. **Select Rotate All Layers if desired.**

   If you have an image with layers and you want all of them rotated, check this option.

4. **Draw a line in your image to represent the new straight edge.**

   Your image is then straightened and, if you chose either of the crop options in Step 2, also cropped.

Using the Straighten menu commands

In addition to the Straighten tool, you can also straighten your images by using two commands in the Image menu, in either Standard Edit or Quick Fix modes, as follows:

- ✔ To automatically straighten an image without cropping, which will leave the canvas remaining around the image, choose Image➪Rotate➪Straighten Image.

- ✔ To automatically straighten and crop the image simultaneously, choose Image➪Rotate➪Straighten and Crop Image.

Using the Divide Scanned Photos command

The Divide Scanned Photos command is great if you want to save time by scanning multiple photos into one document. Cram all the photos you can on your scanning bed and get one initial scan. Just make sure there is a clear separation between each of the images. Then choose Image➪Divide Scanned Photos in either Standard Edit or Quick Fix mode. Elements divides the images and places each one in a separate file, as shown in Figure 9-3. Note that if you have images with a lot of white in them, such as snow, you should cover the scanner with a piece of dark paper to better delineate the boundaries of each image.

Corbis Digital Stock

Figure 9-3: Save time by scanning several images at once and then applying the Divide Scanned Photos command.

Employing One-Step Auto Fixes

Elements has five automatic lighting, contrast, and color correction tools that can improve the appearance of your images with just one menu command. These commands are available in either the Standard Edit or Quick Fix modes, and they're all in the Enhance menu. For more on Quick Fix mode, see the upcoming section.

The advantage of these one-step correctors is that they are extremely easy to use. You don't need to have one iota of knowledge about color or contrast to use them. The downside to using them is that sometimes the result isn't as good as you could get via a manual color correction method. And sometimes these correctors may even make your image look worse than before by giving you weird color shifts. But because they are quick and easy, give them a try on an image that needs some help. Usually, you won't want to use more than one of the auto fixes. If one doesn't work on your image, undo and try another. If you still don't like the result, then move on to one of the manual methods described in Chapter 10.

Auto Smart Fix

This all-in-one command is touted to adjust it all. It is designed to improve lighting, improve the details in shadow and highlight areas, and correct the color balance, as shown in Figure 9-4. The overexposed image on the left was improved quite nicely with the Auto Smart Fix command.

The Auto Smart Fix command is available in the Organizer, where you can apply this command to several selected images simultaneously. It is also now available in the Slide Show editor as well.

If the Auto Smart Fix was just too "auto" for you, you can crank it up a notch and try Adjust Smart Fix. This command is similar to the Auto Smart Fix, but gives you a slider where you, not Elements, controls the amount of correction applied to the image.

Figure 9-4: In a hurry? Apply the Auto Smart Fix command to quickly improve an image.

Auto Levels

The Auto Levels command adjusts the overall contrast of an image. This command works best on images that have pretty good contrast (detail in the shadow, highlight, and midtone areas) to begin with and need just a minor amount of adjustment. Auto Levels works by mapping, or converting, the lightest and darkest pixels in your image to black and white, thereby making highlights appear lighter and shadows appear darker, as shown in Figure 9-5.

Although Auto Levels can improve your contrast, it may also produce an unwanted colorcast (a slight trace of color). If this happens, undo the command and try the Auto Contrast command instead. If that still doesn't improve the contrast, it's time to bring out the big guns. Try the Levels command described in Chapter 10.

Figure 9-5: Auto Levels adjusts the overall contrast of an image.

Auto Contrast

The Auto Contrast command is designed to adjust the overall contrast in an image without adjusting its color. This command may not do as good a job at improving contrast as the Auto Levels command, but it does do a better job at retaining the color balance of an image. It usually doesn't cause the funky colorcasts that can occur when using Auto Levels. This command works great on images with a haze, as shown in Figure 9-6.

PhotoDisc/Getty Images

Figure 9-6: The Auto Contrast command works wonders on hazy images.

Auto Color Correction

The Auto Color Correction command adjusts both the color and contrast of an image, based on the shadows, midtones, and highlights it finds in the image and a default set of values. These values adjust the amount of black and white pixels that Elements removes from the darkest and lightest areas of the image. You usually use this command to remove a colorcast or to balance the color in your image, as shown in Figure 9-7. Occasionally, this command can also be useful in correcting oversaturated or undersaturated colors.

Figure 9-7: Use Auto Color Correction to remove a colorcast.

Auto Red Eye Fix

This new command is pretty self-explanatory. The Auto Red Eye Fix command automatically detects and eliminates red eye in an image. Red eye happens when the person or animal looks directly into the flash. Many cameras have a red-eye prevention mode, which is a pre-flash that causes the subjects' irises to contract, making their pupils smaller when the real flash goes off. Other cameras mount the flash high or to side of the lens, which also reduces the chance of red eye. But if you have neither of these camera options, or if it just happened, it isn't difficult to rectify demonic red eye after the fact.

The Auto Red Eye Fix command is also available in the Organizer, where you can apply this command to several selected images simultaneously. You can also automatically apply this fix when you acquire your images. Check the Automatically Fix Red Eyes option in the File⇨Get Photos dialog box. And like Auto Smart Fix, you can now access this tool in the Slide Show editor as well.

If for some reason, the Auto Red Eye Fix didn't quite do the trick, you can always reach for the Red Eye Removal tool in the Tools palette. Here's how to remove red eye manually:

1. Select the Red Eye Removal tool from the Tools palette.

Using the default settings, click the red portion of the eye in your image. This one-click tool darkens the pupil, while retaining the tonality and texture of the rest of the eye, as shown in Figure 9-8.

Figure 9-8: The Auto Red Eye Fix and the Red Eye Removal tool detect and destroy dreaded red eye.

2. **If you're unhappy with the fix, adjust one or both of the following options:**

    • **Pupil Size:** Use the slider to increase or decrease the size of the pupil.

    • **Darken Pupil:** Use the slider to darken or lighten the color of the pupil.

Editing with Quick Fix

If you use the Auto Fixes we cover in the preceding section while in Quick Fix mode, you may find all you need to repair and enhance your images and rarely visit Standard Edit mode. And so in this section, we offer a closer look at Quick Fix mode.

Quick Fix mode is a pared-down version of Standard Edit mode that conveniently provides basic fixing tools, plus tosses in a few unique features as well, such as a before and after preview of your image.

Here is a step-by-step workflow that you can follow in Quick Fix mode to repair your photos:

1. **Select one or more photos in the Organizer and then choose Go to Quick Fix from the Edit menu or the Shortcuts bar. Or if you are in**

Standard Edit mode, click the Quick Fix button in the top right of the application window.

If you happen to be in Standard Edit mode with an image already open, this image will be transported into the Quick Fix mode. Note that you can also open images by simply using the File⇨Open menu command.

2. **Specify your preview preference from the View pop-up menu at the bottom of the application window.**

You choose to view just your original image (before), your fixed image (after), or both side by side in either portrait or landscape orientations, as shown in Figure 9-9.

3. **Use the Zoom and Hand tools to magnify and navigate around your image. See Chapter 5 for more on these tools.**

You can also specify the Zoom percentage by using the Zoom slider at the bottom of the application window.

4. **Crop your image by using the Crop tool in the Tools palette.**

You can also use any of the methods described earlier, in the "Cropping and Straightening Images" section, except for the Straighten tool, which is exclusive to Standard Edit mode.

Figure 9-9: Quick Fix mode enables you to view before and after previews of your image.

5. **To rotate the image in 90-degree increments, click the Rotate Left or Rotate Right button at the bottom of the application window.**

6. **Use the Red Eye tool to remove the red from your subjects' eyes.**

   Note that you can also automatically fix red eye by clicking the Auto button under Red Eye Fix in the General Fixes palette on the right side of the application window. Both of these methods are described earlier, in the section, "Auto Red Eye Fix."

7. **Apply any necessary auto fixes, such as Auto Smart Fix, Auto Levels, Auto Contrast, and Auto Color Correction.**

   All these commands are found under the Enhance menu or in the General Fixes, Lighting, and Color palettes on the right side of the application window.

   Each of these fixes is described in detail earlier in this chapter. Remember, usually one of the fixes is enough. Don't stack them one onto another. If one doesn't work, click the Reset button near the image preview and try another. If you're not happy, go to Step 8.

8. **If the auto fixes didn't quite cut it, you'll get more control by using the sliders available for Smart Fix, Contrast, and Color, located in the palettes on the right of the application window. If auto fixes did create a result you're happy with, skip to Step 9.**

   Here's a brief description of each available adjustment:

   - **Lighten Shadows:** Drag the slider to the right to lighten the darker areas of your image without adjusting the highlights.

   - **Darken Highlights:** Drag the slider to the right to darken the lighter areas of your image without adjusting the shadows.

   - **Midtone Contrast:** Adjusts the contrast of the middle (gray) values, while leaving the highlights and shadows as is.

   - **Saturation:** Adjusts the intensity of the colors.

   - **Hue:** Changes all the colors in an image. Make a selection first to change the color of just one or more elements. Otherwise, use restraint with this adjustment.

   - **Temperature:** Adjusts the colors warmer (red) or cooler (blue). This adjustment can be used to correct skin tones or to correct overly cool images (such as snowy winter photos) or overly warm images (such as photos shot at sunset or sunrise).

   - **Tint:** Adjust the tint after you have adjusted temperature to make the color more green or magenta.

   If you still don't get the results you need, move on to one of the more manual adjustments, described in Chapter 10.

   Note that you can also apply fixes to just selected portions of your image. Quick Fix mode offers the Selection Brush and Magic Selection Brush tools for your selection tasks. For details on using these tools, see Chapter 7.

9. **Finally, sharpen your image either automatically, by clicking the Auto button, or manually, by dragging the slider in the Sharpen palette.**

   Sharpening gives the illusion of increased focus by increasing the contrast between pixels. This fix should always be the last adjustment you make on your image.

Cloning with the Clone Stamp Tool

Elements enables you to clone elements without the hassle of genetically engineering DNA. In fact, the Clone Stamp tool works by just taking sampled pixels from one area and copying, or cloning, them onto another area. The advantage of cloning over making a selection and copying and pasting is that it is easier to realistically retain soft-edged elements such as shadows, as shown in Figure 9-10.

PhotoSpin

Figure 9-10: The Clone Stamp tool enables you to realistically duplicate soft-edged elements, such as shadows.

The Clone Stamp doesn't stop there. You can also use this tool when fixing flaws, such as scratches, bruises, and other minor imperfections. Although the birth of the healing tools (discussed later in this chapter) has somewhat pushed the Clone Stamp tool out of the retouching arena, it can still do a good repair job in many instances.

Here's how to use the Clone Stamp tool:

1. **Choose the Clone Stamp tool from the Tools palette in Standard Edit mode.**

   You can also press the S key.

2. **In the Options bar, choose a brush from the Brush Presets drop-down menu. Use the brush as is or adjust its size with the Size slider.**

   Keep in mind that the size of the brush you specify should be appropriate for what you are trying to clone or retouch. If you are cloning a large object, use a larger brush. For repairing small flaws, use a smaller brush. Cloning with a soft-edged brush usually produces more natural results. For details on brushes, see Chapter 12.

3. **Choose your desired blend mode and opacity percentage.**

   For more on blend modes, see Chapter 11. To make your cloned image appear ghosted, use an opacity percentage of less than 100 percent.

4. **Select or deselect the Aligned option.**

   With Aligned selected, the clone source moves when you move your cursor to a different location. If you want to clone multiple times from the same location, leave the Aligned option deselected.

5. **Select or deselect the Sample All Layers option.**

   This option enables you to sample pixels from all the visible layers for the clone. If deselected, the Clone Stamp tool clones only from the active layer. Check out Chapter 8 for details about working with layers.

6. **Alt-click the area of your image that you want to clone to define the *source* of the clone.**

7. **Click or drag along the area where you want the clone to appear, as shown in Figure 9-11.**

   As you drag, Elements displays a crosshair icon along with your Clone Stamp cursor. The crosshair is the source you are cloning from, while the Clone Stamp cursor is where the clone is being applied. As you move the mouse, the crosshair moves as well. This provides a continuous reference to the area of your image that you're cloning. Watch the crosshair, or you may clone something you don't want.

Figure 9-11: The crosshair and Clone Stamp cursor in action.

If you're cloning an element, it's best to try and clone it without lifting your mouse. Also, when retouching a flaw, try not to overdo it. One or two clicks on each flaw is usually plenty. If you're heavy-handed with the Clone Stamp, you'll get a blotchy effect that is a telltale sign that something has been retouched.

You can also clone patterns by using the Pattern Stamp tool, which shares a flyout menu with the Clone Stamp tool. Select a pattern from the Pattern picker drop-down palette in the Options bar. Drag with the tool to clone a pattern onto your image.

Retouching with the Healing Brush

The Healing Brush tool is similar to the Clone Stamp tool in that you clone pixels from one area onto another area. But the Healing Brush is superior in that it takes into account the tonality (highlights, midtones, and shadows) of the flawed area. The Healing Brush clones by using the *texture* from the sampled area (the source) and then using the *colors* around the brush stroke as you paint over the flawed area (the destination). The highlights, midtones, and shadow areas remain intact, making the repair more realistic and natural and not as blotchy or miscolored as the Clone Stamp tool.

Here are the steps to heal a photo:

1. **Open an image in need of a makeover and select the Healing Brush tool from the Tools palette in Standard Edit mode.**

    You can also heal between two images, but be sure that they have the same color mode, for example, both RGB. We chose a guy who looks like he might like to lose a few years, as shown in Figure 9-12.

2. **Specify a diameter and hardness for your brush tip from the Brush picker drop-down palette in the Options bar.**

    You can also adjust the spacing, angle, and roundness. For details on these options, see Chapter 12. Don't be shy. Be sure and adjust the size of your brush as needed. Using the appropriate brush size for the flaw you are retouching is critical to creating a realistic effect.

3. **Choose your desired blend mode.**

    For most retouching jobs, you'll probably want to leave it on Normal. The Replace mode preserves textures, such as noise or film grain, around the edges of your strokes.

4. **Choose one of the following Source options:**

    • **Sampled:** Uses the pixels from the image. This is your choice for the majority of your repairs.

    • **Pattern:** Uses pixels from a pattern chosen from the Pattern picker drop-down palette.

5. **Select or deselect the Aligned option on the Options bar.**

    For most retouching tasks, you'll probably want to leave it on Aligned.

    • **If Aligned is selected:** When you click or drag with the Healing Brush, Elements displays a crosshair along with the Healing Brush cursor. The crosshair represents the sampling point, also known as the *source.* As you move the Healing Brush tool, the crosshair also moves, providing a constant reference to the area that you are sampling.

- **If you deselect the Aligned option:** Elements applies the source pixels from your initial sampling point, no matter how many times you stop and start dragging.

6. **Select the Sample All Layers option to heal an image using all visible layers.**

    If this option is unselected, you heal only from the active layer.

To ensure the maximum editing flexibility later on, select the Sample All Layers option and add a new, blank layer above the image you want to heal. When you heal the image, the pixels appear on the new layer and not on the image itself. This enables you to adjust opacity and blend modes and to make other adjustment to the healed layer.

7. **Establish the sampling point by Alt-clicking. Make sure to click on the area of your image you want to clone *from*.**

    In our example, we clicked a smooth area of the forehead.

8. **Release the Alt key and click or drag over a flawed area of your image.**

    Make sure to keep an eye on the crosshair because that's the area you are healing from. We brushed over the wrinkles under and around the eyes and on the forehead, as shown in Figure 9-12. This guy never looked so good, and there was absolutely no recovery time.

PhotoSpin

Figure 9-12: Wipe out ten years in two minutes with the Healing Brush tool.

Zeroing In with the Spot Healing Brush

Whereas the Healing Brush is designed to fix larger flawed areas, the Spot Healing Brush is great for smaller imperfections. The Spot Healing Brush doesn't require you to specify a sampling source. It automatically takes a sample from around the area to be retouched. It's quick and easy and often effective. But it doesn't give you control over the sampling source, so keep an eye out for less-than-desirable fixes.

Here's how to quickly fix small flaws with the Spot Healing Brush tool:

1. **Open your image and grab the Spot Healing Brush tool in Standard Edit mode.**

   The moles on this guy's face, shown in Figure 9-13, are no match for the Spot Healing Brush.

2. **In the Options bar, click the Brush Preset picker and select a desired diameter and hardness for your brush tip from the drop-down palette.**

   It's best to select a brush that is a little larger than the flawed area you're fixing.

3. **Choose a blend mode from the Options bar.**

   As with the Healing Brush, the most likely mode is Normal.

PhotoSpin

Figure 9-13: Now you see it (left), and now you don't (right).

4. **Choose a type from the Options bar:**

   • **Proximity Match:** Samples the pixels around the edge of the selection to fix the flawed area.

   • **Create Texture:** Uses all the pixels in the selection to create a texture to fix the flaw.

   Try Proximity Match first, and if it doesn't work, undo and try Create Texture.

5. **Choose Sample All Layers to heal an image using all visible layers.**

   If left unselected, you heal only from the active layer.

6. **Click or drag on the area you want to fix.**

   We clicked on the moles with the Spot Healing Brush. But for the wrinkles around the eyes, we broke out the Healing Brush. We needed more control of the sampling source to achieve realistic results.

Lightening and Darkening with Dodge and Burn Tools

The techniques of dodging and burning originated in the darkroom, where photographers fixed negatives that had overly dark or light areas by adding or subtracting exposure, using holes and paddles as an enlarger made prints. The Dodge and Burn tools in Elements are even better than their analog ancestors in that they're more flexible and a lot more precise. In Elements, you can specify the size and softness of your tool by simply selecting from one of the many brush tips. You can also limit the correction to various tonal ranges in your image — shadows, midtones, or highlights. And finally, you can adjust the amount of correction applied by specifying an exposure percentage.

Use these tools only on small areas, such as the girl's face in Figure 9-14, and in moderation. Also keep in mind that you can't add detail that isn't there to begin with. If you try to lighten extremely dark shadows that contain little detail, you will get gray areas. If you try to darken overly light highlights, you'll just end up with white blobs.

Follow these steps to dodge or burn an image:

1. **Choose either the Dodge or Burn tool (or press O) from the Tools palette in Standard Edit mode.**

2. **Select a brush from the Brushes preset picker drop-down palette and also adjust the Brush size if necessary.**

Larger, softer brushes spread the dodging or burning effect over a larger area, making blending with the surrounding area easier.

3. **From the Range pop-up menu, select Shadows, Midtones, or Highlights.**

Use Shadows to darken or lighten the darker areas of your image. Use Midtones to adjust the tones of average darkness. Choose Highlights to make the light areas lighter or darker.

In Figure 9-14, the original image had mostly dark areas, so we dodged the shadows.

Figure 9-14: Use the Dodge and Burn tools to lighten and darken small areas.

4. **Choose the amount of correction you want to apply with each stroke by adjusting the Exposure setting in the Options bar.**

Start with a lower percentage to better control the amount of darkening or lightening. Exposure is similar to the Opacity setting you use with the regular Brush tool. We used a percentage of 10 percent.

5. **Paint over the areas you want to lighten or darken.**

6. **If you overdo it, press Ctrl+Z to undo the stroke.**

Smudging Away Rough Spots

The Smudge tool, one of the focus tools, pushes your pixels around using the color that is under the cursor when you start to drag. Think of it as dragging a brush through wet paint. You can use this tool to create a variety of effects. When it's used to the extreme, you can create a warped effect. When it's used more subtly, you can soften the edges of objects in a more natural fashion than with the Blur tool. Or you can create images that take on a painterly effect, as shown in Figure 9-15. Keep an eye on your image as you paint, however, because you can start to eliminate detail and wreak havoc if you're not careful with the Smudge tool.

PhotoSpin

Figure 9-15: The Smudge tool can make your images appear to be painted.

To use the Smudge tool, follow these steps:

1. **Choose the Smudge tool from the Tools palette in Standard Edit mode.**

   You can also press the R key (press Shift+R to cycle through the available focus tools).

2. **Select a brush from the Brushes presets drop-down palette.**

   Use a small brush for smudging tiny areas, such as edges. Larger brushes produce more extreme effects.

3. **Choose a blending mode from the Mode pop-up menu.**

4. **Choose the strength of the smudging effect with the Strength slider or text box.**

   The lower the value, the lighter the effect.

5. **If your image has multiple layers, select Sample All Layers, and Elements will use pixels from all the visible layers to produce the effect.**

   The smudge still appears only on the active layer, but the look is a bit different, depending on the colors of the underlying layers.

6. **Use the Finger Painting option to begin the smudge using the foreground color.**

   Instead of using the color under your cursor, this option smears your foreground color at the start of each stroke. If you want the best of both worlds, you can quickly switch into Finger Painting mode by pressing the Alt key as you drag. Release Alt to go back to Normal mode.

7. **Paint over the areas you want to smudge.**

   Pay attention to your strokes because this tool can radically change your image. If you don't like the results, press Ctrl+Z to undo and then lower your Strength percentage even more.

Softening with the Blur Tool

The Blur tool can be used both for repair and for more artistic endeavors. You can use the Blur tool to soften a small flaw or part of a rough edge. You can add a little blur to an element to make it appear as if it were moving when photographed. You can also blur portions of your image to emphasize your focal point, as shown in Figure 9-16, where we blurred everything but the girl's face. The Blur tool works by decreasing the contrast among adjacent pixels in the area blurred.

The mechanics of using the Blur tool and its options are similar to those of the Smudge tool, described earlier in this chapter. You obviously just won't find the Finger Painting option with the Blur tool. When using the Blur tool, be sure to use a small brush for smaller areas of blur.

PhotoSpin

Figure 9-16: The Blur tool can soften just the edges of a larger portion of an image element.

Focusing with the Sharpen Tool

If the Blur tool is Yin, then the Sharpen tool is Yang. The Sharpen tool increases the contrast among adjacent pixels to give the illusion that things are sharper. This tool needs to be used with restraint, however. Sharpen can quickly give way to overly grainy and noisy images if you're not cautious.

It is best to use a light hand and keep the areas you sharpen small. Sometimes, the eyes in a soft portrait can benefit from a little sharpening, as shown in Figure 9-17. You can also slightly sharpen an area to emphasize it against a less than sharp background.

PhotoSpin

Figure 9-17: Reserve the Sharpen tool for small areas, such as eyes.

To use the Sharpen tool, grab the tool from the Tools palette and follow the steps provided for the Smudge tool. In addition, here are some tips for using the Sharpen tool:

- ✔ Use a lower value, around 25 percent or less.

- ✔ Remember that you want to gradually sharpen your element to avoid the nasty noisy grain that can occur from over sharpening.

- ✔ Because sharpening increases contrast, if you use other contrast adjustments, such as Levels, you will boost the contrast of the sharpened area even more.

If you need to sharpen your overall image, try using the Unsharp Mask filter instead. It offers more options and better control.

Sponging Color On and Off

The Sponge tool soaks up color or squeezes it out. In more technical terms, this tool reduces or increases the intensity, or saturation, of color in both color and grayscale images. Yes, the Sponge tool also works in grayscale mode by darkening or lightening the brightness value of those pixels.

As with the Blur and Sharpen tools, you can use the Sponge tool to reduce or increase the saturation in selected areas in order to draw attention to or away from those areas.

Follow these steps to sponge color on or off your image:

1. **Choose the Sponge tool from the Tools palette in Standard Edit mode.**

   Press the O key or press Shift+O to cycle through the Sponge, Dodge, and Burn tools.

2. **Select a brush from the Brushes preset drop-down palette.**

   Use large, soft brushes to saturate or desaturate a larger area.

3. **Choose either Desaturate or Saturate from the Mode pop-up menu to decrease or increase color intensity, respectively.**

4. **Choose a Flow rate with the Flow slider or text box.**

   The flow rate is the speed with which the saturation or desaturation effect builds as you paint.

5. **Paint carefully over the areas you want to saturate or desaturate with color.**

   In our example in Figure 9-18, we saturated one of the kids to make her more of a focal point and desaturated the others.

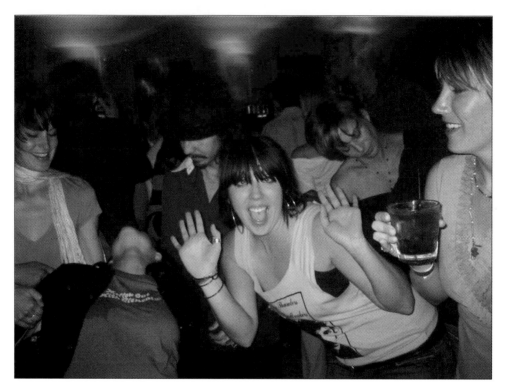

PhotoSpin

Figure 9-18: The Sponge tool increases or decreases the intensity of the color in your image.

Replacing One Color with Another

The Color Replacement tool allows you to replace the original color of an image with the foreground color. You can use this tool in a multitude of ways:

- Colorize a grayscale image to create the look of a hand-painted photo.
- Completely change the color of an element, or elements, in your image, as shown in Figure 9-19.
- Eliminate red eye if other, more automated methods don't work to your satisfaction.

What we particularly like about the Color Replacement tool is that it preserves all the tones of the image. The color applied is not like the opaque paint that is applied when painting with the Brush tool. When you are replacing color, the midtones, shadows, and highlights are retained. The Color Replacement tool works by first sampling the original colors in the image and then replacing those colors with the foreground color. By specifying different sampling methods, limits, and tolerance settings, you can control the range of colors that Elements replaces.

Follow these steps to replace existing color with your foreground color:

1. **Select the Color Replacement tool from the Tools palette in Standard Edit mode. It shares a flyout menu with the Brush and Pencil tools.**

   Alternatively, press the B (or Shift+B) key.

2. **Specify your desired brush tip diameter and hardness from the Brush preset picker drop-down palette.**

3. **Choose your desired blend mode. Here is a brief rundown of each:**

   - **Color:** The default, this mode works well for most jobs. This mode works great when eliminating red eye.

   - **Hue:** Similar to color, this mode is less intense and provides a subtler effect.

   - **Saturation:** This is the mode to use to convert your color image to grayscale. Set your foreground color to Black in the Tools palette.

   - **Luminosity:** This is the opposite of Color and doesn't provide much of an effect.

4. **Choose your sampling method (represented by the icons):**

   - **Continuous:** Samples and replaces color continuously as you drag your mouse.

   - **Once:** Replaces colors only in areas that contain the color you first sampled when you initially clicked.

   - **Background Swatch:** Replaces colors only in areas containing your current Background color.

5. **Select your limits mode:**

   - **Contiguous:** Replaces the color of adjacent pixels containing the sampled color.

   - **Discontiguous:** Replaces the color of the pixels containing the sampled color, whether or not they are adjacent.

6. **Set your tolerance percentage.**

   Tolerance refers to a range of color. The higher the value, the broader range of color that will be sampled, and vice versa.

7. **Select anti-aliasing.**

   Anti-aliasing slightly softens the edges of the sampled areas.

8. **Click or drag on your image.**

   The foreground color replaces the original colors of the sampled areas. In our example, shown in Figure 9-19, we used a foreground color of black.

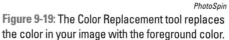

PhotoSpin

Figure 9-19: The Color Replacement tool replaces the color in your image with the foreground color.

10

Correcting Contrast, Color, and Clarity

. . . .

In This Chapter

▶ Correcting shadows and highlights

▶ Fixing contrast

▶ Removing color casts

▶ Adjusting hue and saturation

▶ Removing and replacing color

▶ Adjusting skin tones

▶ Working with Color Variations

▶ Sharpening and blurring your image

▶ Removing noise and artifacts

▶ Eliminating dust, scratches, and tears

. . . .

*1*f you've tried the quick and easy automatic fixes on your images and they didn't quite do the job, you've come to the right place. The great thing about Elements is that it offers multiple ways and multiple levels of repairing and enhancing your images. If an auto fix didn't cut it, then move on to a manual fix. If you're still not happy, you could consider shooting in Camera Raw format, provided your camera is able to do so. Elements has wonderful Camera Raw support, enabling you to process your images to your exact specifications. Chances are that if you can't find the tools to correct and repair your images in Elements, they're probably beyond salvaging.

That being said, and with information in Chapter 9 and this chapter at your fingertips, you'll want to try and employ some kind of logical workflow when tackling the correction and repair of your images:

1. **Make sure and first crop, straighten, and resize your images if necessary.**

2. **After you have them in their proper physical state, then correct the lighting and establish good tonal range for your shadows, highlights, and midtones in order to display the greatest detail possible.**

   Often just correcting the lighting will solve minor color problems. If not, move on to adjusting the color balance.

3. **Eliminate any color casts and adjust the saturation if necessary.**

4. **Then grab the retouching tools, such as the healing tools and filters, to retouch any flaws.**

5. **Finally, sharpen your image if you feel that it could use a boost in clarity and sharpness.**

   By following these steps and allocating a few minutes of your time, you should be able to get all your images in shape to print, post, and share with family and friends.

Adjusting Lighting

Elements has several simple, manual tools you can use to fix lighting if the Auto tools, described in Chapter 9, didn't work or were just too, well, automatic, for you. You'll find that the manual tools offer more control over adjusting overall contrast as well as bringing out details in shadow, midtones, and highlight areas of your images.

Fixing lighting with Shadows/Highlights

The Shadow/Highlight command offers a quick and easy method of correcting over- and underexposed areas. This feature works especially well with images shot in bright, overhead light or in light coming from the back (backlit). These images usually suffer from having the subject partially or completely enveloped in shadows, such as the original image (left) in Figure 10-1.

To use the Shadow/Highlight adjustment, follow these steps:

1. **In Standard Edit mode, choose Enhance⇨Adjust Lighting⇨ Shadows/Highlights. Make sure that Preview is checked.**

   In either Quick Fix or Standard Edit mode, when the dialog box appears, the correction is automatically applied in your preview.

2. **If the automatic adjustment doesn't quite do the job, move the sliders (or enter a value) to adjust the amount of correction for your Shadows (dark areas), Highlights (light areas), and Midtones (middle toned areas).**

   Remember that you want to try and reveal more detail in the dark and light areas of your image. If after you do so, your image still looks like it needs more correction, add or delete contrast in your midtone areas.

Before

Adjusted with the
Shadows/Highlights command

Figure 10-1: Correct the lighting in your images with the Shadows/Highlights adjustment.

3. Click OK to apply the adjustment and exit the dialog box.

If you want to start over, press Alt and click the Reset button (previously the Cancel button).

Using Brightness/Contrast

Despite its aptly descriptive moniker, the Brightness/Contrast command doesn't do that great of a job brightening (making an image darker or lighter) or adding or deleting contrast. Initially, users tend to be drawn to this command because of its appropriate name and ease of use. But once users realize its limitations, they move on to better tools with more controls such as Shadows/Highlights and Levels.

The problem with the Brightness/Contrast command is that it applies the adjustment equally to all areas of your image. For example, you may have a photo that has some highlights that need darkening but all the midtones and shadows are perfect. The Brightness slider isn't smart enough to recognize that. So when you start to darken your highlights, your midtones and shadows also become darker as well. To compensate for the unwanted darkening, you try and adjust the Contrast, which won't fix the problem.

The moral is if you want to use the Brightness/Contrast command, select only the areas that need the correction (for more on selections, see Chapter 7), as shown in Figure 10-2. Then choose Enhance➪Adjust Lighting➪Brightness/Contrast.

Figure 10-2: The Brightness/Contrast adjustment is best reserved for correcting selected areas (left), rather than the entire image (right).

Pinpointing proper contrast with Levels

If you want real horsepower when it comes to correcting the brightness and contrast (and even the color) in your image, look no further than the Levels command. Granted, the dialog box is a tad more complex than what you find with the other lighting and color adjustment commands, but when you understand how it works, it can be downright user friendly.

You can get a taste of what Levels can do by using Auto Levels, detailed in Chapter 9. The Levels command, its manual cousin, offers much more control. And unlike the primitive Brightness/Contrast control, Levels enables you to darken or lighten 256 different tones. Keep in mind that Levels can be used on your entire image, a single layer, or a selected area. You can also apply the Levels command by using an adjustment layer, as described in Chapter 8.

If you're serious about image editing, the Levels command is one tool you want to seriously figure out how to use. Here's how it works:

1. **In Standard Edit mode, choose Enhance➪Adjust Lighting➪Levels.**

   The Levels dialog box appears, displaying a graph called a *histogram*. The histogram displays how the pixels of the image are distributed at each of the 256 available brightness levels. Shadows are shown in the left of the histogram, midtones are in the middle, and highlights are on the right. Note that, in addition to viewing the histogram of the composite RGB channel (the entire image), you can view the histogram of just the Red, Green, or Blue channel by selecting one of them from the Channel pop-up menu.

Although you generally make changes to the entire document by using the RGB channel, you can apply changes to any one of an image's component color channels by selecting the specific channel in the Channel pop-up menu. You can also make adjustments to just selected areas. This can be helpful when one area of your image needs adjusting, while others don't.

2. **In Standard Edit mode, choose Window⇨Info to open your Info palette.**

3. **Set the black and white points manually using the Eyedroppers in the dialog box. Select the White Eyedropper tool and move the cursor over the image.**

4. **Look at your Info palette and try to find the lightest white in the image. Select that point by clicking.**

5. **Repeat Steps 3 and 4 using the Black Eyedropper tool and trying to find the darkest black in the image.**

   By setting the pure black and pure white points, the remaining pixels will be redistributed between those two points.

   You can also reset the white and black points by moving the position of the white and black triangles on the input sliders (just under the histogram). Or you can enter values in the Input Levels boxes. The three boxes represent the black, gray, and white triangles, respectively. Use the numbers 0 to 255 in the white and black boxes.

6. **Use the Gray Eyedropper tool to remove any colorcasts. Select a neutral gray portion of your image, one in which the Info palette shows equal values of red, green, and blue.**

   If your image is grayscale, you can't use the Gray Eyedropper tool.

   If you're not sure where there's a neutral gray, you can also remove a color cast by choosing a color channel from the Channel pop-up menu and doing one of the following:

   • Choose the Red channel and drag the midtone slider to the right to add cyan or to the left to add red.

   • Choose the Green channel and drag the midtone slider to the right to add magenta or to the left to add green.

   • Choose the Blue channel and drag the midtone slider to the right to add yellow or to the left to add blue.

7. **If your image requires it, adjust the output sliders at the very bottom of the Levels dialog box.**

   Moving the black triangle to the right reduces the contrast in the shadows and lightens the image. Moving the white triangle to the left reduces the contrast in the highlights and darkens the image.

8. **Adjust the midtones (or gamma values) with the gray triangle input slider.**

   The default value for gamma is 1.0. Drag the triangle left to lighten midtones, drag right to darken them. You can also enter a value.

9. **Click OK to apply your settings and exit the dialog box.**

   Your image should be greatly improved, as shown in Figure 10-3.

When you click the Auto button, Elements applies the same adjustments as the Auto Levels command, explained in Chapter 9. Note the changes, and subsequent pixel redistribution, made to the histogram after clicking.

Figure 10-3: Improve the contrast of an image with the intelligent Levels command.

Adjusting Color

Getting the color you want sometimes seems about as unattainable as winning the state lottery. Sometimes unexpected color casts (a shift in color) can be avoided at the shooting stage, for example by using (or not using, in some cases) a flash or lens filter. After the fact, you can usually do a pretty good job correcting the color with one of the many Elements adjustments. Occasionally, you may want to change the color of your images to create a certain special effect. Conversely, you also may want to strip the color out of your image altogether to create a vintage feel. Remember that all these color adjustments can be applied to your entire image, a single layer, or just a selection. Whatever your color needs, they'll no doubt be met in Elements.

If you shoot your photos in the Camera Raw file format, you can open and fix your files in the Camera Raw dialog box. Remember that Camera Raw files haven't been processed by your camera. You're in total control of the color and the exposure. For more on Camera Raw, see Chapter 4.

Removing color casts automatically

If you've ever taken a photo in an office or classroom and got a funky green tinge in your image, it's probably the result of the overhead fluorescent lighting. To eliminate this green color cast, you can apply the Color Cast command. This feature is designed to adjust the image's overall color and remove the cast.

Follow the short steps below to correct your image:

1. **Choose Enhance⇨Adjust Color⇨Remove Color Cast in either Quick Fix or Standard Edit mode**.

   The Remove Color Cast dialog box appears. Move the dialog box to better view your image.

2. **Click an area in your photo that should be white, black, or neutral gray, as shown in Figure 10-4. In our example, we clicked the sky in the image on the left.**

   The colors in the image will adjust according to the color you choose. Which color should you choose? This depends on the subject matter of your image. Feel free to experiment. Your adjustment is merely a preview at this point and won't be applied until you click OK. If you really goof up, click the Reset button, and your image will revert back to its unadjusted state.

3. **If you're satisfied with the adjustment, click OK to accept it and exit the dialog box.**

If the Remove Color Cast command didn't cut it, try applying a photo filter (described in the later section, "Adjusting color temperature with photo filters"). For example, if your photo has too much green, try applying a magenta filter.

Figure 10-4: Get rid of nasty color shifts with the Remove Color Cast command.

Adjusting with Hue/Saturation

The Hue/Saturation command enables you to adjust the colors in your image based on their hue, saturation, and lightness. Hue is the color in your image. Saturation is the intensity or richness of that color. And Lightness controls the brightness value.

Follow these steps to adjust color using the Hue/Saturation command:

1. **In either Quick Fix or Standard Edit mode, choose Enhance⇨Adjust Color⇨Adjust Hue/Saturation.**

   The Hue/Saturation dialog box appears. Be sure and check the Preview button so that you can view your adjustments.

2. **Select all the colors (Master) from the Edit pop-up menu, or choose one color to adjust.**

3. **Drag the slider for one or more of the following attributes to adjust the colors as described:**

   • **Hue:** Shifts all the colors clockwise (drag right) or counterclockwise (drag left) around the color wheel.

   • **Saturation:** Increases (drag right) or decreases (drag left) the richness of the colors. Note that dragging all the way to the left gives you the appearance of a grayscale image.

   • **Lightness:** Increases the brightness values by adding white (drag right) or decreases the brightness values by adding black (drag left).

   The top color bar at the bottom of the dialog box represents the colors in their order on the color wheel before you make any changes. The lower color bar displays the colors after you make your adjustments.

   When you select an individual color to adjust, sliders appear between the color bars so that you can define the range of color to be adjusted. You can select, add, or subtract colors from the range by choosing one of the Eyedropper tools and clicking in the image.

   The Hue/Saturation dialog box also lets you colorize images, a useful option for creating sepia colored images.

4. **(Optional) Check the Colorize option to change the colors in your image to a new, single color. Drag the Hue slider to change the color to your desired hue.**

   The pure white and black pixels will remain unchanged, while the intermediate gray pixels will be colorized.

TIP

Use the Hue/Saturation command, with the Colorize option, to create tinted photos, such as the one shown in Figure 10-5. You can also take a grayscale image, make selections, and apply a different tint to each selection. This can be especially fun with portraits. Tinted images can create vintage or moody feels and can transform even mediocre photos into something more special.

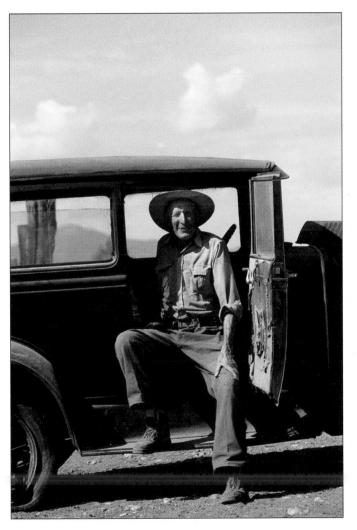

PhotoDisc/Getty Images

Figure 10-5: Adjust the color, the intensity, or the brightness of your image with the Hue/Saturation command.

Eliminating color with Remove Color

With all this talk about color, we realize that there may be times when you don't want any color at all. With Element's Remove Color command, you can easily eliminate all the color out of an image, layer, or selection. In Figure 10-6, we made a selection on the right side of the image and applied the Remove Color command. To use this one step command, simply choose Enhance⇨Adjust Color⇨ Remove Color.

Sometimes stripping away color with this command can leave your image flat or low in contrast. If this is the case, adjust the contrast using one of Element's many lighting fixes such as Auto Levels, Auto Contrast, or Levels.

PhotoDisic/Getty Images

Figure 10-6: Wash away all color with the Remove Color command.

Switching colors with Replace Color

The Replace Color command enables you to replace designated colors in your image with other colors. You first select the colors you want to replace by creating a mask, which is a selection made by designating white (selected), black (unselected), and gray (partially selected) areas. See Chapter 7 for more details on masks. You can then adjust the hue and or saturation of those selected colors.

Follow these steps to get on your way to replacing color:

1. **In Quick Fix or Standard Edit mode, choose Enhance⇨Adjust Color⇨ Replace Color.**

   The Replace Color dialog box appears. Make sure to check Preview.

2. **Choose either Selection or Image:**

   • **Selection:** Shows the mask in the Preview window. The unselected areas are black, partially selected areas are gray, and selected areas are white.

   • **Image:** Shows the actual image in the Preview window.

3. **Click the colors you want to select in either the image or the Preview window.**

4. **Press the Shift key and click, or use the plus (+) Eyedropper tool, to add more colors.**

5. **Press the Alt key or use the minus (–) Eyedropper tool to delete colors.**

6. **To add colors similar to the ones you select, use the Fuzziness slider to fine-tune your selection, adding or deleting from the selection based on the Fuzziness value.**

7. **Move the Hue and or Saturation sliders to change the color or color richness, respectively.**

8. **View the result in your image window. If you're satisfied, click OK to apply the settings and exit the dialog box.**

   Figure 10-7 shows how we substituted the color of our tulips to change them from orange to yellow.

Corbis Digital Stock

Figure 10-7: The Replace Color command enables you to replace one color for another.

Adjusting skin tones

Occasionally, you may find that the loved ones in your photos have taken on a rather sickly shade of green, red, or some other non-flesh colored tone. To rectify that problem, Elements has come up with a command specifically designed to adjust the overall color in the image and get skin tones back to a natural shade.

Here's how to use this new feature:

1. **Open your image in Quick Fix or Standard Edit mode, check Preview, and do one or both of the following:**

   • Select the layer that needs to be adjusted. If you do not have any layers, your entire image will be adjusted.

   • Select your desired areas of skin that need to be adjusted. Only the selected areas will be adjusted. This is a good way to go if you're happy with the color of your other elements and you just want to tweak the skin tones. For more on selection techniques, see Chapter 7.

2. **Choose Enhance⇨Adjust Color⇨Adjust Color for Skin Tone.**

   The Adjust Color for Skin Tone dialog box appears, as shown in Figure 10-8.

3. **In the image window, click the portion of skin that needs to be corrected.**

   The command adjusts the color of the skin tone, as well as the color in the overall image, layer, or selection, depending on what you selected in Step 1.

4. **If you're not satisfied with the results, click on another area or fiddle with the Skin and Ambient Light sliders, as follows:**

   • **Tan:** Adds or removes the amount of brown in the skin.

   • **Blush:** Adds or removes the amount of red in the skin.

   • **Temperature:** Adjusts the overall color of the skin, making it warmer (right towards red) or cooler (left towards blue).

5. **When you're happy with the correction, click OK to apply the adjustment and exit the dialog box.**

   To start anew, click the Reset button. And of course, to bail out completely, click Cancel.

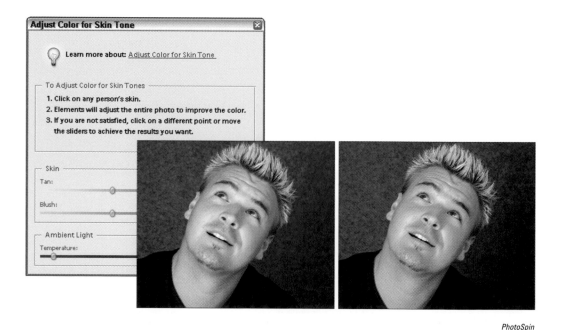

PhotoSpin

Figure 10-8: Give your friends and family a complexion makeover with the new Adjust Color for Skin Tone command.

Defringing layers

A tell-tale sign of haphazardly com-posited images is selections with fringe. I don't mean the cute kind hanging from your leather jacket or upholstery. I mean the unattractive kind that consists of those back-ground pixels that surround the edges of your selections, as shown in Figure 10-9. Inevitably, when you move or paste a selection, some of the background pixels are bound to go along for the ride. These pixels

Fringe   Defringed

PhotoSpin

Figure 10-9: Remove the colored halo around your selections with the Defringe command.

are referred to as a *fringe* or *halo*. Luckily, the new Defringe command replaces the color of the fringe pixels with the colors of neighboring pixels that do not contain the background color. In our example, we plucked the boat out of a white studio background and placed it on an image of water. Some of the background pixels were included in our selection and appear as a white fringe. When we apply the Defringe command, those white fringe pixels are changed to colors of nearby pixels, such as bluc or red, as shown in Figure 10-9.

Here are the steps to defringe your selection:

1. **In Quick Fix or Standard Edit mode, Copy and Paste a selection onto a new or existing layer, or drag and drop a selection onto a new document.**

   For more on selections, see Chapter 7.

2. **Choose Enhance⇨Adjust Color⇨Defringe Layer.**

   The Defringe dialog box appears.

3. **Enter a value for the number of pixels that need to be converted.**

   Try 1 or 2 at first to see if that does the trick. If not, you may need to enter a slightly higher value.

4. **Click OK to accept the value and exit the dialog box.**

Correcting with Color Variations

Although we've already given you several ways to eliminate color casts in an image, we are going to throw in one more. The Variations command is a digital color correction feature that has been around for years and is largely unchanged. That's probably because it is one of those great features that is easy to use, easy to understand, and works. The command works by enabling you to make corrections by visually comparing thumbnails of color variations of your image. You might use this command when you're not quite sure what's wrong with the color or what kind of color cast your image has.

Here's how to use the Color Variations command:

1. **Choose Enhance➪Adjust Color➪Color Variations in Quick Fix or Standard Edit mode.**

   The Color Variations dialog box appears, displaying a preview of your original image (before) and the corrected image (after), as shown in Figure 10-10.

2. **Select your desired tonal range or color richness. If you're unsure which range to select, start with the Midtones. Options are as follows:**

   • **Shadows, Midtones, Highlights:** Adjusts the dark, middle, or light areas in the image, respectively.

   • **Saturation:** Adjusts the color intensity or richness, making colors more intense (saturated) or less intense (desaturated). If your image is faded from time, be sure and increase the saturation after you've corrected any color cast issues.

   Usually, just correcting the Midtones will be enough to get your image's color in order, but if not, you can always adjust the Shadows and Highlights as well.

3. **Specify how much adjustment you want with the Adjust Color slider.**

PhotoSpin

Figure 10-10: Color Variations enables you to visually correct your images by comparing thumbnails.

Drag left to decrease the amount of adjustment, and drag right to increase the amount.

4. **If you selected Midtones, Shadows, or Highlights in Step 2, adjust your color by clicking on the various Increase or Decrease (color) buttons. Click more than once if your initial application wasn't sufficient to correct the problem.**

   Be sure to keep an eye on the After thumbnail, which reflects your corrections as you make them.

5. **Click the Darken or Lighten buttons to make the colors a little darker or lighter.**

6. **If you selected Saturation in Step 2, click the Less Saturation or More Saturation buttons.**

7. **If you've made a mistake, or several mistakes for that matter, click the Undo button.**

   The Color Variations dialog box supports multiple levels of undo. If you've really botched it, you can always click the Reset Image button to start again. Keep in mind that you cannot undo the Reset Image command after you've clicked it. Click Cancel to bail out entirely.

8. **To apply your color adjustments and exit the dialog box, click OK.**

The Variations command is a great tool to correct those old, faded, green (or some other unwanted color) tinted circa yesteryear photos. Variations allows you to easily correct the color and saturation of these precious, but damaged, images. Remember to either decrease the offending color or add the color that is the opposite of the cast in the image. If it is too red, add green and vice versa.

Adjusting color temperature with photo filters

Light has its own color temperature. A photo shot in a higher color temperature of light makes an image blue. Conversely, an image shot in a lower color temperature makes a photo yellow. In the old days, photographers used to place a colored glass filter in front of their camera lens to adjust the color temperature of the light. This would be done to either warm up or cool down a photo, or to just add a hint of color for a subtle special effect. Elements gives you the digital version of these filters with the Photo Filter command.

To apply the Photo Filter adjustment, follow these steps:

1. **Choose Filter➪Adjustments➪Photo Filter in the Standard Edit mode.**

   The Photo Filter dialog box appears.

   Note that you can also apply the photo filter to an individual layer by creating a photo filter adjustment layer. For details, see Chapter 8.

2. **In the dialog box, select Filter to choose a preset filter from the drop-down list, or select Color to select your own filter color from the Color Picker.**

   Here is a brief description of each of the preset filters:

   - **Warming Filter (85), (81), and (LBA):** Adjusts the white balance in an image to make the colors warmer, or more yellow. Filter (81) is like (85) and (LBA), but is best used for minor adjustments. In our example in Figure 10-11, we used the Warming Filter (85) to warm up an overly cool winter shot.

   - **Cooling Filter (80), (82), and (LBB):** Also adjusts the white balance, but instead makes the colors cooler, or bluer. Filter (82) is like (80) and (LBB), but is designed for slight adjustments.

   - **Red, Orange, Yellow, and so on:** The various color filters adjust the hue, or color, of a photo. Choose a color filter to try and eliminate a color cast or for a special effect.

3. **Adjust the Density option to specify the amount of color applied to your image.**

4. **Check Preserve Luminosity to prevent the photo filter from darkening your image.**

5. **Click OK to apply your filter and exit the dialog box.**

Figure 10-11: Apply a Photo Filter to adjust the color temperature of an image.

Mapping your colors

Elements provides some commands referred to as color mappers, which change the colors in your image by mapping them to other values. The color mappers are found under the Filter➪Adjustments submenu. Figure 10-12 shows an example of each command, which is also briefly described in the following subsections.

Equalize

Invert

Threshold

Posterize

PhotoSpin

Figure 10-12: Change the colors in your image by remapping them to other values.

Equalize

This mapper first locates the lightest and darkest pixels in the image and assigns them values of white and black. It then redistributes all the remaining pixels among the grayscale values. The exact effect depends on your individual image.

Invert

This command reverses all the colors in your image, creating a kind of negative. Black reverses to white, colors convert to their complementary hues (blue goes to yellow, red goes to green, and so on).

Threshold

Threshold makes your image black and white, with all pixels that are brighter than a value you specify represented as white, and all pixels that are darker than that value as black. You can change the threshold level to achieve different high-contrast effects.

 The Threshold command can come in handy when you need to clean up scans of line art, such as hand-drawn sketches, people's signatures, pages from a book, or even sheet music. Often when scanning things on paper, the slight color from the paper appears as a dull gray background in the scan. By applying the Threshold command, you can adjust the tones in your image to black and white and drop out the gray. Simply move the slider to get your desired balance of white and black areas.

Posterize

This command reduces the number of colors in your image. Choose a value between 2 and 255 colors. Lower values create an illustrative, poster look, while higher values produce a more photo-realistic image.

Adjusting Clarity

After your image has the right contrast and color, and you've fixed any flaws, as described in Chapter 9, you're ready to finally work on the overall clarity of that image. Although you may have fixed the nitpicky little blemishes with the healing tools, if your image suffers from an overall problem like dust, scratches, or artifacts (blocky pixels or halos), you may need to employ the help of a filter. After you've totally cleaned up your image, the last chore is to give it a good sharpening. Why wait until the bitter end to do so? That's because sometimes, while you're improving the contrast and color and getting rid of flaws, you can reduce the clarity and sharpness of an image. So you want to be sure that your image is as soft as it's going to get before you tackle your sharpening tasks. On the other hand, also be aware that sharpening itself increases contrast, so depending on how much of your image you are sharpening, you may need to go back and fine-tune your image using the lighting adjustments described previously in this chapter.

Finally, with all this talk about sharpening, we know you might find it strange when we say you may also need to occasionally blur your image. Blurring can be done to eliminate unpleasant patterns that occur during scanning, soften distracting backgrounds to give a better focal point, or even to create the illusion of motion.

Removing noise, artifacts, dust, and scratches

Surprisingly, the tools you want to use to eliminate junk from your images are found in the Filter➪Noise filter submenu in Standard Edit mode. With the exception of the Add Noise filter, the others help to hide noise, dust, scratches, and artifacts. Here's the list of junk removers:

- **Despeckle:** Decreases the contrast, without affecting the edges, to make the dust in your image less pronounced. You may notice a slight blurring of your image (that's what's hiding the junk), but hopefully, the edges are still sharp.

- **Dust & Scratches:** The name says it all. This filter hides dust and scratches by blurring those areas of your image that contain the nastiness (it looks for harsh transitions in tone). Specify your desired Radius value, which is the size of the area to be blurred. Also specify the Threshold value, which determines how much contrast between pixels must be present before they are blurred.

  Use this filter with restraint, because it can obliterate detail and make your image go from bad to worse.

- **Median:** Reduces contrast around dust spots. The process the filter goes through is rather technical, so suffice it to say that the light spots darken, the dark spots lighten, and the rest of the image isn't changed. Specify your desired Radius, which is the size of the area to be adjusted.

- **Reduce Noise:** This filter, which we used to correct the original image (left) in Figure 10-13, is designed to remove luminance noise and artifacts from your images. *Luminance noise* is grayscale noise that makes images look overly grainy. Specify these options to reduce the noise in your image:

  - **Strength:** Specify the amount of noise reduction.

  - **Preserve Details:** A higher percentage preserves edges and details but reduces the amount of noise removed.

  - **Reduce Color Noise:** Removes random colored pixels.

  - **Remove JPEG Artifact:** Removes the blocks and halos that can occur from low-quality JPEG compression.

Figure 10-13: Use the Reduce Noise filter to remove noise and artifacts.

Blurring when you need to

It may sound odd that anyone would intentionally want to blur an image. But if you have a photo that is overly grainy or suffers from a nasty moiré pattern (described in the following list), you may need to blur the image to correct the problem. And occasionally, you may even want to blur the background of an image to deemphasize distractions or to make the foreground elements appear sharper and provide a better focal point.

All your blurring tools are found in the Filter➪Blur menu in Standard Edit mode, with the exception of the Blur tool, which is explained in Chapter 9:

- **Average:** This one-step filter calculates the average value of the image or selection and fills the area with that average value. You can use it for smoothing overly noisy areas in your image.

- **Blur:** Another one-step filter, this one applies a fixed amount of blurring to the whole image.

- **Blur More:** The last one-step blur filter gives the same effect as Blur, but more intensely.

- **Motion Blur:** This filter mimics the blur given off by moving objects. Specify the angle of motion and the distance of the blur. Make sure and check Preview to see the effect as you enter your values.

- **Radial Blur:** Need to simulate a moving Ferris wheel or some other round object? This filter produces a circular blur effect. Specify the amount of blur you want. Choose the Spin method to blur along concentric circular lines, as shown in the thumbnail. Or choose Zoom to blur along radial lines and mimic the effect of zooming into your image. Specify your desired Quality. Because the Radial Blur filter is notoriously slow, Elements gives you the option of Draft (fast but grainy) or Good and Best (slower but smoother). The difference between Good and Best is only evident on larger, higher-resolution images. Finally, indicate where you would like the center of your blur by moving the blur diagram thumbnail.

✔ **Smart Blur:** This filter provides several options to enable you to specify how the blur is applied. Specify a value for the Radius and Threshold, both defined later in the "Sharpening for better focus" section. Start with a lower value for both and adjust from there. Choose a quality setting from the pop-up menu. Choose a mode setting. Normal blurs the entire image or selection. Edge Only blurs only the edges of your elements and uses black and white in the blurred pixels. Overlay Edge also blurs just the edges, but it applies only white to the blurred pixels.

✔ **Gaussian Blur:** The last Blur filter to discuss is probably the one you'll use most often. It offers a Radius setting to let you adjust the amount of blurring you desire.

Use the Gaussian Blur filter to camouflage moiré patterns on scanned images. A *moiré pattern* is caused when you scan halftone images. A *halftone* is created when a continuous tone image, such as a photo, is digitized and converted into a screen pattern of repeating lines (usually between 85 and 150 lines per inch) and printed. When you then scan that halftone, a second pattern results and is overlaid on the original pattern. These two different patterns bump heads and create a nasty moiré pattern. The Gaussian Blur filter doesn't eliminate the moiré, it simply merges the dots and reduces the appearance of the pattern, as shown in Figure 10-14. Play with the Radius slider until you get an acceptable trade off between less moiré and less focus. If you happen to have a descreen filter built into your scanning software, you can use that as well during the actual scanning of the halftone image.

Figure 10-14: Use the Gaussian Blur filter to reduce moiré patterns caused by scanning halftones.

Sharpening for better focus

Of course, if your images don't need any contrast, color, and flaw fixing, feel free to jump right into sharpening. Sometimes, images captured by a scanner or a digital camera are a little soft, and it's not due to any tonal adjustments. Occasionally, you may even want to sharpen a selected area in your image just so that it stands out more.

First, let us say that you can't really improve the focus of an image after it's captured. But you can do a pretty good job faking it. All sharpening tools work by increasing the contrast between adjacent pixels. This increased contrast causes the edges to appear more distinct, thereby giving the illusion that the focus is improved, as shown in Figure 10-15.

Elements provides several sharpening tools all found in the Filter⇨Sharpen menu. You can also use the Sharpen tool for small areas, as described in Chapter 9. Here's a description of each of the sharpen filters:

Figure 10-15: Sharpening mimics an increase in focus by increasing contrast between adjacent pixels.

> ✔ **Sharpen:** This one-step filter increases the contrast between all the pixels in the image or selection. It's best reserved for small areas because it has a tendency to make solid-colored areas that aren't part of the edges appear grainy.

> ✔ **Sharpen Edges:** Another one-step filter that focuses on the edges of the elements in your image, adding sharpness while avoiding adding grain. It's better than Sharpen and Sharpen More, but not as good as Unsharp Mask.

✔ **Sharpen More:** The last one-step filter is similar to Sharpen but increases the contrast between pixels even more. Again, use it for minor touch ups and avoid it for large areas.

✔ **Unsharp Mask:** This filter, which gets its odd name from a darkroom technique, is your sharpening tool of choice. Unsharp Mask gives you several options that enable you to control the amount of sharpening and the width of the areas to be sharpened. Use them to pinpoint your desired sharpening:

  • **Amount:** Specify your desired amount (from 1 to 500%) of edge sharpening. The higher the value, the more contrast between pixels around the edges. Start with a value of 100% (or less), which usually gives good contrast without appearing overly grainy.

  • **Radius:** Specify the width (from .1 to 250 pixels) of the edges that the filter will sharpen. The higher the value, the wider the edge. The value you use is largely based on the resolution of your image. Low-resolution images require a smaller radius value. High-resolution images require a higher value.

    Be warned that specifying a value that is too high will overemphasize the edges of your image and make it appear too contrasty or even goopy around the edges.

    A good guideline in selecting a starting radius value is to divide your image's resolution by 150. For example, if you have a 300 ppi image, set the radius at 2 and then adjust by your eye from there.

  • **Threshold:** Specify the difference in brightness (from 0 to 255) that must be present between adjacent pixels before the edge is sharpened. A lower value sharpens edges with very little contrast difference. Higher values only sharpen when adjacent pixels are very different in contrast. We recommend leaving Threshold set at 0 unless your image is very grainy. Increasing the value too high can cause unnatural transitions between sharpened and unsharpened areas.

Occasionally, the values you enter in the Amount and Radius may sharpen the image effectively, but in turn create excess grain, or noise, in your image. You can sometimes reduce this noise by increasing the Threshold value.

Part IV
Exploring Your Inner Artist

The 5th Wave   By Rich Tennant

"Hey- let's put scanned photos of ourselves through a ripple filter and see if we can make ourselves look weird."

In this part . . .

*I*n addition to correcting photos to improve their appearance, you can delve into the world of the Photoshop Elements artist, where you can use tools to draw and paint on existing photos or create new blank documents and create your own drawings. The tools available to you rival an artist's analog tools, and Photoshop Elements' capabilities are limited only by one's imagination. In this part, you discover how to apply different artistic effects by using many tools and how to customize tools for your own use, and you get some helpful tips to create some dazzling images.

In addition to the artistic effects you can apply to your photos, this section also handles working with text. When it comes time to create a poster, an advertisement, or some Web icons, the text features in Elements offer you many options for creating headline type, body copy, and special type effects.

Playing with Filters, Effects, Styles, and More

After giving your images a makeover — cropped, color corrected, flaws repaired, sharpened — you may want to get them all gussied up for a night out on the town. You can do just that with filters, effects, Layer Styles, and Blend Modes. These tools enable you to add that touch of emphasis, drama, whimsy, or just plain goofy fun. I'll be the first to admit that often the simplest art (and that includes photographs) is the best. That gorgeous landscape shot or the portrait that perfectly captures the expression on a child's happy face is something you may want to leave unembellished. But for the times when a little artistic experimentation is order, turn to this chapter as your guide.

Having Fun with Filters

Filters have been around since the early days of digital imaging, when Elements was just a little bitty program. Filters, also called *plug-ins* because they can be installed or removed independently, change the look of your image in a variety of ways, as shown in Figure 11-1. They can correct less-than-perfect images by making them appear sharper or by covering up flaws, as described in Chapter 10. Or they can enhance your images by making them appear as though they were painted, tiled, photocopied, or lit by spotlights. Just make sure to create a backup of your original image if you plan on saving your filtered ones. This section gives you the basics on how to apply a filter and gives a few filtering tips.

| Original | Unsharp Mask filter | Water Paper filter |

Figure 11-1: Use filters to correct image imperfections or to completely transform them.

Applying filters

You can apply a filter in three ways:

- ✔ In either Standard Edit or Quick Fix modes, go to the Filter menu, choose your desired filter category, and then select a specific filter.

- ✔ In Standard Edit mode only, choose Window➪Styles and Effects to open the palette. Choose Filters from the drop-down list in the top-left corner of the palette. Choose your filter category from the drop-down list in the top-right corner of the palette. Double-click the thumbnail of your desired filter or drag the filter onto your image window.

- ✔ In either Standard Edit or Quick Fix modes, choose Filter➪Filter Gallery to apply one or more filters in a flexible editing environment. The Filter Gallery is described later in this chapter.

Note that you cannot apply filters to images that are in Bitmap or Index Color mode. And some filters don't work on images in Grayscale mode. For a refresher on color modes, see Chapter 3.

Corrective or destructive filters

Although there are no hard and fast rules, most digital-imaging folks classify filters into two basic categories, *corrective* and *destructive:*

- **Corrective filters** usually fix some kind of image problem. They adjust color, improve focus, remove dust or artifacts, and so on. Don't get me wrong — pixels are still modified. It's just that the basic appearance of the image remains the same, albeit hopefully improved. Two of the most popular corrective filters, Sharpen and Blur, are covered in Chapter 10.

- **Destructive filters** are used to create some kind of special effect. Pixels are also modified, but the image may look quite a bit different than its original. These kinds of filters create effects such as textures, brush strokes, mosaics, lights, and clouds. They can also distort an image with waves, spheres, and ripples.

One-step or multistep filters

All corrective and destructive filters are either one-step filters or multistep filters. One-step filters have no options and no dialog boxes; select the filter and watch the magic happen. Multistep filters act almost like mini-applications. Choose the filter and you are presented with a dialog box with options to specify. The options vary widely depending on the filter, but most come equipped with at least one option to control the intensity of the filter. Multi-step filters appear in the menus with an ellipsis following their names, indicating that a dialog box follows the execution of the command.

Giving a filter an encore

If you like the filter you applied so much that you want to reapply it, either to the same image or to a different one, all you have to do is either press Ctrl+F or choose the name of the filter from the Filter menu. Either way, your last filter, with the same settings, is reapplied to your image. You might want to reapply a filter to make the effect more pronounced. Or maybe you want to apply the same filter with the same settings to a series of different images. If you want to reapply the filter, but need to tweak the settings, press Ctrl+Alt+F, which brings up the last applied filter's dialog box.

Fading a filter

Sometimes you don't want the full effects of a filter applied to your image. Sometimes fading a filter a bit softens the effect and makes it look less "computer-ish." Here's what you can do:

1. **Choose Layer⇨Duplicate Layer. Click OK when the dialog box appears.**

2. **Apply your desired filter to the duplicate layer.**

3. **Use the blend modes and opacity settings located in the Layers palette to merge the filtered layer with the original unfiltered image.**

4. **(Optional) Using the Eraser tool, selectively erase portions of your filtered image to enable the unfiltered image to show through.**

   For example, if you applied a Gaussian Blur filter to soften a harshly lit portrait, try erasing the blurred portion that covers the subject's eyes to let the unblurred eyes of the layer below show through, as shown in Figure 11-2. The sharply focused eyes provide a natural focal point.

PhotoSpin

Figure 11-2: Fading a filter allows you to mix the filtered and unfiltered images.

Selectively applying a filter

Up to this point, we've been referring to applying filters to your *images*. But really, we've been using this word rather loosely. You don't necessarily have to apply filters to your entire image. You can apply filters to individual layers, or even to selections. You can often get better effects when you apply a filter just to a portion of an image or layer. For example, you can blur a distracting background so the person in your image gets due attention. Or, as shown in Figure 11-3, you can apply an Ocean Ripple or Wave filter to the ocean, leaving your surfer unfiltered to avoid that overly "Photoshopped" effect.

Exercising a little restraint when applying filters usually produces a more attractive image.

Corbis Digital Stock

Figure 11-3: Selectively applying a filter can avoid an image looking overly manipulated.

Working in the Filter Gallery

Don't be surprised if, when you apply a filter, you are presented with a gargantuan dialog box. This *editing window,* as it's officially called, is the Filter Gallery. You can also access it by choosing Filter➪Filter Gallery. In the flexible Filter Gallery, you can apply multiple filters as well as edit them *ad nauseum.*

Even when using the Filter Gallery, remember to make a backup copy of your image or at least create a duplicate layer before you apply filters. Filters change the pixels of an image permanently, and when you exit the Filter Gallery, the filters that are applied can't be removed.

Follow these steps to work in the Filter Gallery:

1. **Choose Filter➪Filter Gallery in either Standard Edit or Quick Fix modes.**

   The Filter Gallery editing window appears, as shown in Figure 11-4.

2. **In the center of the editing window, click your desired filter category folder.**

   The folder expands and shows the filters in that category. A thumbnail displays each filter's effect.

3. **Select your desired filter.**

   You get a large dynamic preview of your image on the left side of the dialog box. To preview a different filter, just select it. Use the magnification controls to zoom in and out of the preview. To hide the Filter menu and get a larger preview box, click the arrow to the left of the OK button.

PhotoSpin

Figure 11-4: Apply and edit multiple filters in the Filter Gallery.

4. **Specify any settings associated with the filter.**

   The preview updates accordingly.

5. **When you are happy with the results, click OK to apply the filter and exit the editing window.**

6. **If you want to apply another filter, click the New Effect Layer button at the bottom of the editing window.**

   This duplicates the existing filter.

7. **Choose your desired new filter, which then replaces the duplicate in the applied filters area of the dialog box.**

   Each of the filters you apply is displayed in the bottom right of the Filter Gallery dialog box. To delete a filter, select it and click the Delete Effect Layer button. To edit a filter's settings, select it in the list and make any changes. Keep in mind that when you edit a filter's settings, that edit may affect the look of any subsequent filters you have applied. Finally, you can rearrange the order of the applied filters. But doing so changes the overall effect.

8. **When you're completely done, click OK to apply the filters and exit the editing window.**

Distorting with the Liquify filter

The Liquify filter is really much more than a filter. It's a distortion that allows you to manipulate an image as though it were warm taffy. You can interactively twist, pull, twirl, pinch, and bloat parts of your image. You can apply this distort filter on the entire image, on a layer, or on a selection. This *über-filter* comes equipped with a mega dialog box with its own set of tools (on the left) and options (on the right), as shown in Figure 11-5.

Follow these steps to turn your image into a melted Dalí-esque wannabe:

1. **Choose Filter⇨Distort⇨Liquify in either Standard Edit or Quick Fix modes.**

   Your image appears in the preview area.

2. **Choose your distortion weapon of choice.**

   You also have a number of tools to help zoom and navigate around your image window.

PhotoSpin

Figure 11-5: The Liquify filter enables you to interactively distort your image.

Here is a description of each tool to help you decide. See Figure 11-6 to get a visual look at the effect of each distortion tool (the letter in parentheses is the keyboard shortcut):

- **Warp (W):** Pushes pixels forward as you drag, creating a stretched effect. Use short strokes or long pushes.

- **Turbulence (T):** Drag to randomly jumble your pixels. Use this tool to re-create maelstroms of air, fire, and water with clouds, flames, and waves. Adjust how smooth the effect is by dragging the Turbulent Jitter slider in the Tool Options area. The higher the value, the smoother the effect.

- **Twirl Clockwise (R) and Twirl Counterclockwise (L):** Rotates pixels either clockwise or counterclockwise. Place the cursor in one spot, hold down the mouse button, and watch the pixels under your brush rotate, or drag the cursor to create a moving twirl effect.

- **Pucker (P):** Press and hold or drag to pinch your pixels toward the center of the area covered by the brush. To reverse the pucker direction (*bloat*), press the Alt key as you hold or drag.

- **Bloat (B):** Press and hold or drag to push pixels toward the edge of the brush area. To reverse the bloat direction (*pucker*), press the Alt key as you hold or drag.

PhotoSpin

Figure 11-6: The Liquify filter can transform a clock into something far from ordinary.

- **Shift Pixels (S):** Moves pixels to the left when you drag the tool straight up. Drag down to move pixels to the right. Drag clockwise to increase the size of the object being distorted. Drag counterclockwise to decrease the size. To reverse any of the directions, press Alt as you hold or drag.

- **Reflection (M):** Drags a reversed image of your pixels at a 90-degree angle to the motion of the brush. Hold down the Alt key to force the reflection in the direction opposite the motion of the brush. Great for making reflections on water.

- **Hand (H):** Works like the Hand tool in the Elements Tools palette. Drag with the Hand tool to move the image around the preview window.

- **Zoom (Z):** Works like the Zoom tool in the Elements Tools palette. Zooms you in and out (hold down the Alt key) so you can better see your distortions. You can also zoom by choosing a magnification percentage from the pop-up menu in the bottom-left corner of the dialog box.

3. **Specify your options in the Tool Options area as follows:**

   - **Brush Size:** Drag the pop-up slider or enter a value from 1 to 600 pixels to specify the width of your brush.

   - **Brush Pressure:** Drag the pop-up slider or enter a value from 1 to 100 to change the pressure. The higher the pressure, the faster the distortion effect is applied.

   - **Turbulent Jitter:** Drag the pop-up slider or enter a value from 1 to 100 to adjust the smoothness when using the Turbulence tool.

   - **Stylus Pressure:** If you're lucky enough to have a graphics tablet and stylus, click this option to select the pressure of your stylus.

4. **Got a little carried away? Select the Reconstruct tool (R) and hold down or drag the mouse on the distorted portions of the image you want to reverse or reconstruct.**

   Note that the reconstruction occurs faster at the center of the brush's diameter. To partially reconstruct your image, set a low brush pressure and watch closely as your mouse drags across the distorted areas.

5. **Click OK to apply the distortions and exit the dialog box.**

   However, if you mucked things up and want to start again, click the Revert button to get your original, unaltered image back. This also resets the tools to their previous settings.

Dressing Up with Effects

In addition to the multitude of filters at your disposal, Elements also provides lots of different effects that you can apply to enhance your photos. Effects are unique in that, depending on the specific effect, each effect can be applied only to a selection, layer, or type. The names of those effects are followed by labels, as follows: (Selection), (Layer), or (Type). To compound the confusion, some effects automatically create a duplicate of the selected layer, whereas other effects can work only on flattened images. (See Chapter 8 for details on layers.) Finally, unlike filters, you cannot preview how the effect will look on your image or type, nor do you have any options to specify.

Here are the very short steps to apply an effect:

1. **Select your desired image or type layer in the Layers palette. Or if you are applying the effect to just a selection, make the selection prior to applying the effect.**

2. **Choose Window⇨Styles and Effects.**

3. **Choose Effects from the drop-down list at the top left of the palette.**

4. **Choose your desired category of effects from the drop-down list at the top right of the palette:**

- **All:** Shows all the effects described in this list

- **Frames:** Includes effects that enhance the edges of the layer or selection.

- **Image Effects:** Includes a wide variety of effects to make your image appear as though it were snowing, made of lizard skin or neon tubes, or painted with oil pastels.

- **Text Effects:** These effects enhance your type with outlines, shadows, spray paint, metal, confetti, or wood, as shown in Figure 11-7. Note that when an effect is applied to type, it becomes *simplified* and looses its editability. For more on type, see Chapter 13.

- **Textures:** Includes textured effects such as bricks, wood, rust, and even slime.

5. **In the Effects palette, double-click your desired effect or drag the effect onto the image.**

   Note that you can view your styles and effects by thumbnails or by list. To change the view, click More at the top-right corner of the palette.

PhotoSpin

Figure 11-7: Enhance your images by adding effects to your image and type layers.

Adding Shadows, Glows, and More

Going hand in hand with filters and effects are Layer Styles. Also designed to enhance your image and type layers, Layer Styles range from simple shadows and bevels to the more complex styles, such as buttons and patterns. The wonderful thing about Layer Styles is that they are completely nondestructive. Unlike filters, Layer Styles don't change your pixel data. You can edit them or even delete them if you're unhappy with the results.

Here are some important facts about Layer Styles:

- **Layer Styles can be applied only to layers.** Therefore, if all you have in your image is a background, be sure and convert it to a layer first.

- **Layer Styles are *dynamically linked* to the contents of a layer.** If you move or edit the contents of the layers, the results are updated.

- **When you apply a Layer Style to a layer, a florin symbol (which looks like a fancy letter *f*) appears next to the layer's name in the Layers palette.** Double-click the florin to bring up the Styles Settings dialog box and perform any editing that's necessary to get the look you want.

Applying Layer Styles

Layer Styles fall into a few different libraries. You can add shadows, glows, beveled and embossed edges, and more complex styles such as neon, plastic, and chrome, as well as various image effects. A sampling of styles is shown in Figure 11-8. Here are the steps to apply a style and a description of each of the style libraries.

1. **Select your desired image or type layer in the Layers palette.**

2. **Choose Window⇨Styles and Effects.**

3. **Choose Layer Styles from the drop-down list at the top left of the palette.**

4. **Choose your desired library of styles from the drop-down list at the top right of the palette:**

   - **Bevels:** Bevels add a three-dimensional edge on the outside or inside edges of the contents of a layer, giving the element some dimension. Emboss styles make elements appear as though they are raising off or are punched into the page. You can change the appearance of these styles by adjusting the lighting angle, shadow distance (how close the shadow is to the layer contents), size of the outer glow and bevel, and bevel direction. The Use Global Light option applies the same lighting angle for all styles and ensures consistency in the light source.

Drop Shadow   Inner Shadow   Bevel

Outer Glow   Inner Glow

Figure 11-8: Add dimension by applying shadows, glows, and bevels to your object or type.

- **Drop and Inner Shadows:** Add a soft drop or inner shadow to a layer. Choose from the garden-variety shadow or one that includes noise, neon, or outlines. You can adjust the lighting angle and shadow distance as desired.

- **Outer and Inner Glows:** Add a soft halo that appears on the outside or inside edges of your layer contents. Adjust the appearance of the glow by changing lighting angle, shadow distance, and the size of the glow.

- **Visibility:** Click Show, Hide, or Ghosted to either display, hide, or partially show the layer contents. The Layer Style remains fully displayed.

- **Complex and others:** The remaining Layer Styles are a cornucopia of different effects ranging from simple glass buttons to the more exotic effects, such as Groovy and Rose Impressions. You can customize all these Layer Styles to a certain extent by adjusting the various settings, which are similar to those for other styles in this list.

5. **In the Layer Styles palette, double-click your desired effect or drag the effect onto the image.**

   The style, with its default settings, is applied to the layer. Note that layer styles are cumulative. You can apply multiple styles, specifically one style from each library, to a single layer.

   To edit the style's settings, either double-click the florin in the Layers palette or choose Layer⇨Layer Style⇨Style Settings.

Working with Layer Styles

Here are a few last tips for working with Layer Styles:

- **Delete a Layer Style(s):** Choose Layer⇨Layer Style⇨Clear Layer Style or drag the florin in the Layers palette to the trash can icon.

- **Copy and paste Layer Styles onto other layers:** Select the layer containing the Layer Style and choose Layer⇨Layer Style⇨Copy Layer Style. Select the layer or layers on which you want to apply the effect and choose Layer⇨Layer Style⇨Paste Layer Style. Easier, you can also just drag and drop an effect from one layer to another while holding down the Alt key.

- **Hide/show Layer Styles:** Choose Layer⇨Layer Style⇨Hide All Effects or Show All Effects.

- **Scale a Layer Style:** Choose Layer⇨Layer Style⇨Scale Effects. Select Preview and enter a value between 1 and 1,000 percent. This allows you to scale the style without scaling the element.

Mixing It Up with Blend Modes

Elements sports a whopping 23 blend modes. Blend modes affect how colors interact between layers and also how colors interact when you apply paint onto a layer. Not only do blend modes create interesting effects, but you can easily apply, edit, or remove blend modes without touching your image pixels.

The various blend modes are located under a pop-up menu at the top of your Layers palette in Standard Edit mode. The best way to get a feel for the effect of blend modes is not to memorize the descriptions we give you in the following section. Instead, grab an image with some layers and apply each of the blend modes to one or more of the layers and see what happens. The exact result will vary depending on the colors in your image layers. Combine these blend modes with varying Opacity settings and who knows what amazing images can materialize?

General blend modes

The Normal blend mode needs no introduction. It's the one you probably use the most. Dissolve is the next one on the list and, ironically, is probably the one you will use the least. Both blend modes are illustrated in Figure 11-9.

- **Normal:** The default mode lets each pixel display unadjusted.

- **Dissolve:** This mode can only be seen on a layer with an opacity setting of less than 100%. It allows some pixels from lower layers, which are randomized, to show through the target (selected) layer.

Normal   Dissolve

Corbis Digital Stock

Figure 11-9: The Dissolve blend mode allows pixels from one layer to peek randomly through another.

Darken blend modes

These blend modes produce effects that darken your image in various ways, as shown in Figure 11-10:

- **Darken:** If the pixels on the target layer are lighter than those below, the lighter pixels turn transparent. If the pixels are darker, they are unchanged.

- **Multiply:** Burns the target layer onto the layers underneath, thereby darkening all colors where they mix. When painting with the Brush or Pencil tool, each stroke creates a darker color, as if drawing with markers.

- **Color Burn:** Darkens the layers underneath the target layer and burns them with color, creating a contrast effect, like applying a dark dye to your image.

- **Linear Burn:** Darkens the layers underneath the target layer by decreasing the brightness. It's like Multiply but often makes parts of your image black.

Corbis Digital Stock

Figure 11-10: These blend modes darken your image layers.

Lighten blend modes

The lighten blend modes are the opposite of the darken blend modes. All these blend modes create lightening effects on your image, as shown in Figure 11-11:

- ✔ **Lighten:** If the pixels on the target layer are darker than those below, the darker pixels turn transparent. If the pixels are lighter, they are unchanged. The opposite of Darken.

- ✔ **Screen:** Lightens the target layer where it mixes with the layers underneath. The opposite of Multiply.

- ✔ **Color Dodge:** Lightens the pixels in the layers underneath the target layer and infuses them with colors from the top layer. Like applying a bleach to your image.

- ✔ **Linear Dodge:** Lightens the layers underneath the target layer by increasing the brightness. Like Screen but often makes parts of your image white.

Lighten	Screen	Color Dodge	Linear Dodge

Corbis Digital Stock

Figure 11-11: These blend modes lighten your image layers.

Lighting blend modes

This group of blend modes plays with the lighting in your layers, as shown in Figure 11-12:

- ✔ **Overlay:** Multiplies the dark pixels in the target layer and screens the light pixels in the underlying layers. Enhances the contrast and saturation of colors.

- ✔ **Soft Light:** Darkens the dark (greater than 50% gray) pixels and lightens the light (less than 50% gray) pixels. Like shining a soft spotlight on the image.

Overlay Soft Light Hard Light Vivid Light

Linear Light Pin Light Hard Mix

Corbis Digital Stock

Figure 11-12: Some blend modes adjust the lighting between your image layers.

✔ **Hard Light:** Multiplies the dark (greater than 50% gray) pixels and screens the light (less than 50% gray) pixels. Like shining a bright, hard spotlight on the image.

✔ **Vivid Light:** If the pixels on the top layer are darker than 50% gray, this mode darkens the colors by increasing the contrast. If the pixels on the top layer are lighter than 50% gray, the mode lightens the colors by decreasing the contrast.

✔ **Linear Light:** If the pixels on the top layer are darker than 50% gray, the mode darkens the colors by decreasing the brightness. If the pixels on the top layer are lighter than 50% gray, the mode lightens the colors by increasing the brightness.

✔ **Pin Light:** If the pixels on the top layer are darker than 50 percent gray, the mode replaces pixels darker than those on the top layer and doesn't change lighter pixels. If the pixels on the top layer are lighter than 50 percent gray, the mode replaces the pixels lighter than those on the top layer, and doesn't change pixels that are darker. Usually reserved for special effects.

✔ **Hard Mix:** Similar to Vivid Light, but reduces the colors to a total of eight — Cyan, Magenta, Yellow, Black, Red, Green, Blue, and White. Creates a posterized effect.

Inverter blend modes

The Inverter blend modes invert your colors and tend to produce some pretty radical effects, as shown in Figure 11-13:

✔ **Difference:** Produces a negative effect according to the brightness values on the top layers. If the pixels on the top layer are black, there is no change on the underlying layers. If the pixels on the top layer are white, the mode inverts the colors of the underlying layers.

✔ **Exclusion:** Like Difference, but less contrast and saturation. If the pixels on the top layer are black, there is no change on the underlying layers. If the pixels on the top layer are white, the mode inverts the colors of the underlying layers. Medium colors blend to create gray.

Difference   Exclusion

Corbis Digital Stock

Figure 11-13: Difference and Exclusion blend modes invert colors.

HSL blend modes

These blend modes use the HSL (Hue, Saturation, Lightness) color model to mix colors, as shown in Figure 11-14:

- **Hue:** Blends the luminance (brightness) and saturation (intensity of the color) of the underlying layers with the hue (color) of the top layer.

- **Saturation:** Blends the luminance and hue of the underlying layers with the saturation of the top layer.

- **Color:** Blends the luminance of the underlying layers with the saturation and hue of the top layer. Enables you to paint color while preserving the shadows, highlights, and details of the underlying layers.

  The Color mode is a great tool for colorizing images. If you've ever admired those hand-tinted black-and-white photos used in greeting cards and posters, you can create the same effect fairly easily. First, make sure your black-and-white image is in RGB mode so it is able to accept color. Create a new layer in the Layer palette and set it to the Color blend mode. Grab the Brush tool (with a soft-edged tip), choose your desired color, and paint over your image. Adjust your opacity to less than 100% to create a softer effect.

- **Luminosity:** The opposite of Color, this mode blends the hue and saturation of the underlying layers with the luminance of the top layer. Preserves the shadows, highlights, and details from the top layer and mixes them with the colors of the underlying layers.

Hue	Saturation	Color	Luminosity

Corbis Digital Stock

Figure 11-14: Some blend modes mix colors based on the actual hue, richness, and brightness of color.

Using Photomerge Panorama

This awesome tool enables you to combine multiple images into a single panoramic image, as shown in Figure 11-15. From skylines to mountain ranges, you can take several overlapping shots and stitch them together into one.

PhotoSpin

Figure 11-15: Combine multiple images into a single panorama with Photomerge.

To be successful at merging photos into a panorama, you need to start with good source files. First of all, make sure that when you shoot your photos, you overlap your individual images by 15 to 40 percent, but no more than 50 percent. Then, avoid using distortion lenses (such as fish-eye) and your camera's zoom setting. Also try to keep the same exposure settings for even lighting. Lastly, try to stay in the same position and keep your camera at the same level for each photo. Using a tripod and rotating the head can help you get shots at the same camera level.

Follow these steps to create a Photomerge Panorama image:

1. **Choose File⇨New⇨Photomerge Panorama in Standard Edit mode.**

   Note that you can also select this command in the Organizer.

2. **In the first Photomerge dialog box, choose your source files. Click the Browse button and navigate to where your files are located.**

3. **After you have selected all applicable images, click OK.**

   Elements opens and automatically assembles the source files to create the composite panorama in the work area of the dialog box. If it looks good, skip to Step 6.

Elements alerts you if it cannot automatically composite your source files. You then have to assemble the images manually.

4. **To manually assemble your panorama, drag the image thumbnails from the lightbox area onto the work area with the Select Image tool (the arrow) or simply double-click the lightbox thumbnail to add it to the composition.**

5. **Arrange and position your images:**

   • Position the images by using the Select Image tool.

   • Use the Rotate Image tool to make rotations.

   • Use the Zoom and Move View tools to help view and navigate around your panorama.

   You can also use the Navigator view box to zoom in and out of your composition by dragging the slider.

   • Select the Snap to Image option to enable overlapping images to automatically snap into place.

6. **To adjust the Vanishing Point, first select the Perspective option in the Settings area. Click your desired image with the Set Vanishing Point tool.**

   Elements changes the perspective of the composition. By default, Elements selects the center image as the vanishing point. If necessary, you can move the other images.

   Note that when you select the Perspective setting, Elements links non-Vanishing Point images to the Vanishing Point image. To break the link, click the Normal Setting button or separate the images in the work area.

7. **Adjust the blending of the composition.**

   Select the Perspective setting first and then choose Cylindrical Mapping to reduce the bowed distortion you can get when you add perspective to your composition.

   If you have some color inconsistencies from having photos with different exposures, select Advanced Blending to blend the different colors and tones.

   Click Preview to view your settings. Click Exit Preview to return to the Edit mode.

8. **Select the Keep as Layers option to save each image in the composite as an individual layer.**

9. **Click OK to create the panorama.**

   It opens as a new Photoshop Elements (.psd) file.

Drawing and Painting

*E*lements is such a deluxe, full-service image editing program that it doesn't just stop at giving you tools to select, repair, organize, and share your images. It figures you may need to add a swash of color, either freeform with a brush or pencil or in the form of a geometric or organic shape. Don't worry, this drawing and painting business isn't just for those with innate artistic talent. In fact, Elements gives you plenty of preset brushes and shapes that you can use. If you can pick a tool and drag your mouse, you can draw and paint.

Choosing Color

Before you start drawing or painting, you may want to change your color to something other than the default black. By now, I'm sure you've checked out the Elements Tools palette and noticed the two overlapping color swatches at the bottom of the palette. These two swatches represent two categories of color — *foreground color* and *background color*. Here's a quick look at how they work with different tools:

🖊 When you add type, paint with the Brush tool, or create a shape, you are using the foreground color.

🖊 When you erase with the Eraser tool, or when you increase the size of your canvas, you are accessing the background color.

✔ And when you drag with the Gradient tool, provided your gradient is set to the default, you are laying down a blend of color from foreground to the background.

Elements gives you three ways to choose your foreground and background colors — the Color Picker, the Color Swatches, and the Eyedropper tool, which samples color in an image. In the following sections, we explore each one.

Working with the Color Picker

By default, Elements uses a black foreground color and a white background color. If you're experimenting with color and want to go back to the default color, press the D key. If you want to switch between foreground and background colors, press the X key. If you want any other color of the rainbow, click your desired swatch to change either the foreground or background color. This action transports you to the Color Picker, shown in Figure 12-1.

Here are the steps to choose your color via the Color Picker:

1. **Click either the Foreground or Background color swatch in the Tools palette.**

   The Color Picker appears.

Figure 12-1: The Color Picker.

2. **Drag the color slider or click in the color bar to get close to the general color you desire.**

3. **Choose the exact color you want by clicking in the large square, called a *color field,* on the left.**

   The circle icon targets your selected color. The two swatches in the top-right corner of the dialog box represent your newly selected color and the original foreground or background color.

   The numeric values on the right side of the dialog box also change according to the color you have selected. If you happen to know the values of your desired color, you may also enter them in the text boxes. Remember, RGB values are based on brightness levels, from 0 (black) to 255 (white). You can also enter HSB (Hue, Saturation, Brightness) values or the hexadecimal formula for Web-safe colors.

4. **When you're happy with your color, click OK.**

Dipping into the Color Swatches palette

Another way Elements enables you to choose a foreground or background color is by selecting a color in the Swatches palette. The Swatches palette is a digital version of the artist's paint palette. In addition to the preset colors, you can mix and store your own colors for use now and later. You can have several palettes for certain types of projects or images. For example, you might want a palette of skin tones for retouching portraits. Choose Window➪Color Swatches to bring up the palette, shown in Figure 12-2.

To grab a color from the Color Swatches palette, just click the color swatch you want. By the way, it doesn't matter which tool you currently have. As soon as you move the tool over the palette, it temporarily converts to an eyedropper that samples the color and makes it your new foreground or background color.

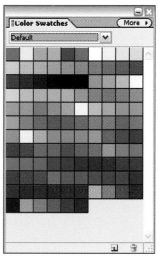

Figure 12-2: The Swatches palette

Although the Color Swatches palette is a breeze to use, here are a few tips to help you along:

✔ **Change the background color.** Either first select the background swatch in the Tools palette or Ctrl+click a swatch.

✔ **Use preset colors.** To load a particular preset swatch library, choose it from the Color Swatches palette drop-down list. Elements offers libraries specific to Web graphics, photo filters, and Windows systems.

✔ **Add a color to the Color Swatches palette.** To add a color to the Swatches palette, choose New Swatch from the More pop-up menu. Name your swatch and click OK.

✔ **Save swatches.** Choose Save Swatches from the More pop-up menu in the top-right corner of the palette. We recommend saving the swatch library in the default Color Swatches folder in the Presets folder. If by chance this folder doesn't come up by default, just navigate to the Color Swatches folder by following this path: `Adobe Elements 4.0\Presets\Color Swatches`.

The Save Swatches for Exchange command enables you to save swatch libraries that can be shared with other Adobe applications, such as Photoshop, InDesign, and Illustrator.

✔ **Load swatches.** If you want to load a custom library created by you or by someone else, choose More➪Load Swatches. In the dialog box, select your desired library from the Color Swatches folder. The new library will be appended (added) to your current library.

You can also work with swatches by using the Preset Manager. For more on the Preset Manager, see Chapter 2.

✔ **Delete swatches.** To delete a swatch, drag it to the trash can at the bottom of the palette or Alt+click the swatch.

✔ **Change the palette's appearance.** Click the More button in the upper right to choose from Small or Large Thumbnail (swatch squares) or Small or Large List (swatch squares with a name).

✔ **Replace your current swatch library with a different library.** Choose Replace Swatches from the More pop-up menu. Choose a library from the Color Swatches folder.

Sampling with the Eyedropper tool

The last way that Elements enables you to choose color is via the Eyedropper tool. The Eyedropper tool comes in handy when you want to sample an existing color in an image and use it for another element. For example, let's say we want our text to be the same color as the green background in our image, shown in Figure 12-3. We grab the Eyedropper tool (or press I) and click a shade of green in the background. The tool samples the color and makes it our new foreground color. We then create the type with our new foreground color.

Here are few things to remember when using the Eyedropper tool:

✔ **Sample a new foreground or background color.** Obviously, you can select either the foreground or background swatch in the Tools palette before you sample a color. But if the foreground color swatch is active, pressing the Alt key will sample a new background color, and vice versa.

✔ **Choose a color from any open image.** If you have multiple images open, you can even sample a color from an image that you're not working on!

✔ **Choose your sample size in the Options bar.** You have the option of selecting the color of just the single pixel you click (Point Sample), or Elements can average the colors of the pixels in a 3-x-3- or 5-x-5-pixel area.

✔ **Make colors Web safe.** If you right-click your image to bring up the context menu, you have a hidden option — Copy Color as HTML. This option provides the Web-safe hexadecimal color formula for that sampled color and copies it to the Clipboard. You can then paste that formula into an HTML file or grab the Type tool and choose Edit⇨Paste to view the formula in your image.

✔ **Toggle between the Eyedropper and other tools.** Elements, being the multitasker that it is, enables you to temporarily access the Eyedropper tool when you're using the Brush, Pencil, Color Replacement, Gradient, Paint Bucket, Cookie Cutter, or Shape tools. Simply press the Alt key to access the Eyedropper. Release Alt and you're back to your original tool.

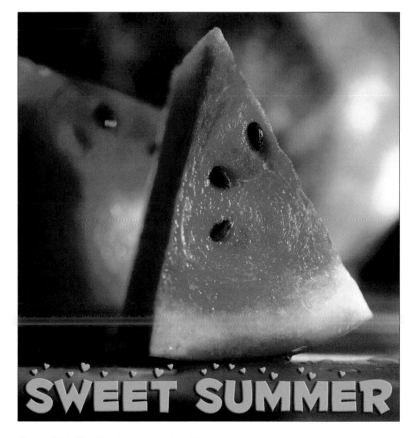

Figure 12-3: The Eyedropper tool enables you to sample color from your image to use with other elements, such as type.

Getting Artsy with the Pencil and Brush Tools

Now that you've been thoroughly doused with every way to choose a color, you probably want to find out how to paint and draw with that color. The Pencil and Brush tools give you the power to put your creative abilities to work, and the following sections show you how.

These are two tools that benefit immensely from the use of a pressure-sensitive digital drawing tablet. The awkwardness of trying to draw or paint with a mouse disappears and leaves you with tools that behave much closer to their analog ancestors.

Drawing with the Pencil tool

Drawing with the Pencil tool creates hard edges. You can't get the soft, feathery edges that you can with the Brush tool. In fact, the edges of a pencil stroke cannot even be anti-aliased (for more on anti-aliasing, see the section, "Painting with the Brush tool"). So keep in mind that if you draw anything other than vertical or horizontal lines, your lines will have some jaggies when viewed up close. But hey, don't diss the Pencil just yet. Those hard-edged strokes can be perfect for Web graphics. And what's more, the Pencil tool has the ability to erase itself, and it's great for digital sketches, as shown in Figure 12-4.

Figure 12-4: The Pencil tool can be used for digital drawings.

Follow these steps to become familiar with the Pencil tool:

1. **Select the Pencil tool from the Tools palette.**

   You can also press the N key. By default, the Pencil tool's brush tip is the 1-pixel brush. Yes, even though the Pencil tip is hard-edged, we still refer to it as a brush.

2. **On the Options bar, choose your desired pencil options, beginning with a brush preset. Click the arrow and select your desired brush from the Brush Preset Picker drop-down palette.**

   To load another preset library, click the Brushes menu at the top of the palette.

Remember, you aren't limited to the standard old brush strokes. Check out the Assorted and Special Effects brushes. You'll be surprised at some of the interesting brushes lurking in these palettes. Use them to create stand-alone images or to enhance your photographic creations.

Access the pop-up menu on the drop-down palette to save, rename, or delete individual brushes and also save, load, and reset brush libraries. For more on these operations, see the upcoming section, "Painting with the Brush tool."

3. **Choose your brush size.**

   A preset brush's pixel diameters are shown as text below a thumbnail image of the brush shape. If you want to change the size of that brush tip, drag the slider or enter a value.

4. **Select a blending mode.**

   You can find more about blend modes in Chapter 11.

5. **If you want the background to show through your strokes, adjust the Opacity by dragging the slider or entering an opacity percentage less than 100 percent.**

   The lower the percentage, the more the background images show through.

   Your strokes must be on a separate layer above your images for you to be able to adjust the opacity and blend modes after you've drawn them. For more on layers, see Chapter 8.

6. **Select Auto Erase if you want to enable that option.**

   This option removes portions of your pencil strokes. For example, if my foreground color is black and my background color is white and I apply some black strokes, with Auto Erase enabled, if I drag back over my black strokes, I apply white. If I drag over my white background, I apply black.

7. **Click and drag with the mouse to create your freeform lines.**

   To draw straight lines, click at a starting point, release the mouse button, and then Shift+click at a second point.

Painting with the Brush tool

The Brush tool creates soft-edged strokes. How soft those strokes are depends on what brush you use. By default, even the hardest brush has a slightly soft edge because it is *anti-aliased*. Remember, anti-aliasing creates a single row of partially filled pixels along the edges to produce the illusion of a smooth edge. You can also get even softer brushes, which employ feathering. For details on feathering, see Chapter 7.

The Brush tool shares most of the options found in the Pencil tool, except the Auto Erase feature isn't available. Here is the lowdown on the unique Brush options:

- **Airbrush:** Click the Airbrush button on the Options bar to apply the Airbrush mode. In this mode, the longer you hold down the mouse button, the more paint pumps out of the Brush, and the wider the airbrush effect spreads.

- **Tablet Options:** If you're using a pressure-sensitive digital drawing tablet, check the settings you want the tablet to control, including size, scatter, opacity, roundness, and hue jitter. The harder you press with the stylus, the greater the effect of these options.

- **More Options:** Click the brush icon to the right of the More Options label to access the additional options below. These options, referred to as brush *dynamics,* change while you apply your stroke. See Figure 12-5 for an example of each.

    - **Spacing:** The higher the number, the more space between marks.

    - **Fade:** The lower the value, the quicker the stroke fades. Zero, however, creates no fade.

    - **Hue Jitter:** Varies the stroke between the foreground and background colors. The higher the value, the more frequent the variation.

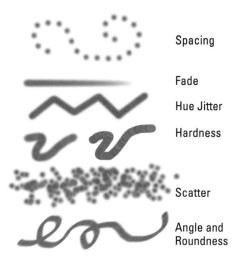

Spacing

Fade

Hue Jitter

Hardness

Scatter

Angle and Roundness

Figure 12-5: Change brush options to create a custom brush.

    - **Hardness:** The higher the value, the harder the brush.

    - **Scatter:** The higher the value, the higher the number of brush marks and the farther apart they are.

    - **Angle:** If you have created an oval brush by adjusting the roundness (see the next bullet), this option controls the angle of that oval brush stroke. It's so much easier to drag the points and the arrow on the diagram rather than guesstimating values in the text boxes.

- **Roundness:** A setting of 100 percent is totally circular. The lower the percentage, the more oval your brush becomes.

- **Keep These Settings for All Brushes:** You can lock in these brush dynamics by checking this option. This ensures that every brush you choose adopts these settings.

Like the Pencil tool, additional features for the Brush tool appear under the pop-up menu on the Brush Preset Picker drop-down palette. Here's a quick description of each:

- **Save Brush:** This command allows you to save a custom brush as a preset. See "Creating your own brush" for details.

- **Rename Brush:** Don't like your brush's moniker? Change it with this option.

- **Reset Brushes:** Reverts your current brush library back to the default.

- **Save Brushes:** Saves custom brushes in a separate library.

- **Load Brushes:** Loads a preset or custom brush library.

- **The display options:** This isn't a single command but rather a set of commands that enable you to change the way your brush tips are displayed. These commands include Text Only and Small Thumbnail.

You can also manage brush tip libraries by using the Preset Manager. See Chapter 2 for information on using the Preset Manager.

Creating your own brush

After playing with all the various options, if you really like the Frankenbrush that you have created, feel free to save it as a preset that you can access again in the future. Choose Save Brush from the pop-up menu on the Brush Preset Picker palette. Name the Brush and click OK. Your new custom brush will show up at the bottom of the Brush Preset Picker drop-down palette.

There is one additional way to create a brush. Elements allows you to create a brush from all or part of your image. The image could be a photograph or it could be something you have painted or drawn.

Here's how to create a brush from your image:

1. **Select part of your image with any of the selection tools. If you want to use the entire image or entire layer, *deselect* everything.**

   For more on selections, see Chapter 7.

2. **Choose Edit⇨Define Brush or Edit⇨Define Brush from Selection.**

   You see one command or the other, depending on what you do in Step 1.

3. **Name the brush and click OK.**

   The new brush shows up at the bottom of your Brush Preset Picker drop-down palette. Note that your brush is only a grayscale version of your image. When you use the brush, it automatically applies the color you have selected as your foreground color, as shown in Figure 12-6.

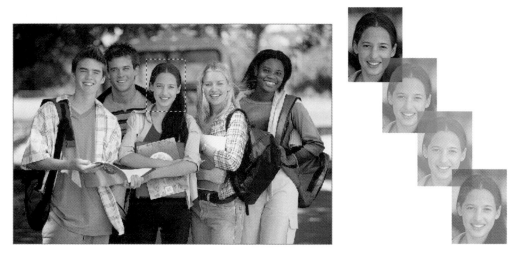

Digital Vision

Figure 12-6: Create a custom brush from a portion of your image.

Using the Impressionist Brush

In this section, we introduce the Impressionist Brush. This tool is designed to paint over your photos in a way that makes it look like a fine art painting. You can set various options that change the style of the brush strokes.

Here's how to use this artistic brush:

1. **Select the Impressionist Brush from the Tools palette.**

   It looks like a brush with a curly *q* next to it.

2. **Set your brush options.**

   The Brushes, Size, Mode, and Opacity options are identical to those found with the Brush tool, described in "Painting with the Brush tool," earlier in this chapter. You can also find some unique options in the More Options palette:

   - **Style:** This drop-down list contains various brush stroke styles, such as dab and tight curl.

   - **Area:** Controls the size of your brush stroke. The larger the value, the larger the area covered.

   - **Tolerance:** Controls how similar color pixels have to be before they are changed by the brush stroke.

3. **Drag on your image and paint with your brush strokes, as shown in Figure 12-7.**

   The best way to get a feel for what this tool does is to open your favorite image, grab the tool, and take it for a test drive.

Figure 12-7: The Impressionist Brush turns your photo into a painting.

Filling and Outlining Selections

There may be times when you want to create an element on your canvas that can't quite be created with a brush or pencil stroke. Maybe it's a perfect circle or five-pointed star. Elements offers a couple of other ways to create these objects. If you have a selection, you can fill or stroke that selection to create that element, rather than drawing or painting it on. The Fill command adds a color or a pattern to the entire selection, whereas the Stroke command applies the color to the edge of the selection border only.

Fill 'er up

You won't find a Fill tool in the Tools palette. Elements decided to avoid the overpopulated palette and placed the Fill and Stroke commands under the Edit menu. Here are the simple steps to fill a selection:

1. **Grab the selection tool of your choice and create your selection on a new layer.**

   Although it isn't mandatory that you create a new layer to make a selection to fill, we recommend it. That way, if you don't like the filled selection, you can delete the layer, and your image or background below it remains safe. See Chapter 7 for more on selections and Chapter 9 for details on working with layers.

2. **Select either the foreground or background color and then choose a fill color.**

   See "Choosing Color," earlier in this chapter, if you need a refresher.

3. **Choose Edit⊏⟩Fill Selection.**

   The Fill Layer dialog box, shown in Figure 12-8, appears.

Figure 12-8: Fill your selection or layer with color or a pattern.

If you want to bypass the Fill dialog box (and the rest of these steps), you can use these handy keyboard shortcuts instead:

- **To fill it with the foreground color,** press Alt+Backspace.

- **To fill the selection with the background color,** press Ctrl+Backspace.

4. **Choose your desired fill from the Use pop-up menu.**

   You can select whether to fill with the foreground or background color. You also can choose Color, Black, 50% Gray, White, or Pattern. If you select Color, you are transported to the Color Picker. If you choose Pattern, you must then choose a Pattern from the Custom Pattern drop-down palette. For more on patterns, see the upcoming section.

If you don't have an active selection border in your image, the command will say Fill Layer, and your entire layer will be filled with your color or pattern.

5. **In the blending area, you can choose whether to Preserve Transparency, which enables you to fill the whole selection or only portions of the selection that contain pixels (the nontransparent areas).**

Although you can also choose a blend mode (how the fill color interacts with colors below it) and opacity percentage, we urge you not to adjust your blend mode and opacity in the Fill Layer dialog box. Make those adjustments on your layer later via the Layer palette commands, where you have more flexibility for editing.

6. **Click OK.**

The color or pattern fills the selection.

Outlining with the Stroke command

Stroking a selection enables you to create colored outlines, or borders, of selections or layers. You can put this border inside, outside, or centered on the selection order.

Here are the steps to stroke a selection:

1. **Choose a foreground color and make a selection.**

2. **Choose Edit➪Stroke (Outline) Selection.**

The Stroke dialog box opens.

3. **Select your desired settings.**

Many settings are the same as those found in the Fill dialog box, explained in the preceding section. Here is a brief rundown of those options unique to strokes:

- **Width:** Enter a width of 1 to 250 pixels for the stroke.

- **Location:** Specify how Elements should apply the stroke: outside the selection, inside the selection, or centered on the selection.

4. **Click OK to apply the stroke.**

I gave a 30-pixel centered stroke to my selection, shown in Figure 12-9.

Figure 12-9: Stroke a selection to create a colored border.

Splashing On Color with the Paint Bucket Tool

The Paint Bucket tool has been a long-time occupant of the Tools palette. This tool, whose icon looks just like a bucket, behaves like a combination of the Fill command and the Magic Wand tool. This means that it makes a selection based on similarly colored pixels and then immediately fills that selection with color or a pattern. Just like the Magic Wand tool, this tool is the most successful when you have a limited number of colors, as shown in Figure 12-10.

To use the Paint Bucket tool, simply click inside the selection you want to fill. Before you click, however, specify your options:

Corbis Digital Stock

Figure 12-10: The Paint Bucket tool makes a selection and fills it at the same time.

- ✔ **Fill:** Choose between a fill of the foreground color or a pattern.

- ✔ **Pattern:** If you choose pattern, select a preset pattern from the drop-down palette. For more details on patterns, see the upcoming section.

- ✔ **Mode:** Select a blending mode to change how your fill color interacts with the color below it.

- ✔ **Opacity:** Adjust the opacity to make your fill more or less transparent.

- ✔ **Tolerance:** Choose a tolerance level that specifies how similar in color a pixel must be before it is selected and then filled. The lower the value, the more similar the color must be. For more on tolerance, see the section on the Magic Wand in Chapter 7.

- ✔ **Anti-alias:** Choose this option to smooth the edges between the filled and unfilled areas.

- ✔ **Contiguous:** If selected, this option selects and fills only pixels that are touching within your selection. If unselected, pixels will be selected and filled wherever they lie within your image.

- ✔ **All Layers:** This option selects and fills pixels in all layers that are within your tolerance level.

Working with Multi-Colored Gradients

If one color isn't enough for you, you'll be pleased to know that Elements enables you to fill a selection or layer with a *gradient*. A gradient is a blend of two or more colors that gradually dissolve from one to another. Elements provides a whole slew of various preset gradients. But creating your own custom gradient is also fun and easy.

Applying a preset gradient

Similar to colors, patterns, and brushes, gradients have a whole slew of presets that you can apply to your selection and layers. You can also load other libraries of gradients from the Gradient palette pop-up menu.

Here's how to apply a preset gradient:

1. **Make the selection you want to fill with a gradient.**

   We recommend making the selection on a new layer so that you can edit the gradient later without harming the underlying image.

   If you don't make a selection, the gradient is applied to the entire layer or background.

2. **Select the Gradient tool from the Tools palette or press the G key.**

3. **In the Options bar, click the downward-pointing arrow in the Gradient Picker drop-down palette and choose a preset gradient.**

   Remember, you can choose other preset libraries from the palette pop-up menu. Libraries like Color Harmonies and Metals contain interesting presets.

4. **Next, choose your desired gradient type by clicking one of the icons. See Figure 12-11 for an example of each type.**

5. **Choose from the following additional options on the Options bar:**

   - **Mode:** Choose a blending mode to change how the color of the gradient interacts with the colors below it.

   - **Opacity:** Choose how opaque or transparent the gradient is.

   - **Reverse:** Reverse the order in which the colors are applied.

   - **Dither:** Add _noise_, or random information, to produce a smoother gradient that prints with less banding (weird stripes due to the printing limitations).

   - **Transparency:** Deselect this option and Elements ignores any transparent areas in the gradient and makes them opaque instead.

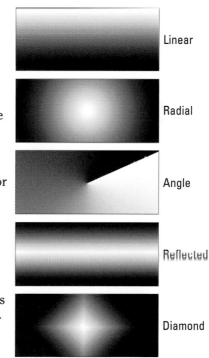

Linear

Radial

Angle

Reflected

Diamond

Figure 12-11: Choose from one of five gradient types.

6. **Position your gradient cursor at your desired starting point within your selection or layer.**

7. **Drag in any direction to your desired end point for the gradient.**

   Longer drags result in a subtler transition between colors, whereas shorter drags result in a more abrupt transition. Hold down the Shift key to restrain the direction of the gradient to a 45-degree angle.

8. **Release the mouse button to apply the gradient.**

   We applied an Orange Yellow radial gradient from the Color Harmonies 2 preset library to a selection of a sun in Figure 12-12. We selected the Reverse option and dragged from the center of the sun to the tip of the top ray.

Figure 12-12: We filled our sun selection with a radial Orange Yellow gradient.

Customizing gradients

If you can't find the exact gradient you need, you can easily create your own. The Gradient Editor lets you create your own custom gradient, using as many colors as you want. After you create a custom gradient, you can save it as a preset to reuse in the future.

Follow these steps to create a custom gradient:

1. **Select the Gradient tool from the Tools palette.**

2. **Click the Edit button in the Options bar.**

   The Gradient Editor dialog box opens, shown in Figure 12-13.

3. **Pick an existing preset to use as the basis for your new gradient.**

Figure 12-13: Use the Gradient Editor to edit and customize gradients.

4. **Choose your Gradient Type, either Solid or Noise, from the pop-up menu.**

   A Noise gradient contains random colors. Interestingly, each time you create a Noise gradient, the result is different.

   Note that as soon as you start to edit the existing gradient, the name of the gradient changes to Custom.

5. **Choose your options for either a Solid or Noise gradient, depending on what you chose in Step 4.**

   • **If you chose Solid:** Adjust the Smoothness percentage to determine how smoothly one color blends into another.

   • **If you chose Noise:** You can choose which Color Model to use to set the color range. You can also adjust the Roughness, which affects how smoothly or abruptly the color transitions from one to another. Click Restrict Colors to avoid oversaturated colors. The Add Transparency option adds transparency to random colors. Click the Randomize button to randomly generate a new gradient. You can then skip down to Step 15 to finish your gradient-making process.

6. **If you are creating a Solid gradient, begin choosing the first color of your gradient by first clicking the left color stop under the gradient bar, shown in Figure 12-13.**

   The triangle on top of the stop turns black to indicate you are working with the starting point of the gradient.

7. **Then, choose the starting color by double-clicking the left color stop and selecting a color from the Color Picker.**

   In the Stops area, you can also click the Color Swatch or choose Foreground, Background, or User Color from the Color pop-up menu. If you select color with the Foreground or Background option when you change either of those colors, the color in the gradient changes automatically for gradients you make. However, when you open the Gradient Editor again, you can revert to your original foreground or background color by selecting the User Color option.

8. **Select the ending color by clicking the right color stop. Repeat Step 7 to define the color.**

9. **Change the percentage of the amount of one color versus the other by moving the starting or ending point's color stop to the left or right. Drag the midpoint slider (a diamond icon) to adjust where the colors mix equally, 50-50.**

   You can also change the position of the midpoint by typing a value into the Location box.

10. **To add another color, click below the gradient bar at the position you want to add the color. Define a color in the same way you did in Step 7.**

11. **Repeat Step 10 to add additional colors.**

12. **To add transparency to your gradient, select an opacity stop, shown in Figure 12-13, and adjust the Opacity slider to specify the amount of transparency you desire.**

By default, a gradient has colors that are 100 percent opaque. You can fade a gradient to transparency so that the portion of the image under the gradient shows through.

You can also add additional opacity stops in the same way you add color stops.

13. **Adjust your color and opacity stops and their midpoint sliders to vary the percentages of each color.**

14. **You can also redefine any of the colors. To delete a color stop, drag it up or down off of the gradient bar.**

15. **When you're done, name your gradient and click the New button.**

Your gradient is added to the Presets menu.

After all that work, you may want to consider saving your gradients for later use. To save a gradient, click the Save button in the Gradient Editor dialog box. Save the current presets, with your new gradient, under the current library's name or a new name altogether. You can then later load that preset library. You can also manage your gradient presets with the Preset Manager, explained in Chapter 2.

Working with Patterns

If you've ever seen someone wearing leopard-print pants with an argyle sweater and a plaid blazer, then you're familiar with patterns. Not always pretty when used without restraint, patterns can be used to occasionally fill selections or layers. You can also stamp your image by using the Pattern Stamp tool. You can even retouch by using a pattern with the Healing Brush tool. Elements offers lots of preset patterns to keep you happy. And if you're not, you can, of course, create your own.

Applying a preset pattern

Although you can apply patterns by using many different tools, this chapter sticks with applying patterns as fills. To fill a layer or selection with a preset pattern, follow these steps.

1. **Choose the layer or selection you want to fill with a pattern.**

Again, we recommend making your selection on a new layer above your image for more flexible editing later on.

2. **Choose Edit⇨Fill Selection or Fill Layer and select Pattern from the Use pop-up menu.**

3. Click the downward-pointing arrow and select a pattern from the Custom Pattern drop-down palette, as shown in Figure 12-14.

If you don't see a pattern to your liking, choose another preset library by clicking the palette pop-up menu and selecting another preset library at the bottom of the sub-menu.

Figure 12-14: Fill your selection with one of Elements' many preset patterns.

4. Choose any other fill options you want to apply, such as Mode, Opacity, or Preserve Transparency.

For details on these options, see the section "Filling and Outlining Selections," earlier in this chapter.

5. Click OK to fill the layer or selection with the chosen pattern.

Creating a new pattern

You may someday want to create your own pattern. Patterns can be easily created from any existing photo or painting you've created in Elements. You can even scan your signature or logo, define it as a pattern, and use it with the Pattern Stamp tool to sign all your work.

To create your own pattern, follow these steps:

1. Open the photographic, painted, or scanned image that contains the area you want to use as a pattern.

2. **Use the Rectangular Marquee tool to select the area you want to convert into a pattern. Make sure that your Feather option is set to 0.**

   If you don't make a selection, Elements uses your entire layer as a basis for the pattern.

3. **Choose Edit➪Define Pattern from Selection or Edit➪Define Pattern.**

4. **Enter a name for your pattern in the Pattern Name dialog box.**

   Your new pattern will now appear in every Pattern palette, wherever it may lurk in Elements.

In addition to filling your selection with a pattern, you can also stamp on a pattern with the Pattern Stamp tool. For details, see Chapter 9.

Creating Shapes of All Sorts

In this section, we leave the land of pixels and head into uncharted territory — Vectorville. Before we discuss the ins and outs of creating shapes, here's a little overview that explains the difference between pixels and vectors:

- **Pixel images** describe a shape in terms of a grid of pixels. When you increase the size of a pixel-based image, it loses quality and begins to look blocky, mushy, and otherwise nasty. For more details on resizing pixel-based images and the ramifications of doing so, see Chapter 3.

- **Vectors** describe a shape mathematically. The shapes comprise paths made up of lines, curves, and anchor points. Because vector shapes are math-based, you can resize them without any loss of quality whatsoever.

In Figure 12-15, you can see both types of images.

Figure 12-15: Elements images can be vector-based (left) or pixel-based (right).

When you create a shape in Elements, you are creating a vector-based element. Shapes reside on a special kind of layer called, not surprisingly, a shape layer. Use shapes to create simple logos, Web buttons, and other small spot illustrations.

Drawing a shape

Elements offers an assortment of shape tools for you to choose from. Follow these steps to draw a shape in your document:

1. **Choose your desired shape tool from the Tools palette.**

   You can also press the U key and choose the shape tool from the Options bar. All the following tools have associated geometry options, which are described in an upcoming section. Here are the tools that are available:

   - **Rectangle and Ellipse:** Like their Marquee counterparts, you can hold down the Shift key while dragging to produce a square or circle; hold down the Alt key to draw the shape from the center outward.

   - **Rounded Rectangle:** Works like the regular Rectangle but with the addition of a radius value used to round off the corners of the rectangle.

   - **Polygon:** Creates a polygon with a specified number of sides, from 3 to 100.

   - **Line:** Draw a line with a width from 1 to 1000 pixels. You can also add arrowheads at either end.

   - **Custom:** The most varied shape tool of all. You have numerous preset custom shapes to choose from. As with any shape, hold down Shift to constrain proportions or Alt to draw from the center out.

2. **Select your desired color from the Color drop-down palette in the Options bar.**

   Click the More Colors button to access the Color Picker for additional color choices.

3. **Select a style from the Style drop-down palette.**

   To jazz up the shape with bevels and other fancy edges, choose a style from the palette. For more on styles, see Chapter 11.

4. **Click the downward-pointing arrow just to the right of the Shape tools to specify your geometry options.**

For detailed explanations on the various geometry options, see the upcoming sections.

If you chose the Custom Shape tool in Step 1, click the downward-pointing arrow to access the drop-down shapes palette and choose your desired shape. You can access more preset shape libraries via the pop-up menu at the top of the palette.

5. **Drag in the document to draw the shape you've defined.**

   The shape appears in the image window on its own shape layer. Check out the Layers palette to see this phenomenon. Figure 12-16 shows our shape, a Japanese hairstyle, which we add to in the next section.

Figure 12-16: Custom shapes run the gamut from the ordinary to the exotic, such as this hairstyle.

Drawing multiple shapes

After you create a shape layer, you can draw additional shapes to that layer. You can add, subtract, overlap, and intersect shapes in exactly the same way you do with selections (see Chapter 7). Just follow these steps:

1. **Select your desired state button in the Options bar. You can choose from the following options:**

   - **New Shape Layer:** Creates your initial shape layer.

   - **Add to shape area:** Combines and joins two or more shapes.

   - **Subtract from shape area:** Subtracts one shape from another shape.

   - **Intersect shape areas:** Creates a shape only from the areas that overlap.

   - **Exclude overlapping shape areas:** Creates a shape only from the areas that do not overlap.

2. **Choose your desired Shape tool and draw the next shape.**

   I completed my shape by adding the face, shown in Figure 12-17.

Figure 12-17: Add to your shape layer by pressing the Shift key.

Specifying geometry options

Geometry options help define how your shapes look. Click the downward-pointing arrow on the Options bar to access the geometry options described in the sections that follow.

Rectangle and Rounded Rectangle geometry options

Here are the Geometry options for the rectangle and rounded rectangle shapes:

- **Unconstrained:** Enables you to have free reign to draw a rectangle at any size or shape.

- **Square:** Constrains the shape to a perfect square.

- **Fixed Size:** Lets you draw rectangles in fixed sizes, as specified by your width and height values.

- **Proportional:** Allows you to define a proportion for the rectangle. For example, specifying 2W and 1H makes a rectangle twice as wide as it is high.

- **From Center:** Enables you to draw from the center out.

- **Snap to Pixels:** Aligns the shape to the pixels on your screen.

- **Radius:** For Rounded Rectangles, you can enter the radius of a circle used to round off the corners.

Ellipse geometry options

The ellipse shape has the same options that are available for rectangles except for the Snap to Pixels option. The only differences are instead of being able to create a perfect square, you can create a perfect circle.

Polygon geometry options

The geometry options for the Polygon shape are as follows:

- **Radius:** Enter the radius of a circle used to round off the corners of a polygon when you have the Smooth Corners option selected.

- **Smooth Corners:** Round off the corners.

- **Star:** Creates an inward-pointing polygon called a star.

- **Indent Sides By:** Determines the amount the sides indent inward.

- **Smooth Indents:** Rounds off the inner corners of indented sides.

- **Sides:** Specifies the number of sides for your polygon or the number of points for your star.

Line geometry options

The line's geometry settings include whether to put arrowheads at the start and/or end of the line. You can also adjust the width, length, and concavity settings to change the arrowhead shapes.

Custom shape geometry options

The custom shape options are similar to those you find for the other shapes, but with a couple unique options:

- **Defined Proportions:** Draws a shape based on the original proportions you used when you created it.
- **Defined Size:** Draws a shape based on its original size when you created it.

Editing shapes

You can edit shapes you create by using a variety of tools and techniques. Here's a list of the things you can do to modify your shapes:

- **Select:** Choose the Shape Selection tool to move one or more shapes in their layers. This tool shares a flyout menu with the Shapes tools.
- **Move:** Choose the Move tool (press V) to move the entire contents of the shape layer.
- **Delete:** Select a shape and press Delete to remove it.
- **Transform shapes:** Choose the Shape Selection tool and select your shape. Choose Image⇨Transform Shape and choose your desired transformation.
- **Change the color:** Double-click the thumbnail of the shape layer in the Layers palette. This transports you to the Color Picker, where you can choose a new color.
- **Clone a shape:** Press Alt and move the shape with the Move tool.

To convert your vector-based shape into a pixel-based shape, click the Simplify button in the Options bar or choose Layer⇨Simplify Layer. Note that you cannot edit a shape after you simplify it, except to modify the pixels.

13

Working with Type

Although we've spouted on about how a picture says a thousand words, we'd be terribly negligent if we didn't at least give a nod to the power of the written word as well. You may find that you never need to go near the type tools. That's fine. We won't be offended if you skip right past this chapter.

But then again, you may have an occasional need to add a caption or headline or maybe even a short paragraph to an image. Although it is by no means a word-processing or even page-layout program, Elements does give you ample tools for creating, editing, stylizing, and even distorting type.

Understanding Type Basics

Elements has four type tools. Two of them are for entering horizontally oriented type, and two are for entering vertically oriented type. Don't worry about the vertical type tools. Although you can use them, they are really designed for the Asian market, to enter Chinese and Japanese characters. The horizontal and vertical type tools are identical in their attributes, so we just cover the two horizontal type tools from here on, and, for the sake of simplicity, we just call them the Type and Type Mask tools:

✔ **Type tool:** Use this tool to enter type. This type is created on its own type layer except when used in Bitmap or Indexed Color modes, which don't support layers.

We refer to layers a lot in this chapter, so if your layer knowledge is rusty, check out Chapter 9.

✔ **Type Mask tool:** This tool does not create actual type; instead, it creates a selection border in the shape of the type you want to enter. The selection border is added to the currently active layer. You can do anything with a type selection that you can do with any other selection.

We also talk more about selections in this chapter, so for more details on selections, see Chapter 7.

You can enter text in Elements in two different modes: point type and paragraph type. Both the Type and Type Mask tools can enter either. Here is a brief description of each. For the step-by-step process of creating the text, see the following sections.

✔ **Point type:** Use this mode if all you want to enter is a few words or so. To create point type, select the Type tool, click in your image, and . . . well . . . type. The text appears as you type and continues to grow. In fact, it will even continue past the boundary of your image! Remember that point type *never* wraps around to a new line. To wrap to the next line, you must press Enter.

✔ **Paragraph type:** Use this mode to enter longer chunks of text on an image. To create paragraph type, click and drag your type tool to create a text bounding box and then type. All the text is entered in this resizable bounding box. If a line of text is too long, Elements automatically wraps it around to the next line.

Elements is capable of displaying and printing type in two different formats. Each format has its pros and cons, and which format you use depends on your needs. Here's the lowdown on each format:

✔ **Vector type:** All text in Elements is initially created as *vector* type. Vector type provides scalable outlines that you can resize without producing jaggy edges in the diagonal strokes. Vector type remains fully editable and always prints with optimum quality, appearing crisp and clean. Vector type is the default type format in Elements.

✔ **Raster type:** When Elements converts vector type into pixels, the text is *rasterized*. Elements refers to this rasterization process as *simplifying*. When text is simplified, it is no longer editable but is converted into a graphic image. You usually simplify your vector type when you want to apply filters to the type to produce a special effect or when you want to merge the type with the image. You can't resize simplified type without losing some quality or risking jagged edges. For more details, see "Simplifying Type," later in this chapter.

Creating Point Type

The majority of your type entry will most likely be in point type mode. Point type is great for short chunks of text like headlines, labels, logos, and headings for Web pages.

Point type is so called because it is preceded by a single anchor point. Remember, point type lines don't wrap automatically, as shown in Figure 13-1.

Figure 13-1: Point type doesn't wrap automatically, but instead can run off your image into a type neverland.

Follow these steps to create point type:

1. **Open an image or create a new blank Elements document.**

2. **Select the Type tool from the Tools palette.**

   You can also press the T key.

3. **On the image, click where you want to insert your text**

   Your cursor is called an *I-beam*. When you click, you make an insertion point.

   A small horizontal line about one-third of the way up the I-beam shows the *baseline* (the line on which the text sits) for horizontal type.

4. **Specify your type options from the Options bar.**

   All the options are described in detail in the section, "Specifying Type Options," later in this chapter.

5. **Type your text. Press Enter to begin a new line.**

   When you press Enter, you insert a hard return that doesn't move.

6. **When you finish entering the text, click the Commit button (check icon) on the Options bar.**

   You can also commit the type by pressing Enter on the numeric keypad or by clicking any other tool in the Tools palette. A new type layer with your text is created. Type layers appear in your Layers palette and are indicated by the T icon.

Creating Paragraph Type

If you have larger chunks of text, it is more practical to enter the text as paragraph type. Entering paragraph type is similar to entering text in a word-processing or page-layout program, except that it's contained inside a bounding box. As you type and come to the end of the bounding box, Elements automatically wraps the text to the next line.

To enter paragraph type, follow these steps:

1. **Open an image or create a new blank Elements document.**

2. **Select the Type tool from the Tools palette or press the T key.**

3. **On the image, insert and size the bounding box by using one of two methods:**

   • Drag to create a bounding box close to your desired size. After you release the mouse button, you can drag any of the handles at the corners and sides of the box to resize the box.

   • Hold down the Alt key and click the image. The Paragraph Text Size dialog box appears. Enter the exact dimensions of your desired bounding box. When you click OK, your specified box appears, complete with handles for resizing later, if necessary.

4. **Specify your type options from the Options bar.**

   Options are described in detail in the "Specifying Type Options" section, later in this chapter.

5. **Enter your text. To start a new paragraph, press Enter.**

   Each line wraps around to fit inside the bounding box, as you can see in Figure 13-2.

   If you type more text than can squeeze into the text box, an overflow icon appears. Just resize the text box by dragging any of the bounding box handles.

6. **Click the Commit button (check icon) on the Options bar or press Enter on the numeric keypad.**

   Elements creates a new type layer.

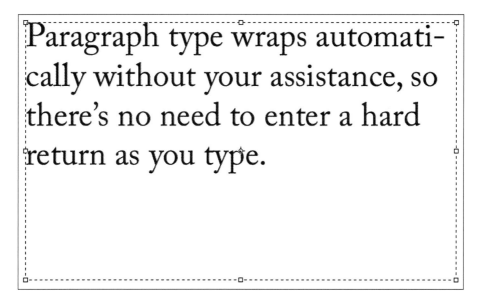

Figure 13-2: Paragraph type automatically wraps to fit within your bounding box.

Specifying Type Options

You can find several character and paragraph type settings in the Options bar, shown in Figure 13-3. Although you don't have some of the more specialized options, such as small caps and superscript, you do have access to the most commonly used options, and they should be more than sufficient if all you want to do is pair a small amount of type with your images.

Figure 13-3: Specify your type options, such as font family and size, before you type.

Here is an explanation of each available option on the Options bar, from left to right:

- ✔ **Type tools:** You can choose your flavor of type tool from the Options bar as well as from the Tools palette.

- ✔ **Font family:** Select the font you want from the drop-down list. Elements 4.0 provides a WYSIWYG (What You See Is What You Get) font menu. After each font name, the word *Sample* is rendered in the actual font — no more choosing a font without knowing what it really looks like. You also find one of these abbreviations before each font name to let you know what type of font it is:

   - *a* for Adobe Type 1 (PostScript) fonts

   - *TT* for TrueType fonts

   - *O* for OpenType fonts

   - Those with no abbreviation are Bitmapped fonts.

- **Font style:** Some font families have additional styles, such as light or condensed. Only the styles available for a particular font appear in the list. This is also now a WYSIWYG menu.

- **Font size:** Select your type size from the drop-down list or just type a size in the text box. Note that type size is most commonly measured in points (72 points equals about 1 inch at a resolution of 72 ppi). You can switch to millimeters or pixels by choosing Edit➪Preferences➪Units and Rulers.

- **Anti-aliasing:** Select Anti-aliasing to slightly smooth out the edges of your text. Anti-aliasing softens that edge by 1 pixel, as shown in Figure 13-4. For the most part, you want to keep this option on. The one occasion in which you may want it off is when you are creating small type to be displayed on-screen, such as on Web pages. The soft edges can sometimes be tough to read easily.

- **Faux Bold:** Use this option to create a fake bold style when a real bold style (which you would choose under Font Style) doesn't exist. Be warned that although the sky won't fall, applying faux styles can distort the proportions of a font. It's best to use fonts with real styles, and if they don't exist, oh well.

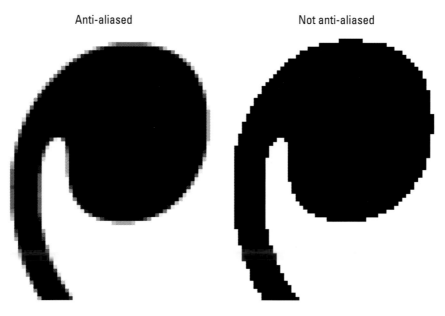

Anti-aliased   Not anti-aliased

Figure 13-4: Anti-aliasing softens the edges of your type.

- **Faux Italic:** This option creates a phony italic style and carries the same warning as the Faux Bold option.

- **Underline:** This setting obviously underlines your type, like <u>this</u>.

- **Strikethrough:** Choose this option to apply a ~~strikethrough~~ style to your text.

- **Text alignment:** These three options align your horizontal text on the left, center, or right. If you happen to have vertical text, these options rotate 90 degrees clockwise and change into Top, Center Vertical, and Bottom settings.

- **Leading:** Leading (pronounced "ledding") is the amount of space between the *baselines* of lines of type. A *baseline* is the imaginary line on which a line of type sits. You can choose Auto Leading or you can specify the amount of leading to apply. When you choose Auto Leading, Elements uses a value of 120 percent of your type point size. Therefore, 10-point type gets 12 points of leading. Elements adds that extra 20 percent so that the bottoms of the lowest letters don't crash into the tops of the tallest letters on the line below them.

- **Text Color:** Click the color swatch to select a color for your type from the Color Picker. You can also choose a color from the Swatches palette.

- **Style:** Click this option to access a drop-down palette of preset styles that you can apply to your type. For more on this option and the next one, see "Stylizing and Warping Type," later in this chapter.

- **Create Warped Text:** This fun option lets you distort type in more than a dozen ways.

- **Change the Text Orientation:** Select your type layer and then click this option to switch between vertical and horizontal type orientations.

- **Cancel:** Click this button (or press Esc) to cancel the type from being entered. You only use this option, and the Commit option, after you have clicked the type tool on your canvas.

- **Commit:** Click this button to apply the type onto your canvas.

Editing Text

Now that we've slogged through all the available options for type in Elements, just remember that you can apply these settings before you enter your text or after. To correct typos, add and delete type, or change any of the type options, simply follow these steps:

1. Select the Type tool from the Tools palette.

2. **Select your desired type layer in the Layers palette or click within the text to automatically select the type layer.**

3. **Do one of the following:**

    - **To change the font family, size, color, or other type option:** If you want to change all the text, simply select that type layer in the Layers palette. To select only portions of the text, highlight the text by dragging across it with the I-beam of the Type tool.

    - **To delete text:** Highlight the text by dragging across it with the I-beam of the Type tool. Then press the Backspace key.

    - **To add text:** Make an insertion point by clicking your I-beam within the line of text. Then type your new text.

4. **When you're done editing your text, click the Commit button.**

You may also occasionally need to transform your text. To do so, make sure the type layer is selected in the Layers palette. Then choose Image⇔Transform⇔ Free Transform. Grab a handle on the bounding box and drag to rotate or scale. Press Ctrl and drag a handle to distort. When you're done, double-click inside the bounding box to commit the transformation. For more details on transformations, see Chapter 9.

Simplifying Type

As we explain way back in the section "Understanding Type Basics," Elements can display and print type in two different formats — vector and raster. Remember that as long as you keep type in a vector format in a type layer, you can edit and resize that type all day long.

Occasionally, however, you may find the need to *simplify* your type — to convert your type into pixels. After they're simplified, you can apply filters, paint on the type, and apply gradients and patterns. If you're working with layers and you flatten your image (merge your layers into a single background image), your type layer is also simplified and merged with the other pixels in your image. By the way, if you try to apply a filter to a type layer, Elements barks at you that the type layer must be simplified before proceeding and gives you the opportunity to click OK (if you want to simplify) or Cancel.

To simplify your type, select the type layer in the Layers palette and choose Layer⇔Simplify Layer. Your type layer is then converted (the T icon disappears) into a regular layer on which your type is now pixels against a transparent background, as shown in Figure 13-5.

WARNING!

To avoid re-creating your type from scratch, be sure to make all your necessary edits prior to simplifying. This includes sizing your text. After you simplify your type, you cannot resize your text without risking the dreaded jaggies. The other down side to remember about simplified type is that, although it looks identical to vector type onscreen, it will never print as crisply and cleanly as vector type. Even at higher resolution settings, there will always be a slight jagged edge to simplified type. So if you're experimenting with painting or filters on your type, just make a duplicate of your type layer prior to simplifying it and then hide that layer.

Simplified pixel type

Vector type

Figure 13-5: Simplifying your type layer converts vector type into pixels.

Masking with Type

Using the Type Mask tool epitomizes the combination of type and image. Unlike its conventional cousin, the Type Mask tool doesn't create a new layer. Instead, it creates a selection on the currently active layer. This is the tool of choice for filling text with an image or cutting text out of an image so the background shows through, as shown in Figure 13-6.

REMEMBER

Remember, a selection is a selection, no matter how it was created. So even though they look like letters, they act like selections. You can move, modify, and save them.

Here are the steps to create a type mask:

1. **Open the image of your choice.**

   We selected a stone texture.

2. **Convert your background into a layer by double-clicking the word *Background* in the Layers palette. Click OK.**

   This enables us to jazz up the type with styles later on.

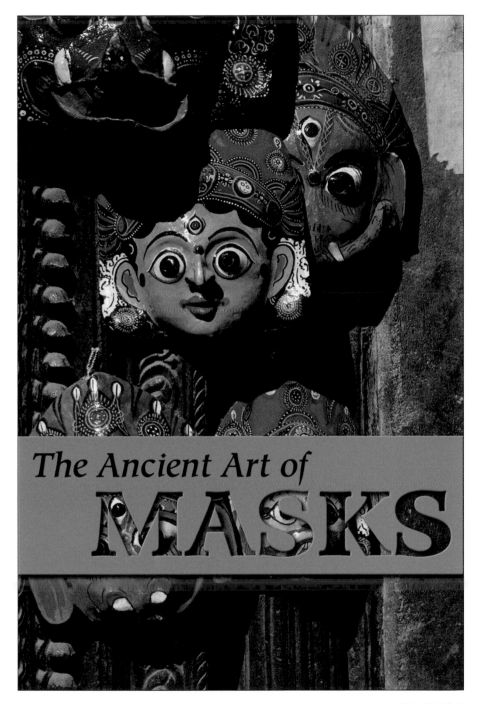

Corbis Digital Stock

Figure 13-6: The Type Mask tool enables you to cut type out of solid color or image layers.

3. **Choose the Horizontal Type Mask tool from the Tools palette and then click on the image where you would like your text.**

4. **Specify your type options, such as font family, style, and size, in the Options bar.**

5. **Type your desired text, and when you're done, click the Commit button on the Options bar.**

   A selection border in the shape of your type appears on your image.

6. **Choose Select⇨Inverse, which deselects your letter selections and selects everything else.**

7. **Press the Backspace key to delete everything outside your selection border.**

   Your type is now filled with your image.

8. **Choose Select⇨Deselect.**

9. **Experiment with applying Layer Styles to your type.**

   If the Layer Styles palette isn't visible, choose Window⇨Styles and Effects. Choose Layer Styles from the drop-down list in the palette. Choose the style of your choice. We used a drop shadow and inner bevel in Figure 13-7. You can find more details about Layer Styles in Chapter 11.

Corbis Digital Stock

Figure 13-7: Fill type with imagery by using the Type Mask tool.

If you want to admire your type against a solid background, as we did, create a new layer and then choose Edit⇨Fill Layer and choose your desired color from the Use pop-up menu.

Stylizing and Warping Type

If you tried your hand at creating a type mask in the preceding section, you know that Elements is capable of much more than just throwing a few black letters at the bottom of your image. With a few clicks here and there, you can warp, distort, enhance, and stylize your type. If you're not careful, your creative typography could outshine your image.

Adjusting type opacity

If you checked out Chapter 9 before you came here, you know that layers are a digital version of the old analog transparency sheets. You can change the opacity of elements on layers to enable the underlying layer to show through in varying degrees. This is also possible on a type layer. Peek at Figure 13-8 to see how varying the percentage of opacity of our type layer makes more of the underlying layer of water show through.

To change the opacity of a type layer, simply select the layer in the Layers palette, click the arrow to the right of the Opacity setting, and drag the slider. The lower the percentage, the less opaque the type (and the more the underlying layer shows through).

100% opacity

80% opacity

60% opacity

40% opacity

20% opacity

Corbis Digital Stock

Figure 13-8: You can vary the opacity of type layers to allow the underlying layer to peek through.

Applying filters to your type

One of the most interesting things you can do with type in Elements that you can't do in a word-processing or page-layout program is apply special effects, such as filters. You can make type look like it's on fire, underwater, or on the move, as shown in Figure 13-9, where we've applied a motion blur. The only caveat, as we mention earlier, is that type has to be simplified first before a filter can be applied. So be sure you do all your text editing before you get to the filtering stage. Actually applying the filter is as easy as just selecting the simplified type layer in the Layers palette and selecting a filter from the Filter menu. For more on filters, see Chapter 11.

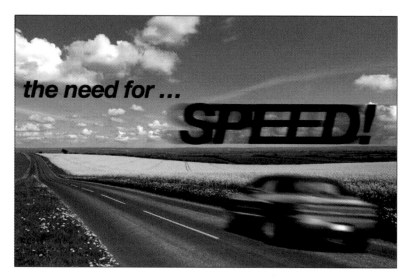

Corbis Digital Stock

Figure 13-9: Applying a Motion Blur to type can make it appear as fast as the car.

Painting your type with color and gradients

Changing the color of text is as easy as highlighting it and choosing a color from the Color Picker. But what if you want to do something a little more unconventional, like apply brush strokes of paint randomly across the type, like we did in the first image in Figure 13-10? It's really easier than it looks. Again, like with applying filters to text, the only criterion is that the type has to be simplified first. After that's done, choose a color, grab the Brush tool with settings of your choice, and paint. In our example, we used the Granite Flow brush found under the Special Effect Brushes presets. We used a diameter of 39, 15, and 6 pixels and just swiped our type a few times.

Figure 13-10: Bring your type to life with color (left) or a gradient (right).

If you want the color or gradient to be confined to the type area only, you can either select the text by Ctrl+clicking the layer containing the text or by locking the transparency of the layer in the Layers palette.

You can also apply a gradient to your type. Here are the steps to follow after simplifying your type:

1. **Select the Gradient tool from the Tools palette.**

2. **In the Options bar, click the downward-pointing arrow next to the Gradient Picker to access the Gradient Picker drop-down palette.**

3. **Choose your desired gradient.**

   If you want to create a custom gradient, find out how in Chapter 12.

4. **Position your gradient cursor on the text where you want your gradient to start and drag to where you want your gradient to end.**

   Don't like the results? Drag again until you get the look you want. Remember, you can drag at any angle and to any length, even outside your type. In the second image in Figure 13-10, we used the copper gradient and just dragged from the top of the letters to the bottom.

Warping your type

If horizontal or vertical text is just way too regimented for you, try out some of the distortions you can apply to your type with the Warp feature. The best part about the distortions you apply to the type is that the text remains fully editable. This feature is fun and easy to use. Click the Create Warped Text button at the far left of the Options bar. (It's the T with a curved line under it.) This opens the Warp Text dialog box, where you'll find a vast array of distortions under the Style pop-up menu with descriptive names like Bulge, Inflate, and Squeeze.

After choosing a warp style, you can adjust the orientation, amount of bend, and degree of distortion by dragging the sliders. The Bend setting affects the amount of warp and the Horizontal and Vertical Distortions apply perspective to that warp. Luckily, you can also view the results as you adjust. We could give you technical explanations of these adjustments, but really the best way to see what they do is to just play with them. See Figure 13-11 to get a quick look at a few of the warp styles. The names speak for themselves.

Figure 13-11: Text remains fully editable even after applying distortions with the Warp command.

Part V
Printing, Creating, Sharing

The 5th Wave   By Rich Tennant

"Mary—Jo, come here quick! Look at this special effect I learned with the new Photoshop software!"

In this part . . .

If you learn much of what is contained in the
first four parts of this book, this last part finishes up with photo output and deployment. As is
the case with so many other editing features, you
have an abundance of opportunities for outputting
your files. Beginning with the most familiar, which
is simply printing to your desktop color printer,
we talk about how to get the best results on your
printed images. We start with printing to your personal desktop printer and then cover issues related
to submitting photos to commercial photo labs
and service centers.

In addition to printing, you have a number of different options for sharing images, and these are
all covered in the final chapters, where you find
out about slide shows, videodiscs, Web hosting,
e-mailing, and sharing via online services. The
opportunities are enormous, and you'll want to
look over all Photoshop Elements has to offer
related to photo output and file sharing.

Getting It on Paper

*P*erhaps the greatest challenge to individuals using programs like Photoshop Elements, and even the professionals who use its granddaddy Adobe Photoshop, is getting what you see on your monitor to render a reasonable facsimile on a printed page. You can find all sorts of books on color printing — how to get color right, how to calibrate your equipment, and how to create and use color profiles — all for the purpose of getting a good match between your computer monitor and your printer. It's downright discouraging to spend a lot of time tweaking an image so that all the brilliant blue colors jump out of your computer monitor only to find that all those blues turn to murky purples when the photo is printed.

If you've already read Chapters 2 and 3, you're ahead of the game because you know a little bit about color management, color profiles, and printer resolutions. After you check out those chapters, your next step is to get to know your printer or your print service center and understand how to correctly print your pictures.

To reliably print files on your personal desktop printer or on commercial printing machines at service centers, there is no magic formula we can give you. If you want to produce the correct print the first time and every time, you need to prepare yourself for testing, testing, and more testing. If you're satisfied with much less, then you can visit the print dialog box, click a few buttons, and be done with it. But if you take the time to look over some of the options we talk about in this chapter and run some tests, you can be certain that your final printed images will look much better than if you had just pushed a few buttons in the Print dialog box.

In this chapter, we talk about options — many options — for setting print attributes for printing to your own color printer, and we toss in some tips on how to get better results when using print service centers. If you need to, reread this chapter a few times just to be certain you understand the process for printing good-quality images. A little time spent here will hopefully save you some headaches down the road.

Setting Up Your Printer

Setting up your printer is your first step toward good-looking printouts. To set up your printer within Elements, you need to complete a few tasks before you ever launch the program:

- ✒ **Hook up your desktop color printer to your computer and turn it on.**

- ✒ **Make sure the computer sees the printer.** To be sure, open the Printers and Faxes area of Windows and see if your printer appears. If not, click Add a Printer and follow the wizard.

- ✒ **Remove the shrink-wrap from the printer's user manual and browse through it.**

- ✒ **If you have it, install your printer software on your computer.**

With all these bases covered, you're ready to set up your printer in Elements. Just follow these steps:

1. **Choose File⇨Print or press Ctrl+P.**

   The Print dialog box opens. We talk about that dialog box a little later.

2. **For now, click the Page Setup button.**

3. **Click the Printer button.**

   When you do, another Page Setup dialog box opens, as shown in Figure 14-1. You use this Page Setup dialog box to select your printer.

Figure 14-1: Click Printer in the Page Setup dialog box to open another Page Setup dialog box where you can select your target printer.

1. **Look for your printer in the Name drop-down list and select the printer you intend to print your files to. Click OK when you're done.**

   If you have only one printer installed on your computer, you may see only one choice in the Name drop-down menu. If you don't see your printer, you need to go back to the printer installation guide and retrace the steps required to setup your printer.

Printing from the Organizer

Although you can print files from the Organizer or the editing modes, we recommend you stick with the Organizer. Wherever you print, you can access all the print options, but in the Organizer, the options are easier to navigate: You can easily select one or more files to print and simply follow the steps.

 In addition to setting all the print options for printing a photo, you need to prepare your images properly before printing. With all your options, it's easy to get confused and not know where to start. What you need is a procedure to follow consistently each time you want to print your photos to your desktop printer. Here's a procedure we recommend you follow when printing photos:

1. **Set your color management preferences to Adobe RGB (1998).**
2. **Edit your photos.**
3. **Save your edits.**
4. **Click the Photo Browser button to switch to the Organizer.**
5. **Tag images for printing.**
6. **Select the files you want to print.**
7. **Choose File➪Print in the Organizer.**
8. **Click Page Setup and select your page setup options.**
9. **Set your print options in the Print Selected Files dialog box.**
10. **Click More Options to select the correct color profile, among other options.**
11. **Click Print in the Print Selected Files dialog box.**

In the sections that follow, we introduce the interface and break down these steps to explain each in detail. Refer back to this section every time you print to make sure you don't miss a step. Doing so will help you get stellar-looking prints every time — and avoid wasting expensive photo paper.

Checking out Elements' print shop

Elements offers so many options for printing, it's like having a mini print shop that you operate from your computer (although the pros obviously can do a lot more than a consumer inkjet printer can). If you select one or more files and choose File⇨Print in the Organizer, the Print Selected Files dialog box pops onto the screen, looking something like Figure 14-2. Before you get started printing, here are some basics to help familiarize you with this dialog box:

- ✔ **Image thumbnails:** The left pane shows thumbnail images of the photos selected for printing.

- ✔ **Scroll selected images:** Click the left and right arrows to scroll the selected photos and see print previews in the Print Preview area. Note that changing the Print Preview can only be accomplished by clicking the arrows. Selecting thumbnails in the Image thumbnails pane won't change the Print Preview.

Image thumbnails   Print preview

Scroll selected images

Figure 14-2: Open the Organizer and select one or more files. Choose File⇨Print to open the Print Selected Files dialog box.

↙ **Paper size:** Below the arrows, you see the current selected paper size.

↙ **Print preview:** The window shows you how your photo will print on the selected page size.

Stepping through a print job with Print Selected Files

You have your images loaded into Elements and are ready to get them on paper. As we mention earlier in this chapter, this is the section that breaks down the standard procedure for printing into all the details. Read through the following sections to find out what you need to know to print your photos.

Steps 1–3: Prepping a photo for printing

These steps involve all the things you do before you print so that your print-outs look their best:

1. **Set your color management preferences to Adobe RGB (1998) by choosing Edit⇨Color Settings in any workspace.**

   Alternatively, you can press Shift+Ctrl+K or (Ctrl+Alt+G if printing from the Organizer). The Color Settings dialog box opens.

2. **Select the Always Optimize for Printing radio button.**

   See Chapter 2 for more information on Color Management.

3. **Open the photos you want to print in Standard Edit mode and apply image enhancement edits according to the needs of each individual image, as we describe in Chapter 10.**

   Edit image brightness, color balance, clarity, and sharpness as needed.

4. **Choose Image⇨Resize⇨Image Size.**

   The Image Size dialog box opens, where you can set the resolution to the optimum printer resolution and type the width or height that matches the output dimensions in the respective text boxes.

   Be certain you only downsample images and do not upsample them in the Image Size dialog box. (See Chapter 3 for more information about resolution, resampling, and resizing images.)

   You can size images freely in the Print Selected Files dialog box. However, doing so puts an extra burden on your computer and printer. You'll find printing is much faster when you size images in Standard Edit mode to a 1:1 ratio between the image size and the print size.

5. **If you need to crop the image, use the Crop tool.**

   You may find it easier to use the Crop tool either before or after visiting the Image Size dialog box, depending on the photo and what needs to be cropped. (See Chapter 9 for more information on cropping images.)

6. **Save your edits by choosing File⇨Save or File⇨Save As to overwrite the existing file or save a copy of the file, respectively. Be certain to check the box for Include in the Organizer when saving the files so the edited photos will be added to the current catalog.**

   Anything you do to a photo should be saved before printing the image. If Elements quits unexpectedly, you'll loose all the edits you made if you don't first save the file.

Steps 4–6: Selecting photos you want to print

With your edited files ready to go, it's time to select them for printing. Here are the details:

1. **If you're not already in the Organizer, click the Photo Browser button to open it.**

2. **Tag images (optional).**

   If you have few images in an Organizer window, you can skip this step.

   If you have a large number of files, you might find it easier to locate your files to print if you tag them.

   a. Open the Tags palette, create a new tag, and name the tag — something like **Files to Print**. (See Chapter 6 for more information on creating tags and tagging files.)

   b. Drag the tag to the files you edited for printing.

   c. Click the square adjacent to the tag name, and the Organizer window changes to show only your tagged photos.

3. **Select the files you want to print.**

   If you want to print all the tagged files, press Ctrl+A or use the Edit⇨Select All menu command. If you want to eliminate files from the selected group, press the Ctrl key and click the selected images to deselect them.

Steps 7–8: Choosing your Page Setup options

With your files selected, you're ready to choose all the Page Setup options. You can do this in a number of ways, but sticking to one area for all your printing options simplifies the process and helps ensure that you don't miss any important steps. The following steps walk you through all the options available and explain what they mean:

1. **Choose File⇨Print to open the Print Selected Files dialog box.**

2. **At the bottom of the Print Selected Files dialog box, click Page Setup.**

   The Page Setup dialog box opens.

   This dialog box will be different for each printer because the properties are choices you make for your specific printer. For example, in Figure 14-3, the printer is an Epson desktop color printer. Most Epson printers have similar settings options. If you use a printer from a different manufacturer, you may see some different choices, but the important attributes for selecting a paper type and variations of color printing choices are fairly standard among all desktop color printers.

Figure 14-3: Click Properties in the second Page Setup dialog box to open the Properties dialog box, where attributes specific to your printer are selected.

3. **Select the quality type, based on the paper you use and the image content.**

   In Figure 14-3, you could choose either Photo or Best Photo for printing photo images. If using a photo-quality paper, you want to select the Best Photo option.

4. **Select a paper type.**

   This option is found with most desktop color printers, and it's one of the most critical choices you need to make. Be certain the paper type selection from a radio button, check box, or drop-down menu matches the paper you use to print the file. You'll see noticeable differences in prints if the proper paper selection is not made.

5. **Depending on your printer and the recommendations made in the user manual, make any other necessary adjustments.**

   For example, you may have many other options for photo enhancements, sharpening, reversing print order, checking ink levels, running routine maintenance, and so on. Be certain to refer to the user guide to become familiar with other options.

6. **After you gain a little experience, check out advanced options if your printer supports them.**

You may include adjustments for brightness and color rendering, such as those found with the Epson printer shown in Figure 14-4. If your printer consistently prints with a *color shift* (changing color from your monitor appearance to the printed piece), you may be able to make some corrections in the advanced settings. Don't attempt this until you are completely familiar with your printer. When you feel you're ready, experiment and play with the settings after thoroughly reviewing the printer's user guide.

Figure 14-4: Open an advanced properties dialog box and look over options choices available for advanced settings.

7. **Click OK in the Page Setup dialog box to return to the Print Selected Files dialog box.**

Step 9: Selecting your print options

After choosing your Page Setup options, you jump back to the Print Selected Files dialog box (refer to Figure 14-2), where you can choose print options.

You may want to review the images you selected on the left side of the dialog box to double-check that you're printing all the images you want, no more and no less:

✔ **To add more photos** to the Image thumbnails, click the Add (+) symbol for additional files to print.

✔ **To delete a file** from the list, select a thumbnail and click the minus (–) symbol. Deleting a file here does not delete the file from the Organizer.

On the right side of the Print Selected Files dialog box, you see a set of steps that walk you through all the print options — well, sort of. Some of the options are more self-explanatory than others. The following steps mirror the steps you'll find in the dialog box, but with a bit more explanation of the options:

1. Select Printer.

Select your target printer from the drop-down menu. This option is the same as selecting your printer in the Page Setup dialog box.

Other options you can choose from in this area include:

- **Check or adjust your printer preferences:** Click the icon adjacent to the Select Printer drop-down menu and you open the Printer preferences, the same as when selecting Properties in the Page Setup dialog box.

- **Select Print Image Matching (P.I.M.):** Print Image Matching ensures that a P.I.M.-enabled digital camera and printer work together to produce the best possible color. Check this box if your camera supports P.I.M. To learn more about P.I.M., click the light bulb icon to the right of the check box.

- **Select Exif Print:** This option is available only if your photos have Exif data. Exif Print is a format that allows additional information to be recorded with digital camera data. Among the data recorded by the camera are color profile and print optimization information. If your digital camera supports Exif Print, check this box. Note that this option is not available for files in which Exif data was not recorded.

A lot of information on Print Image Matching technology and Exif Print is available. To find out more about getting your camera and printer in sync using P.I.M., check out a Web site dedicated to providing information on this technology. Open your Web browser and browse to `www.printimage matching.com`. For more information on Exif Print, search the Internet and locate information on the current version of the Exif Print format.

2. Select Type of Print.

From the drop-down menu, select the type of prints you want. When printing individual images on your printer, use the Individual Prints menu command. You also have options for Contact Sheets, Picture Package, and Labels (see sections later in this chapter for printing with these other options).

3. Select Print Size and Options.

From a drop-down menu, you have options for the image size printed on paper. You can select from fixed print options common for photo print sizes, such as $3\frac{1}{2} \times 5$, 4×6, 8×10, and so on, or you can edit the width and height dimensions of the final print to create a custom size.

You must have sufficient resolution to produce quality prints. Therefore, you can't size a small 2-×-3 photo to an 11-×-17-inch print size. For more information on printing and resolution, see Chapter 3.

You also find a few other options in this area:

- **One Photo Per Page:** If this check box is checked, only a single photo in the selected group prints to a page. Uncheck the box and you can print as many selected photos as you can fit on one page.

- **Use each photo __ times:** If you want multiple copies of the same image, type a value in this text box.

- **Crop to fit:** This option is grayed out if you select Actual Size from the Select Print Size and Options drop-down menu. For all other sizes you select from the menu commands, you can check the box to crop images to fit the selected print size. When the check box is checked, the print fits the paper at the horizontal or vertical size (whichever is smaller) and the excess (horizontal or vertical) is cut off.

Step 10: Working in the More Options dialog box

Opening the More Options dialog box and making some choices before printing files to your printer is critical. This dialog box contains choices for some optional items and a selection for using a color profile.

Click More Options in the Print Selected Files dialog box, and the More Options dialog box, shown in Figure 14-5, opens. Choices in the More Options dialog box include:

- **Label:** Check the boxes for labels you want printed outside the image area.

- **Other:** If you want to print iron-on transfers for T-shirts and other types of items that accept transfer material, check the box for Invert Image (Transfer Printing).

  Crop marks are lines that identify where a print is cut when printing images on paper larger than the image size. Check the box if you have some white area on the edges of an image and your print doesn't show you a clear area where a print needs to be cut. Using crop marks

Figure 14-5: Click More Options in the Print Selected Files dialog box to open the More Options dialog box.

shows you where to cut a print to eliminate any white border that may appear on the final print.

- ✓ **Border:** Select a size from the drop-down menu or edit the text box to determine the line width for a border. If you don't want a border printed around the image, uncheck the box for Add a Border.

  Click the color swatch to open the Color Picker, where you can select a color for a border.

- ✓ **Color Management:** The Print Space drop-down menu lists a number of different color profiles. If you have a color profile that was installed with your printer software, the profile is listed in this menu. Be certain to use a printer profile when printing to your printer. When you select a profile, the color from your monitor viewing color space is converted to the printer color space. Without getting too technical, you generally see much better prints when using a color profile designed for your printer. (For more information on color profiles and color management, see Chapter 2.)

After making choices in the More Options dialog box, click OK and you return to the Print Selected Files dialog box.

Step 11: Sending images to your printer

This last step is easy. After you've selected all your options, click the Print button and your file is printed using all the choices you made.

Consistency is your best means for committing complex procedures to memory. If you prefer printing from one of the edit modes, then by all means, do it. Just be certain you are consistent in using the same mode and the same dialog boxes for printing until you've mastered all the options and you can predict the print results before exploring different alternatives.

Printing a video image

If you have video clips in your Organizer window, you can print the first frame in a video image. The video frame must be printed from the Organizer window. You cannot open audio files, video frames, or Creations in either editing mode.

Select a video clip and choose File⇨Print. The same Print Selected Photos dialog box opens as when selecting photos for printing. Choose the same options for printing the file as you do for printing photos and click the Print button.

Note that video frames are low resolution, and the quality is likely to be poor when printing the first frame in a video clip at full size. If you want to print thumbnail images, you can reduce the image size in the Print Selected Files dialog box, and the quality will improve as the image size is reduced.

Printing a contact sheet

In the same way that you can get contact sheets from photo labs when sub-mitting film-processing orders, Elements provides you a means for printing contact sheets from selected photos:

1. **Select the photos you want to print as a contact sheet and choose File⇨Print.**

2. **Make all the choices discussed earlier for printing selected photos.**

3. **From the Select Type of Print drop-down menu in the Print Selected Files dialog box, select Contact Sheet.**

4. **Use the check boxes to add labels.**

When printing a contact sheet, it's helpful to add label information. As soon as you select the Contact Sheet menu option, check boxes appear for adding labels, as you see in Figure 14-6.

Figure 14-6: Select Contact Sheet from the Select Type of Print drop-down menu, select the number of columns, and check the boxes for label information.

5. **If you like, edit the Columns text box to select the number of columns you want to appear on the contact sheet.**

   As fewer columns are selected, the resultant image sizes become larger. The Print Preview area shows you a preview of the contact sheet.

6. **After setting the print attributes, click Print.**

   The images are printed on individual sheets of paper according to the number of selected files and the number of pages required to print all files.

Packaging pictures

Picture packages are also similar to orders you can place at photo labs; a package might include one photo in several different sizes printed on one piece of photo paper or multiple images printed at different sizes on one piece of photo paper.

In addition to the choices you have for print sizes, Elements offers you many choices for framing images. In Figure 14-7, you can see a choice made for printing two 3-x-5 prints, and an Antique Oval was selected as the frame.

Figure 14-7: Picture packages offer options for image sizes and frame choices.

Like printing contact sheets, you make the Picture Package selection in the Select Type of Print drop-down menu. Frame options are selected from the Select a Frame drop-down menu.

If you want the same image printed at different sizes, select an option for the size from the Select a Layout drop-down menu and check the Fill Page With First Photo box. If this check box is checked, each image is printed at different sizes on the same sheet of paper. Unchecking the box prints selected images distributed at different sizes on the same sheet of paper.

In Figure 14-8, multiple image sizes appear on one sheet of paper, and with the Fill Page With First Photo check box checked, the same image is set to print on the same sheet of paper. Note that the frame option Antique Rectangle 1 is selected from the Select a Frame drop-down menu.

Figure 14-8: Check Fill Page With First Photo and the same image prints on one sheet of paper at sizes determined by the selection made in the Select a Layout drop-down menu.

Printing Avery label sizes

Elements provides you an option for printing Avery labels at preset sizes. Open the Select Type of Print drop-down menu and select Labels. The Select a Layout drop-down menu lists four label sizes and the Avery label code for each size.

When you purchase labels at your local office supply store, be certain to jot down the codes and sizes on a piece of paper. Purchase the label sizes according to the product code, and you're ready to print labels from Elements.

Printing Creations with Adobe Reader

In Chapter 16, we talk about making creations in Photoshop Elements. All the to-dos and know-hows are addressed in that chapter. However, because we're talking about printing in this chapter, we thought you might like to know how to print creations, such as photo albums, greeting cards, and calendars.

The reason printing creations is different from printing your photos is that many creations are exported to Adobe PDF format. After your creation is packaged for output as a PDF, you can't use the print options in Elements to print your creation files. You need to use Adobe Reader instead.

Adobe Reader is installed with your Elements installation, but you may want to check the version of the Reader program and upgrade your free Adobe Reader to the most current version. The Elements 4 CD installer provides you with Adobe Reader 7. Be certain to install this version if you have an older version installed on your computer.

Adobe Reader offers two ways to go about printing your creations, each with its own advantages:

- **The Print and Page Setup dialog boxes** offer a multitude of options that you can tweak to your heart's content. In particular, the Page Scaling options enable you to customize the layout of the printed page.

- **The Picture Tasks bar** doesn't have all the options of the Print dialog box but does offer a wizard that walks you through the print setup and includes templates you can use for quick and easy page layout. For example, one template sets up a page of wallet-size prints.

Printing with the dialog boxes

Printing from the Adobe Reader Page Setup and Print dialog boxes is much like printing with similar dialog boxes in Elements or even other programs. But some of the options are unique to Adobe Reader, and this section walks you through all of them. When you use this method, you will find that you have lots of options to choose from.

To print using these dialog boxes, follow these steps:

1. **Launch Adobe Reader, choose File➪Open, and open the PDF creation that you want to print.**

   Adobe Reader has a Full Screen mode much like the Elements Full Screen View mode. Many creations you make with Elements that get exported to Adobe PDF open in Adobe Reader's Full Screen Mode.

2. **Bail out of Full Screen Mode by pressing the Esc key.**

   Now you can see the Reader toolbars, which were hidden while in Full Screen Mode. You'll want to use these toolbars when printing files.

3. **Choose File➪Page Setup and select the paper size and orientation in the Page Setup dialog box.**

   Adobe Reader has a nasty habit of returning to default options in the Page Setup dialog box and doesn't remember the last settings you made for printing a file. Make a habit of always opening the Page Setup dialog box and selecting the correct paper size and orientation before opening the Print dialog box each time you print a new file.

4. **Choose File➪Print.**

   The Print dialog box, shown in Figure 14-9, opens. Alternatively, press Ctrl+P.

   Note that the slider at the bottom of the preview image scrolls pages in the PDF file. Move the slider right to advance pages. Note in Figure 14-9 that the preview shows page 5 of 19 pages.

5. **Select your target printer from the Name drop-down menu if it's not already selected.**

6. **Click Properties to open your printer's Properties dialog box, where you can make the same choices covered in "Stepping through a print job with Print Selected Files," earlier in this chapter. Then click OK.**

7. **Back in the Print dialog box, choose Document from the Comments and Forms drop-down menu.**

   The creations you produce in Elements won't have comment notes or form fields. Printing Comments and Form Fields are used with other types of PDF documents, not those created in Elements.

Print

Printer

Name: EPSON Stylus C62 Series ▼   Properties

Status: Ready   Comments and Forms:
Type: EPSON Stylus C62 Series   Document ▼

Print Range   Preview
⊙ All
○ Current view
○ Current page
○ Pages from: 1   to: 19
Subset: All pages in range ▼ ☐ Reverse pages

Page Handling
Copies: 1 ⬍   ☐ Collate

Page Scaling: Fit to Printer Margins ▼

☑ Auto-Rotate and Center

☐ Choose Paper Source by PDF page size

☐ Print to file   Units: Inches   Zoom: 58%

                                     5/19 (5)

Printing Tips   Advanced   OK   Cancel

Figure 14-9: After you choose your options in the Page Setup dialog box, use the Print dialog box to adjust the settings for your printer.

8. **Select a print range by typing in the From and To text boxes the page numbers you want to print. If you want to print all pages, select All.**

9. **In the Page Handling area, select the number of copies you want to print.**

10. **Be certain to choose an appropriate page scaling.**

    • **Fit to Printer Margins** makes pages fit on the selected page size.

    • **Multiple Pages per Sheet** enables you to design your custom layout. In the text boxes that appear, type the number of columns in the first text box and the number of rows in the second text box.

Using the Multiple Pages per Sheet option is a great way to print cards for CD and DVD jewel cases. You can write your creations to CD-ROMs and DVDs and then print a card that fits nicely inside the CD/DVD jewel case.

11. **Select or deselect the following check boxes, depending on your circumstances:**

- If the **Auto Rotate and Center** check box is checked, Reader automatically rotates pages to fit on the paper and centers the page on the paper. Auto rotation is handy if you have both Portrait and Landscape images in the same PDF document.

- **Choose Paper Source by PDF Page Size** is an option you use when you have different page sizes in a single document. In most cases, you won't use this option, so leave it unchecked.

- Selecting **Print to File** sends your file to your hard drive and not to the printer. It can be helpful for those printing to PostScript printers, but for your color desktop printer, make sure this check box remains unchecked.

12. **Click OK and the file is sent to your target printer.**

Be patient and let the printer do its work. Depending on the number of pages, it may take a little time to complete the print job.

If you can't print the PDF file to your printer, go back through all the options in the preceding list, but before you click OK, click the Advanced button to open the Advanced Print Setup dialog box. Here, check the Print as Image check box, as shown in Figure 14-10. Sometimes PDF documents can overload a printer's memory — especially if it uses a lot of fonts. The Print as Image option rasterizes all the page data (see Chapters 3 and 13 for more information on rasterizing data) and simplifies the printing. However, the down side to Print as Image is that the image quality is likely to be noticeably degraded. Use this option only if you cannot print a PDF file on your printer.

Figure 14-10: Check Print as Image in the Advanced Print Setup if you can't print a PDF document to your printer.

Printing with the Picture Tasks tool

The Picture Tasks tool offers an alternative way to print with Adobe Reader. One advantage of using this tool is that you can choose from templates that set up the page in a certain way for you. Here's how you can use the Picture Tasks tool to print a creation you made in Elements:

1. **Export a PDF from one of Elements' creation options and open the creation in Adobe Reader.**

   The Picture Tasks tool is loaded in the Reader Toolbar Well at the top of the Reader window.

2. **Open the drop-down menu from the Picture Tasks tool and select How To . . . Picture Tasks.**

   This menu command opens the How To pane that appears on the right side of the Adobe Reader workspace, as shown in Figure 14-11.

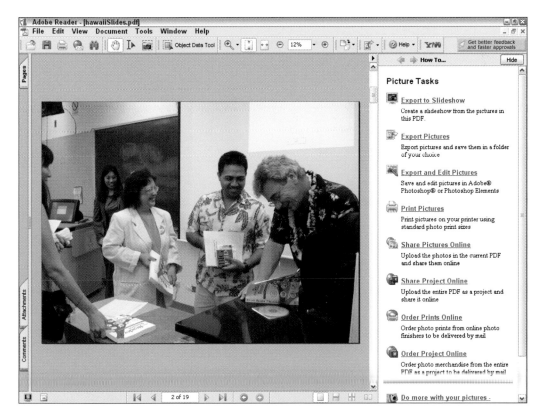

Figure 14-11: Use the Picture Tasks How To pane to select different tasks and find help information.

In the How To pane, you have links that open dialog boxes for performing the various tasks listed. You can also find brief help information that describes what each task does. For printing creations, you click Print Pictures; see the nearby sidebar for more details about all the tasks.

3. **Click Print Pictures in the How To pane.**

   Alternatively, you can open the Picture Tasks drop-down menu and select Print Pictures. The Picture Tasks Print Wizard opens after clicking in the How To pane or selecting the menu command. Note in Figure 14-12 that the Print Wizard from Picture Tasks is different than the Print dialog box you open when choosing File⇨Print in Adobe Reader.

Figure 14-12: The Picture Tasks Print Wizard.

4. **Select the pages to print.**

   Click Select All in the Print Wizard to select all pages to print or individually check and uncheck the boxes to mark those pictures you want to print.

5. **Click Next and select a printing template.**

   You have many options for using a printing template. Notice in Figure 14-13 that the Wallet template is selected, and the preview shows all pages as they will print in wallet sizes. Click a Radio button to select the template you want.

   Although Picture Tasks printing offers you an option to create a picture package like picture packages created in Elements, you have more options available in Elements. You're better off using Elements for this task. However if you lose your original images after making a creation, you can use the option in Adobe Reader.

6. **Click Print to print the pages.**

You may not be familiar with the Picture Tasks tool because it isn't available in a plain PDF document you might download from a Web site or a help file on the Elements installer CD. Only PDF documents that are created from image files — including your Elements creations — support Picture Tasks.

Figure 14-13: Step 2 in the Wizard provides options for selecting a printing template.

Perusing all the Picture Tasks

Options you find for working with Picture Tasks in the How To pane include

✔ **Export to Slideshow:** If you have a slide show or any other PDF document and you want to select some individual pages while eliminating pages from a slide show, click this option. Another dialog box opens where you can make selections for the pages to export, choose from a list of different transition effects, select background music, and set the slide durations.

✔ **Export Pictures:** Any or all pages can be exported back to file formats that you can open directly in Elements.

✔ **Export and Edit Pictures:** Click this link and a dialog box opens, in which you can choose Elements as your photo editor. When you

export pictures, they open directly in Elements.

✔ **Share Pictures Online:** We talk about online sharing in Chapter 16. This option enables you to share pictures through online services.

✔ **Share Project Online:** Projects as well as pictures can be shared online. This is another option you have for online sharing.

✔ **Order Prints Online:** You can order prints of PDF documents online in the same way you order prints from Elements, which we explain later in this chapter.

✔ **Order Project Online:** After a project has been shared, you can order a project from an online sharing service.

Getting Professional

Although you have the tools to create great professional-quality prints, you also have many options for printing your pictures at service centers and discount stores. There are many reasons why turning to a service center may be better than printing photos yourself:

- ✔ **Cost:** In some cases, purchasing photo prints at discount stores is cheaper than buying the materials for your desktop printer.

- ✔ **Printing capabilities:** You may find printing on different kinds of papers and sizes to be more within the capabilities of a service center than you have available using your own equipment.

- ✔ **Longer-lasting prints:** Photo labs and service centers can use different materials and processes than you can use with an inkjet desktop printer. Inasmuch as there have been great advances in printer technology, you still wind up with prints that are ink-based, which can lead to more progressive fading and shorter life expectancies than the prints you order from photo labs. If you take a roll of film to a photo lab or photo service, the film is chemically processed, and the prints are output on machines that use a photo chemical process, exposing the paper and running it through a developer, fixer, and wash. If you take digital-camera images to a photo lab or service center, you get exactly the same kinds of prints as you get from film.

The one disadvantage of ordering prints from a photo service center is that you lose control over the printing process. If you shop at the bargain centers, your images are printed without the intervention of a qualified technician. The average mega-store employee knows very little about color management, profiles, and printing options other than the automated runs they perform on their photo equipment. Therefore, you need to be certain to prepare your files properly before sending them to a service center, and this section shows you how. You also find a handy checklist that can help you make sure your photos are in good shape before you send them off to a photo lab or service center.

Using color profiles with service centers

Although we cover color profiles in detail in Chapter 3, here are some things you should know about color profiles and printing:

- ✔ **Elements can embed one of two color spaces.** When saving a file, you can use sRGB or Adobe RGB (1998) and embed the color profile in your files. These color spaces are monitor color working spaces and are used when you edit files in Photoshop Elements.

- ✔ **When printing to a color printer, you get best results when printing with a printer color profile.** The color profile you use with printing equipment is a printer's profile. When you print a picture to a printing device, your monitor color profile is converted to the printer's color profile.

✔ **When you print files to your desktop printer, you select your printer's profile when you print the file.** In the More Options section of the Print Selected Files dialog box, you select your printer's color profile and print the job. Your monitor color is then converted to the printer color during the print process.

Okay, so all the above is related to what you can control on your printing equipment. If you take your files to a custom photo-finishing lab, the qualified technicians may print your files using their equipment's color profiles. It's all well and good so far.

Now here comes the problem. Your most economical avenue for getting photo prints from a service center is to use a mega-store like Costco, Sam's Club, and FedEx Kinko's. These outlets offer the best prices because they don't use $100-an-hour experienced color technicians, and they don't give you custom printing services. Their service is as automated as possible. Rather than opening a file in Photoshop Elements or Adobe Photoshop and selecting a color profile before printing, the technicians usually download your pictures with a downloader utility, and the file is printed using an embedded color profile. You can't blame the stores. They're offering a product at a very low cost, like less than 10 cents a print for standard 4×6 photo prints.

Your problem, then, is embedding the right profile in your pictures. You know you can't use Elements because Elements can't embed profiles other than sRGB and Adobe RGB (1998). Well, with a little help from some free downloads, you can edit your pictures for the best possible printing, and here's how you do it:

1. **Make all the necessary edits you need to make in Elements and save your files in TIFF format.**

   You must use TIFF format to use the converter we mention in Step 6.

2. **Download color profiles from your providers' Web sites.**

   Almost all service centers post color profiles for their printing equipment. You can visit the Costco Web site at www.costco.com, click the Services link on the home page, and click Photo Center on the next page. You are prompted to set up an account, and then you come to a page where profiles are listed. Costco makes the profiles available for stores in their geographic regions, and usually you find profiles for printing on their equipment and profiles best suited for different papers. This is something you need to observe. If several profiles are available for downloading, be certain to use the right profile for the paper you want your pictures to be printed on.

If you use a photo lab that wants you to embed profiles, you can visit independent lab Web sites and download profiles as well.

3. **Copy the profiles to your system color folder:** `C:\WINDOWS\system32\spool\drivers\color`.

   This is the folder where all your color profiles are stored.

4. **Download a converter by going to** `http://drycreekphoto.com/tools/profile_converter` **and clicking the link for** `ProfileConverterSetup.zip`.

   You need a utility to convert your files that use the Adobe RGB (1998) color space to the color space used by machines at your service center. Fortunately, the Dry Creek Photo converter is a great free tool.

   In addition, the Dry Creek Photo Web site is one of the best sources of information available for color management and color profiling. In addition to offering custom color profiling services, Dry Creek Photo hosts a number of different color profiles for many different commercial printers.

5. **After downloading the file to your hard drive, double-click the Setup file and follow the brief steps in the install wizard.**

6. **Choose Start⇨Programs⇨ Dry Creek Photo⇨Profile Converter⇨ICC Profile Converter.**

   The simple program interface opens, as you see in Figure 14-14.

7. **Click the Source Image ellipsis (. . .) and select the source file.**

   The source file is the file you want to print, saved in TIFF format.

Figure 14-14: Select the options for converting the color profile and check the box for Embed Profile before clicking the Convert button.

8. **Click the Source Color Profile ellipsis and select the source color profile.**

   This is the color profile that is currently embedded in your source file.

9. **Click the Destination Image ellipsis and select the folder where you want to save your file.**

10. **Click the Destination Color Profile ellipsis and select the color profile used by the equipment where you place your order.**

    You saved your color profiles to the Windows Color folder, so be certain to look in this folder for the target printer color profiles.

11. **If you want to process multiple files, check the box for Process Multiple Files.**

12. **Be certain to check the box for Embed Profile in Image and then click the Convert button when all the options have been selected.**

    After you click Convert, the profile converter handles the profile conversion and saves your files to the target folder.

Submitting files to service centers

On provider Web sites, you can usually find guidelines for the file formats acceptable and the recommended resolution and dimensions of your images. If you don't see these guidelines on Web sites, be sure to call and inquire as to what file attributes are acceptable.

As a general rule, here are some things you should consider when submitting files if guidelines are not provided:

- ✔ **Resolution:** For photo printing machines, be certain to submit files at 300 ppi (pixels per inch). See Chapter 3 for more information on image resolution.

- ✔ **Dimensions:** As a general rule, size images to the print size. For example, if you want 4-×-6-inch prints, be certain your images are sized to 4×6 inches at 300 ppi.

- ✔ **File format:** Some centers may take only JPEG images. If TIFF is not acceptable, open the converted images you saved from Dry Creek ICC Profile Converter. Open the TIFF file(s) in Photoshop Elements and choose File⇨Save As. Be certain the check box is checked for ICC Profile in the Save Options

Figure 14-15: You can change file formats from TIFF to JPEG and preserve embedded profiles when saving from Elements.

  in the Save/Save As dialog box. Select JPEG for the format and click Save. Notice that the profile used with the Dry Creek ICC Profile Converter is listed as the ICC Profile. In Figure 14-15, you can see a profile embedded for a Costco print center.

- ✔ **Media storage:** If you walk into a FedEx Kinko's store and go to the self-serve photo printing machines, you won't see support for any external USB hard drives or removable USB drives. All the print centers support a wide range of media cards used by digital cameras. Be certain to use your memory cards and not USB devices when placing orders. If you use Compact Flash II, memory sticks, or other media sources used by digital cameras, copy your files to these sources when you place orders as a walk-in customer.

Vendors that host Web sites with downloadable profiles and order information are likely to accept file uploads online. This saves you the time fighting crowds when placing orders. In some cases, you can have service centers mail your images back to you so you won't need to wait when picking up orders either — but this online ordering stuff is another matter that we talk about in the next section.

Using Online Printing Services

Photoshop Elements supports the Adobe Photoshop Services program that is a joint effort between Adobe Systems and Kodak EasyShare (formerly Ofoto), a division of Kodak. The Services program offers online ordering of prints, sharing of photos and projects, and a huge array of different print products for consumers and professionals.

As of this writing, you get 10 free prints, so it's worth taking a little time to check out the service — especially if you want to order prints and have them mailed directly to your home or office. No lines, no hassles, no fighting high-rising gasoline costs — this service offers great prints and an abundance of convenience.

To use the service, follow these steps:

1. **Select files in the Organizer much like you would select files for printing.**

2. **In either editing mode or the Organizer, choose File⇨Order Prints.**

   The Kodak EasyShare Wizard opens, as shown in Figure 14-16. The first screen you come to in the wizard is a form for you to create an account.

If you try to place an order from your office where your IT department prevents connecting to some external sources, you may need to have your firewall settings adjusted. Talk to your IT department to help you make a connection.

3. **If you haven't set up an account already, fill in the information and step through the wizard by clicking the Next button on each page in the wizard. If you have set up an account, supply your logon information.**

   The selected files in the Organizer are automatically loaded in Step 1 of the wizard order page.

4. **You can modify your order by deleting files from the order and specifying different print sizes and quantities of prints.**

Figure 14-16: Choose File➪Order Prints and the Kodak EasyShare Wizard opens.

One nice feature in the service is the option for sending duplicate prints to another party. You can keep an address book on the provider's Web site and specify whom you want to receive an order. This is a nice feature if you're away spending your children's inheritance on a Caribbean cruise and want to send all the kids photos of the great time you're having. Just pop open your laptop on the pool deck, load up the digital camera images, and connect via a wireless connection. Before you return to Buffalo in mid-winter with a suntan, your kids will be frowning as they fan through the prints they received a week earlier.

5. **Continue stepping through the wizard to upload your files and confirm your order. Click the Finish button on the last pane and your order is complete.**

Showing It on Screen

*E*lements is a great packaging tool you can use to deploy your photos and creations for screen viewing. And that's not just your computer monitor. You can edit photos or assemble creations that are exported for Web viewing, too, and you can even prepare files to show on your television.

In Chapter 3, you find out about resolutions and color modes. The output requirements for printing files, which we cover in Chapter 14, are much different than what you use for images output for screen viewing.

In this chapter, we cover the options for Web and screen viewing that get you started with basics, including saving images for the Web (or screen viewing), setting up a slideshow, and burning your images on CDs or DVDs. If you're looking to take your Elements projects a step further, check out Bonus Chapters 1 and 2 on this book's Web site. Bonus Chapter 1 explains how to create GIF animations and show your images on a TV. Bonus Chapter 2 walks you through the steps for creating a simple photo gallery where you can share your pictures on the Web. (You can find details about the book's Web site in this book's introduction.)

Optimizing Images for the Web

When you show images on the Web, you want the images to look good, but you also want them to download before your visitors lose interest (or patience). Elements makes striking a balance between the two easy.

You may already know that file formats come into play when saving images for the Web. (You can find an overview of file formats in Chapter 3.) The two standard formats for Web images are JPEG and GIF. But if your first inclination is to choose File⇨Save As and select either of these formats, stop! There's a better way.

First, do a little prep work on your files. Then, you get best results if you use Photoshop Elements' special command for saving files for Web images. More options are available to you when using the File⇨Save for Web command than when using other save options. We explain just what you need to know in the sections that follow.

Preparing files for Web hosting

Before you save a file for Web hosting, you need to make some edits and save your file by using the Save or Save As menu command. A few edits made in the Standard Edit mode can save you some time and get the file properly set up before saving in the JPEG or GIF format with the Save for Web menu command.

Here are the edits you need to consider when preparing files for Web viewing:

- ✔ **Adjust dimensions and resolution.** Use the Image Size dialog box we discuss in Chapter 3 to resample images to the dimensions and resolution needed for Web viewing. Resolution should be sampled to 72 ppi, and the dimensions should equal the size you want the image to appear on a Web page.

- ✔ **Change the bit depth to 8-bit.** If you capture images with a digital camera or scan photos in 16- or 32-bit depth, be certain to change the bit depth to 8-bit by choosing Image⇨Mode⇨8 Bits/Channel, as we explain in Chapter 3.

- ✔ **Consider transparency.** You can save files with transparency for Web viewing. If you want to preserve transparent areas in an image, be certain to save files without flattening layers, as we explain in Chapter 8.

You can use the Save for Web dialog box to resample images and make some adjustments that prepare the image for saving for a Web file. However, if your file has a higher bit depth or resolution than is acceptable for Web graphics, a warning dialog box informs you that the image exceeds the size Save for Web was designed for and that you may run out of memory. Therefore, follow the guidelines here and plan on preparing files for Web requirements before you attempt to save a file through the Save for Web command.

Using the Save for Web command

After you prepare an image for Web use, it's time to save the file in either JPEG or GIF format. Because the Save for Web dialog box is loaded with features, here's a quick preview of the more helpful ones:

✔ **Tools:** You can select the Hand tool, the Zoom tool, the Eyedropper tool, or the Eyedropper Color tool from the top-left corner. Use the Hand tool to move the image around when zoomed in. Use the Zoom tool to zoom the preview image, the Eyedropper tool to sample color, and the Eyedropper Color tool to open the color picker.

✔ **File information at a glance:** Information is reported dynamically in the dialog box below the two previews. The image on the left in Figure 15-1 shows the default image size below the image preview. The image on the right side shows the new file size according to the options selected in the Preset area. As you change file attributes, the file size is reported as well as how long the image will take to download on a 28.8 Kbps (Kilobytes per second) modem.

The best thing about saving files for Web and screen views is that what you see is what you get. There's no guesswork when saving files for screen. If the settings you apply in the Save for Web dialog box don't look good on the resultant images, just open the original and save with different settings. You can test and play with the options to determine settings that work best for you and immediately preview your results.

Figure 15-1: Choose File➪Save for Web to save files for Web use.

I've been told PNG works

Yes, PNG (Portable Network Graphics) is a format that was designed specifically for Web use. The limitation is that not all Web browsers support PNG by default. Some browsers need a special plug-in to support viewing PNG files.

Although there are some advantages to saving in PNG format, such as the ability to save 24-bit images (see Chapter 3 for more information on 24-bit images) and support for transparency,

you may want to stay away from this format until you are certain that all Web browsers are upgraded to support PNG. For safe distribution of files to display on the Web and to be certain that all your family and friends can see the images, use either JPEG or GIF — especially if Aunt Sara is still using Windows 98 and an old version of Internet Explorer.

To finish getting your images ready for the Web with the Save for Web command, follow these steps:

1. **Open your image in either the Quick Fix or Standard Edit mode.**

2. **Choose File⇨Save for Web.**

   Alternatively, you can press Alt+Shift+Ctrl+S. The Save for Web dialog box opens (refer to Figure 15-1).

3. **Below the Preset drop-down menu (where you see GIF appear in Figure 15-1), select GIF or JPEG.**

   Because both of these formats are acceptable for Web viewing, the question arises: "What format is best for uploading my photos to a Web site?" Fortunately, you can use a few simple guidelines for deciding which format to choose:

   • **Photos:** If you're saving a photo for Web display, use JPEG as your file format. Continuous-tone images such as photographs appear best when saved as JPEG. Whereas GIF images support a maximum of 256 colors, JPEG supports 24-bit images in which a maximum of 16.7 million colors can be seen.

   • **Artwork:** Artwork, such as logos, illustrations, and designs, that has fewer colors than you see in continuous-tone images is best saved in GIF format. The reason is simple: The fewer colors you save, the smaller the file sizes. You want your images to load quickly in Web browsers, so file size is always a consideration. When saving in JPEG format, you don't have the option for saving fewer colors that the GIF format provides you.

   • **Animation:** If you animate an icon or image, then GIF is your choice for preserving the animated features. See Bonus Chapter 1 for details.

You can also choose one of two PNG formats, but we suggest reading the nearby sidebar "I've been told PNG works" before you go this route.

Alternatively, you can choose a preset for GIF, JPEG, or PNG from the Preset drop-down menu. The Custom option enables you to choose the attributes you want.

4. **If you chose Custom from the Preset drop-down menu, choose the format attributes for whichever format you chose in Step 3 (JPEG or GIF).**

   If you chose JPEG, you have the following format attributes to choose from, as shown in Figure 15-2:

   • **Quality:** Select image compression and a setting for quality consistent with the options we discuss in Chapter 3.

   • **ICC Profile:** This check box enables you to embed a color profile. See Chapter 14 for more information on using color profiles.

Figure 15-2: JPEG options are different than options you use for GIF images.

If you chose GIF, you can adjust the following attributes instead:

- **Color intents:** You have options for Selective, Adaptive, and Restrictive (Web). Use the Restrictive (Web) option (refer to Figure 15-1) to reduce colors to a Web-safe palette, as we describe in Chapter 3. This reduces colors to 216 compatible colors when saving in GIF format.

- **Interlaced:** Use this option to interlace the image, so it appears on a Web page in a slow progression from a faded graphic to the full-resolution image.

- **Colors:** Use the slider to adjust the number of colors in a GIF image. If you have only eight colors shown on a piece of artwork, this text box and slider let you reduce the colors from 256 to 8.

- **Dither:** For best quality, leave the default at 100%. Dithering helps create smooth transitions between colors.

- **Matte:** If you save a file on a layer and don't preserve the transparency, the matte setting turns the transparent areas to the color selected for the matte. You can choose from black, white, a color in the image you sample with the eyedropper tool (seen in the top-left corner of the dialog box), or a custom color you select from the Color Picker. (See Chapter 12 for more information on selecting colors in the Color Picker.)

5. **For either GIF or JPEG, check the Transparency box to preserve transparency. (For JPEG you also have an option for Progressive. Check the Progressive checkbox to save a file that progressively appears in a Web browser as the file downloads from the Web.)**

6. **Click OK to save the file.**

   Another dialog box opens where you can make choices for filename and location.

Although you also have an area for outputting different dimensions in the New Size area, it's better to do your sizing before you use Save for Web. In "Preparing files for Web hosting," earlier in this chapter, we explain how you prepare images at the correct size and resolution before accessing the Save for Web command.

Creating a Slide Show

This *Million Dollar Baby* is no *Mystic River*, it's simply *Absolute Power!* Well . . . maybe you won't travel the same path from Rowdy Yates to multiple Academy Award–winning director and filmmaker Clint Eastwood, but even Mr. Eastwood might be impressed with the options for movie making with Photoshop Elements' slide show creations. When he's not rolling out the Panaflex camera, Mr. Eastwood might just want to take photos of the grandkids and do the directing and producing as well as the editing right in Photoshop Elements.

For the rest of us, we can be our own Clint Eastwood wannabes by using the powerful features of the Photoshop Elements Slide Show Editor to create PDF slide shows and movie files. It's so easy, Elements promises you won't be *Unforgiven*.

Creating a project

You create a project file in the Slide Show Editor and can then export it for a number of different uses. In this section, you find out how to create and save your project. In the next section, you dive into exporting.

Here's how you create a slide show project that you can edit and export at a later time:

1. **Open the Organizer and select the pictures you want to use in your slide show.**

2. **Click the Create button in the Shortcuts bar and select Slide Show when the Creation Setup window opens. Click OK.**

   The Slide Show Preferences dialog box opens. Just about everything in the dialog box can be adjusted in the Slide Show Editor, so don't worry about making choices here. If you want to keep the Slide Show Preferences dialog box from reappearing when you make slide creations, remove the check mark from the Show This Dialog Each Time a New Slide Show Is Created option.

3. **Click OK in the Slide Show Preferences dialog box.**

   The Photoshop Elements Slide Show Editor opens, as shown in Figure 15-3.

4. **If your Slide Show Editor doesn't show you a screen similar to Figure 15-3, maximize the window by clicking the Maximize button in the top-right corner of the Editor window.**

   This way, you can see the Storyboard at the bottom of the screen and the Palette Bin on the right side of the editor.

5. **(Optional) Create a Pan & Zoom view.**

   As slides are shown, you can zoom and pan a slide. Click the check box marked Enable Pan and Zoom and click the Start thumbnail. A rectangle appears in the preview area. Move any one of the four corner handles in or out to resize the rectangle. Moving the cursor inside the rectangle and clicking the mouse button enables you to move the rectangle around the preview.

   For the end zoom position, click the End thumbnail and size the rectangle to a full view or a view you want to stop the zoom. Notice in Figure 15-3 that the Start thumbnail is selected and the rectangle is sized to about 50% in the center of the first slide.

Figure 15-3: Open the Slide Show Editor and choose your options for a slide show.

6. **(Optional) Add a graphic.**

A library of graphics appears in the Extras pane in the Palette Bin. Drag a graphic to a slide. If you want a blank slide to appear first and add text and graphics to the blank slide, click the Add Blank Slide in the Shortcuts Bar at the top of the editor.

7. **(Optional) Add text.**

Click the Text tool in the Extras pane in the Palette Bin and drag a text style to the blank slide or the opening slide in the slide show. After you drag text to a slide, the Text Properties pane opens in the Palette Bin. The text you drag to the slide is placeholder text. To edit the text, click Edit Text in the Properties pane. You can also select a font, a font point size, a color for the text, text alignment, and a font style. After setting the type attributes, click inside the text and move it to position.

8. **(Optional) Set transitions.**

   The icons between the slides in the Storyboard (at the bottom of the Slide Show Editor) indicate a default transition applied to the slide show. You can change transition effects for each slide independently or to all the slides in the show. Click the right-pointing arrow on the right side of a transition icon to open a pop-up menu containing a number of different transitions. If you want to apply the same transition to all slides, select Apply to All from the menu commands.

9. **(Optional) Add audio and media.**

   You can add audio to the slide show by choosing Add Media⇨ Audio from Organizer (or from Folder). Select an audio file and click OK.

   You can also add movie files to your slide show. A movie file can be added on top of a slide or on a new slide. When the slide show is played, the video file plays. Choose Add Media⇨Photos and Media from Organizer (or from Folder).

   This same set of commands can also be used to add additional pictures to the slide show.

10. **(Optional) Record your own sounds.**

    If you want to add narration, click the Narration tool in the Palette Bin, and the Extras pane changes to provide you with tools to record a sound or import a sound file. Note that this option requires you to have a microphone properly configured on your computer.

11. **(Optional) Fit slides to the audio.**

    If you have 3 minutes of audio and the slide duration is 2 minutes 30 seconds, you can, with a single mouse click, fit the slide duration uniformly to fit the 3-minute audio time. Just click the Fit Slides to Audio tool below the preview image.

    If you want to manually adjust time for slide durations, click the down arrow on the time readout below the slide thumbnails in the Storyboard.

12. **Click Save Project in the Shortcuts Bar and, in the dialog box that opens, type a name and click Save.**

    Your project is added to the Organizer and is available for further editing at a later time. Or you can open it to save in a number of different output formats, as we explain in the next section.

13. **Preview the slide show.**

    Before exporting the slide show, you can see a preview by clicking the buttons directly below the image preview area. If you want a full-screen preview, click the Preview button in the Shortcuts Bar and click the play button.

Exporting to slides and video

After creating a project, you have a number of different output options. You can write a project to disc for archival purposes and include slide shows on a video disc or a DVD. You can e-mail a slide show to another user, share a project online, write a project compatible for display on a TV, or save to either a PDF slide show or a Windows movie file.

We talk about e-mailing and sharing projects in Chapter 16. For now, we describe how you create slide shows and movie files and write your creations to a CD or DVD.

To write a PDF slide show or a movie file, do the following:

1. **In the Organizer window, double-click the project thumbnail.**

   The project opens in the Adobe Photoshop Elements Slide Show Editor.

2. **Click the Output tool in the Shortcuts bar.**

   The Slide Show Output Wizard opens, as shown in Figure 15-4.

Figure 15-4: Select Output in the Photoshop Elements Slide Show Editor and the Slide Show Output Wizard opens.

3. **Select the type of file you want to export to.**

   Select Movie File (.wmv) to export a Windows media video file. Your exported video can be viewed in Elements or viewed in the Windows Media Player. You can import the video in all programs that support .wmv files.

Select PDF File (.pdf) if you want to create a PDF slide show. If you create a PDF slide show, some of the animation features, such as zooming slides and transition effects, won't be shown in the resultant PDF document.

4. **In the dialog box that opens, prompting you to add your output file to the Organizer, click Yes.**

   You can now easily view the file by double-clicking it in the Organizer window.

Opening multi-page PDF files in Elements

If you create a slide show and export the slide show to a PDF document, you can open individual PDF pages in Elements. Elements can open any PDF document created from any PDF producer. Here's how:

1. **In the Organizer, select a file to open and click the Standard Edit option in the Shortcuts bar.**

   Remember to select the file and click Standard Edit. Don't double-click the file in the Organizer; that action opens the file in Adobe Reader.

   When the file is opened in Standard Edit mode, the Import PDF dialog box opens, as shown in Figure 15-5.

2. **In the dialog box, you can select one or more pages and specify the resolution and color mode.**

3. **Click OK to open the PDF pages in individual Image windows.**

Figure 15-5: Select a PDF file to open in Elements and the Import PDF dialog box opens.

Writing Creations to CDs and DVDs

You can output creations, such as slide shows and images you've optimized for TV, to a CD or DVD by using the Slide Show Output Wizard. If you have a movie but don't have a DVD burner, most DVD players sold today enable you to view videodiscs written to CDs. The CDs just won't hold as much content as a DVD can.

For writing to a CD or DVD, follow these steps:

1. **Open a project in the Slide Show Output Wizard by choosing File⇨ Open Creation in the Organizer window.**

2. **Click Output in the Slide Show Editor.**

3. **Click Burn to Disc in the Slide Show Output Wizard.**

4. **Select an option for the type of output you want to use — VCD or DVD (Figure 15-6).**

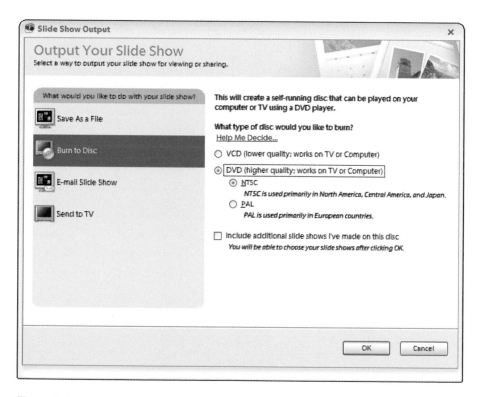

Figure 15-6: Type a name and select the format to export in the Slide Show Output Wizard.

- **If you're creating a CD,** select VCD (Lower Quality; Works on TV or Computer). When you select this option, your project is converted to a movie file (.wmv) during the write process. If you want additional files added to the CD, check the box for Include Additional Slide Shows I've Made on This Disc.

- **To burn a DVD,** check the option DVD (Higher Quality; Works on TV or Computer) in the Slide Show Output window. Using this option requires you to have Adobe Premiere Elements installed on your computer.

5. **Click OK and the Burn dialog box opens, as shown in Figure 15-7.**

6. **Select a CD or DVD drive if you have more than one drive installed on your computer.**

   DVD drives can often write in CD format as well. By default, the AUTO selection is often your best choice for the write speed.

7. **Click the video format (either NTSC or PAL) and click OK.**

   The status bar shows the writing progress.

After the CD or DVD finishes writing, pop open your CD/DVD drive and remove the disc. Place the disc in your DVD player and press Play. The movie automatically starts playing like any commercial videodisc.

Figure 15-7: Click Burn to Disc in the Slide Show Output Wizard to open the Burn dialog box.

16

Making Creations

*A*dobe Photoshop Elements offers you a number of creations that can be shared onscreen or in print. In the Creation Setup window, which is featured throughout this chapter, you have options for creating greeting cards, photo albums, and calendars.

In this chapter, we talk about these creations and all the output options available to you (PDFs, prints, e-mail, and more). It's all here in Elements; but shhhhh . . . don't tell the Photoshop people because Photoshop doesn't have all these wonderful creation features.

Aloha!
Wish you were here

Getting a Grip on Common Output Methods

In Chapter 15, we talk about slide shows, videodiscs, and HTML Photo Galleries. These creations offer different output options, such as e-mailing, burning files to disc, and creating HTML documents, as well as printing and PDF creation.

The remaining creations you work with in the Creation Setup window include Album Pages, Bound Photo Albums, Four-Fold Greeting Cards, Photo Greeting Cards, Calendar Pages, and Bound Calendars. All these creations can be output to PDF files, to your printer, and sent via e-mail. The two bound items (photo books and calendars) can also be output to a sharing service.

For a quick glimpse at what options are available for each type of creation, select Create in the Organizer and click items in the left pane of the Creation Setup window. In the lower-right portion of the window, you see icons for Adobe PDF, a printer, an online sharing service, and e-mail, like those shown in Figure 16-1. As you look over the creations discussed in this chapter, realize that these are the output methods supported by projects discussed here.

Adobe PDF · Online sharing service · Print · E-mail

Figure 16-1: Icons show a project's output options.

Creating the Family Photo Album

Elements provides some fancy ways to create pages for a photo album. Album Pages support all output formats except sharing services. Elements offers options for printing pages that look just like pages in a fancy photo album you might purchase at the local drug store.

Follow these steps to create Album Pages:

1. **Select files in the Organizer and click Create.**

   The procedure for all creations is the same. You first select files in the Organizer (or an editing mode) and then click the Create button in the Shortcuts bar. If you forget files you want to add to a creation, the creation wizards provide options for adding photos.

2. **Select Album Pages in the Creation Setup window and click OK.**

   The Create Album Pages Wizard opens.

3. **Select a template in the right pane of the wizard and click Next Step.**

   Another feature common to these creations is a list of templates from which to choose. From a vast number of predesigned templates, pick the style you want to use and a preview is shown in the window, as you can see in Figure 16-2.

4. **Using the options for arranging photos, you can add, duplicate, and delete photos in the album. When you're done (or if the photos look okay), click the Next Step button to advance to the next pane.**

   Step 3 in the wizard shows you the title page.

5. **Click the placeholder text and type a title.**

6. **From the drop-down menu at the top of the pane, select additional pages to edit the caption on each page.**

7. **Click Next Step when you finish editing your page captions.**

8. **In the next pane, type a filename, check the box for showing the photos in the Organizer, and click Save to save the project.**

Figure 16-2: Almost all creations offer you templates that you can use with your creations.

The final step is the Share pane (Step 5).

9. **Decide what output you want (PDF, print, or e-mail) by clicking the related button.**

   Although you can't share Album Pages online, you can place an online order by clicking the Order Online button.

If you want to update your project, you can open the saved project and add more photos at a later date. A new PDF file should be generated if outputting to PDF. However, if you're printing pages, you can print just the new pages added to the updated file.

Another type of photo album is available in the Creation Setup window — the *Bound Photo Album*. Although this creation offers the same output options as photo album pages, the bound album is a creation you more likely order from an online service provider, which we explain how to do later in this chapter. The photo album pages we explain how to create in this section, however, are easier to output yourself.

Greetings!

You can create one of two types of cards with the Creation Setup window. Both the Four-Fold Card and the Photo Greeting Card follow similar paths through the creation process — that is, you select photos in the Organizer, choose a template, add text, and choose an output format. Both these creations support output for PDF, printing, and e-mailing.

✔ **The Four-Fold Card** is a design that is similar to greeting cards folded twice, creating four panels. On your final design, the folds are marked with dotted lines.

✔ **Photo Greeting Cards** are similar to postcards you pick up at travel destinations — the designs are not intended to be folded. Figure 16-3 shows the results of creating a Photo Greeting Card.

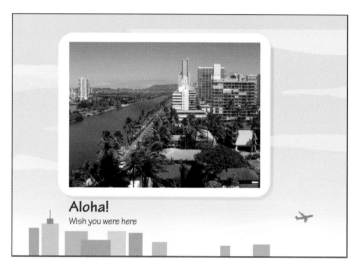

Figure 16-3: Photo Greeting Cards are designed like postcards you pick up at the airport.

Calendars

Create your own personal calendar in Photoshop Elements, and you won't buy any more calendars as each new year rolls around. This is a great tool for creating calendars for the kids — using pictures of their soccer team, the group at the boys and girls club, the 4-H club, that great vacation you took with the family last year — or even for satisfying your own ego by passing out your creations at the office. The calendar options have many uses, limited only by your imagination.

The procedure for making calendars is similar to creating cards:

1. **Select 13 images in the Organizer and click Create.**

   When creating calendars, the first image appears on a title page, and the remaining 12 images appear for each month in the year.

2. **Select either Calendar Pages or Bound Calendar in the Creation Setup window and click OK.**

   Bound Calendars support sharing services, whereas Calendar Pages do not.

Figure 16-4 shows a Calendar Pages creation shown in Adobe Reader with a facing pages view.

3. **Select a template in the right pane of the wizard and click Next Step.**

   You see image thumbnails for the photos that appear according to title page and month.

4. **If you want to rearrange the photos, click and drag them around the Step 2 pane. When you're done, click Next Step.**

5. **In the next step of the wizard, preview the pages placed on the template you chose.**

6. **Click Next Step and type a name for the file to be saved.**

7. **Click Save, and you arrive at the Share pane. Click Create PDF to create a PDF file, Print to print your calendar, or E-mail to send your calendar as an e-mail attachment.**

   Bound Calendars can be exported to PDF, print, or e-mail, as well as for sharing, so that you can order bound, commercially printed calendars.

   Ordering printed calendars results in a professional-looking product. Be certain to use images with at least 300 ppi resolution at 100% size when placing online orders.

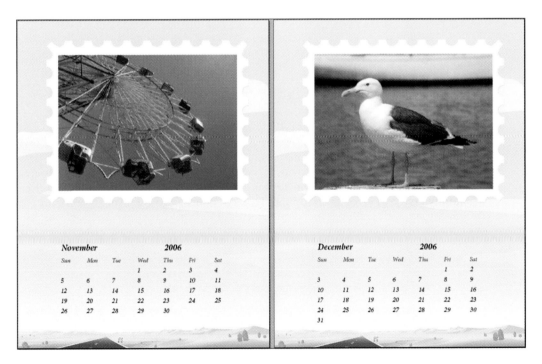

Figure 16-4: A Calendar Pages creation shown in Adobe Reader in a facing pages view.

Spreading the Love through Sharing

Two methods of sharing your creations are available in Elements. You can place orders with online services, specifically the Kodak EasyShare service we talk about in Chapter 14, or you can e-mail your creation to others.

Ordering bound books and calendars online

Using the Kodak EasyShare service makes ordering and distribution very easy. You can place orders for photo books and calendars, and the service takes care of mailing and distributing your creation to friends and family spread around the country or the world.

With both the Bound Photo Book and the Bound Calendar creations, you have options for clicking the Order Online button in the Share step (the last step) in the creation wizards. To set up these creations, you follow the same procedures for selecting photos, templates, adding text, and so on that you can find in "Creating the Family Photo Album," earlier in this chapter. When you get to the last step in the creation wizard, follow these steps to place your online order:

1. **Click Order Online.**

   You need to have an account to place an order.

2. **When you select the online service for the first time, you are prompted to set up an account. After your account is set up or if you already have an account, enter your login information.**

   You find more details about setting up an online account in Chapter 14.

3. **On the order page for the item, make sure you use one of the templates recommended on the help screen.**

   Figure 16-5 shows a help screen for placing an order for Photo Books.

4. **Click Edit Book on the help screen if you need to change the template. When you're ready to proceed, click Purchase Book.**

5. **On the order screen, make some choices, such as book color, for the product you are ordering; set the quantity that you want to purchase; and review the total cost. Click Next when you're finished.**

6. **If you want to share your creation with other users, you can identify users' names and addresses in the Recipients pane in the Order Wizard. Click Next when you're done.**

7. **Follow any remaining steps in the wizard to complete your order.**

Figure 16-5: The Kodak EasyShare help screen provides recommendations for the design of your project.

E-mailing creations

After you put together a creation with the creation wizard, you can e-mail the creation to your friends, family, or whomever you like by clicking the E-mail button in the Share pane in the creation wizard. (We introduce this and other ways to share creations in "Getting a Grip on Common Output Methods," earlier in this chapter.)

When you want to e-mail a creation, follow these steps:

1. **Click E-mail in a creation wizard.**

   The Attach Creation Item to E-mail dialog box opens, as shown in Figure 16-6.

2. **Click the Edit Contacts button.**

3. **In the window that opens, add any contacts you like. Click OK when you're done.**

   You can add a long list of contacts.

Attach Creation Item to E-mail

Items

Select Recipients
- ☑ Obermeier, Barbara
- ☑ Padova, Ted

Attachment
File Name: My Photo Book

Select Size and Quality
- ◉ Optimize for Viewing Onscreen
- ○ Optimize for Printing
- ○ Use Full Resolution

Message
Here are the photos that I want to share with you.

Edit Contacts...

Next   Cancel   Help

Figure 16-6: Click E-mail in a creation wizard, and the Attach Creation Item to E-mail dialog box opens.

4. **Back in the Attach Creation to E-Mail dialog box, just check the boxes beside recipients' names to identify who will receive your creation.**

5. **In the Select Size and Quality area of the dialog box, select your desired output.**

   The first two items, Optimize for Viewing Onscreen and Optimize for Printing, compress and downsample the photos according to the selection you make. Use Full Resolution compresses the photos but does not downsample them. Regardless of which option you choose, your file is converted to a PDF document and downsampled when the PDF is created.

6. **Click Next.**

   A dialog box opens, informing you of the file size and how long the recipient's e-mail will take to download your file, as measured on a 56Kbps (Kilobytes per second) modem.

   Be certain your recipients can receive large file sizes before sending the creation via e-mail.

7. **Click OK in the dialog box that shows file information.**

   Your PDF file is sent to all the recipients you selected.

By default, Elements uses your primary e-mail client application, which may or may not be the e-mail program you use. You can change the default e-mail client by pressing Ctrl+K to open the Preferences dialog box when in the Organizer, and clicking Sharing in the left pane. From a drop-down list in the Sharing preferences, select the e-mail client application you want Elements to use.

Part VI
The Part of Tens

The 5th Wave   By Rich Tennant

"Why don't you try blurring the brimstone and then putting a nice glow effect around the hellfire."

In this part . . .

The Part of Tens offers a couple of fun chapters to help you take your photography and Elements a little further. In Chapter 17, you find our top ten tips for composing better photos. Find out about the rule of thirds, framing, and other simple tricks that will make your photos look better than ever.

Also, in Part V, we introduce the creations that Elements helps you make, but why stop there? Chapter 18 offers even more ideas for projects you can create for your home or work, such as flyers, portfolios, CD and DVD covers, and more.

17

Ten Tips for Composing Better Photos

A few things have to come together to make a great photograph. One is being in the right place at the right time. Another is the ability to tell a story. And yet another is excellent composition. Unfortunately, we can't help with your schedule or storytelling, but we can give you several easy tips on how to take photographs that are interesting and well-composed. Some of these tips overlap and contain common concepts. But they're all free; they don't require any extra money or equipment. All they take are an open mind and an eye that is willing to be trained over time.

Find a Focal Point

One of the most important tools for properly composing a photo is establishing a *focal point* — a main point of interest. If too many elements are competing for attention, a photo probably doesn't have a clearly defined focal point. Your eye, therefore, doesn't know where to look. Too many images without a focal point cause the viewer to tire quickly or lose interest. The eye wants to be drawn to a subject.

Excessive background elements, like furniture, walls, tables, fences, buildings, and even random bystanders, don't add much to the compositional or emotional value of your shot. What you really want to capture are the smiles and expressions of your family and friends.

Keep these tips in mind to help find your focal point:

- ✔ **Pick your subject and then get close to it.**

- ✔ **Include a point of interest in scenic shots.** Sunrises and sunsets are pretty, but after you've seen a few, you've seen them all. Try to capture an early morning fisherman casting his line off the pier or a child checking out a rogue hermit crab at dusk. That once-ho-hum scenic shot now has some visual punch.

- ✔ **When appropriate, try to include an element in the foreground, middle ground, or background to add depth and a sense of scale, as shown in Figure 17-1.** Just make sure it is a meaningful element and not random clutter.

Brand X Pictures

Figure 17-1: Including elements in the foreground adds depth to a photo.

Use the Rule of Thirds

After you've found a focal point for your shot, the next step is to try to put that focal point, or subject, in a prime location within your viewfinder or LCD display. Those prime locations are based on a photographic principle called the *Rule of Thirds*. If you divide an image into a grid of nine equal segments, as shown in Figure 17-2, the elements most appealing to the eye and most likely to be noticed first are those that fall close to one of the four intersections of the dividing lines.

Corbis Digital Stock

Figure 17-2: Position your subject at one of the intersecting points on the Rule of Thirds grid.

When composing your shot, try to mentally divide your frame into vertical and horizontal thirds and position your most important visual element at any intersecting point. When shooting landscapes, remember a low horizon creates a dreamy and spacious feeling, while a high horizon gives an earthy and intimate feeling. For close-up portraits, try putting the face or eyes of a person at one of those points.

If the Rule of Thirds is too hard for you to remember or employ, when you look through the viewfinder, just repeat this mantra, "move from center." We all have a natural tendency to want to center everything. Get it nice and orderly. But centered subjects are often static and boring. Asymmetry often gives us more dynamic and interesting images.

If you have an autofocus camera, you'll need to lock the focus when moving from center because the autofocus sensor locks onto whatever is in the center of the viewfinder — not on your point of interest. Autofocus can also be problematic when trying to do something as simple as photographing two people (in this case, you may want the two people in the center), and your camera keeps focusing on the space in the distance between them. Center your subject in the viewfinder and apply slight pressure to your shutter release button to lock the focus. Then, reposition your subject at an intersecting point on the Rule of Thirds grid and press down all the way to snap the photo.

Cut the Clutter

Contrary to supermarket tabloid covers, those telephone poles, branches, car antennas, and other everyday objects do not naturally grow out of people's heads. Although these *mergers,* as photographers call them, are good for a laugh, they're not good enough to make it into picture frames and scrapbooks.

Here are some ways you can cut the clutter from your background:

- **Get up close and personal.** Most people worry about getting their heads cut off when they get their photos taken. But more often than not, people tend to capture too much boring or distracting background. Fill your viewfinder frame with your subject. Although you can always crop your image later, it's better to try to get your subject to fill the frame when you take the photo.

- **Shoot at a different angle.** Yes, you can turn your camera! Most photos are horizontal just for the mere fact that it is easier to hold the camera that way. That's fine for a lot of shots (such as the requisite group photo and some landscape shots). But other subjects — buildings, trees, waterfalls, mountain peaks, giraffes, Shaquille O'Neal — lend themselves to a vertical format.

- **Move around your subject.** Moving around may help eliminate unwanted clutter. Shoot from below or above your subject if necessary.

- **Move your subject, if possible, to get the optimum background.** Although there are exceptions, an ideal background is usually free from distracting elements like tree branches, poles, wires, chain-link fences, signs, bright lights, lots of loud colors, busy wallpaper, and so on. Only include what complements your subject.

- **Use background elements to enhance, not distract.** On the other hand, if your background is interesting and can make your photo stronger, then include it. You can use famous landmarks, props, and even decorations in the background to give context to images, as shown in Figure 17-3.

- **Use space around a subject to evoke a certain mood.** A lot of space around a person can give a sense of loneliness, just as a closely cropped portrait can create a feeling of intimacy. Just make sure the space is intentionally used in the shot.

Figure 17-3: Use background elements, like decorations, to help define an event and add ambience to the subject.

> ▸ **If you're stuck with a distracting background, you can try blurring it by using a wider aperture (like f/4 instead of f/11 or f/16) on your camera.** This makes the _depth of field_ (areas of sharpness in relation to your focal point) shallower so your subject is in focus, but the background isn't.
>
> Because consumer digital cameras use image sensors that are typically one-third the size of a 35mm frame, the lens is very close to the sensor, which really increases the depth of field. This can make it hard to blur the background. Not a problem — you can also blur the background by making a selection and using the Blur filter in Elements. See Chapters 7 and 10 for more on selections and the Blur filter.

Frame Your Shot

When appropriate, use foreground elements to frame your subject. Frames lead you into a photograph. You can use elements like tree branches, windows, archways, and doorways to frame a wide or long shot, add a feeling of depth, and create a point of reference, as shown in Figure 17-4. You don't have to reserve the use of framing for wide and long shots, however. Close-ups can also be framed. Your framing elements do not always have to be sharply focused. Sometimes, if they're too sharp, they distract from the focal point. And remember to avoid mergers!

ImageState

Figure 17-4: Use elements that frame your subject.

Employ Contrast

Just remember "light on dark, dark on light." A light subject will have more impact and emphasis if it is shot against a dark background, and vice versa, as shown in Figure 17-5. When viewing an image, our eyes go to the area of the most contrast first. Obviously, sometimes finding contrast in the environment is beyond your control. But when setting up a shot, you can certainly try to incorporate this technique. Keep in mind, however, that contrast needs to be used carefully. Sometimes it can be distracting, especially if the high-contrast elements are not your main point of interest.

PhotoDisc, Inc./Getty Images

Figure 17-5: High-contrast shots demand attention.

Using Leading Lines

Leading lines are lines that, either by the actual elements in the image or by the composition of those elements, lead the eye into the picture and hopefully to a point of interest. These lines add dimension, depth and perspective by carrying the eye through the photo:

- ✔ Diagonal lines are dynamic and evoke movement.

- ✔ Curves are graceful and harmonious.

- ✔ Horizontal lines are peaceful and give a feeling of balance.

- ✔ Vertical lines are direct and active.

The best leading lines are those that enter the image from the lower left corner. Many elements provide natural leading lines, especially in scenic or landscape photos such as roads, walls, fences, rivers, shadows, skyscrapers, and bridges. The photo in Figure 17-6 of the Great Wall of China is an example of curved leading lines.

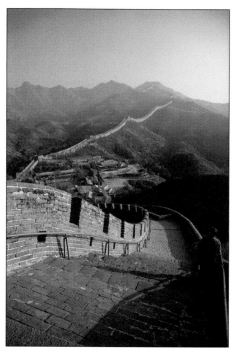

Flat Earth

Figure 17-6: You don't have to trek to China to find leading lines, although you may not find a longer unbroken curve than the Great Wall.

Experiment with Viewpoints

Not much in the world looks fascinating photographed from a height of 5 to 6 feet off the ground. Unfortunately, this is the viewpoint of "Snapshotville." Try to break out of this mode by taking photos from another vantage point. Experiment with taking a photo from above (bird's-eye view) or below (worm's-eye view) the subject. A different angle may provide a more interesting image:

- ✔ **Unexpected angles can exaggerate the size of the subject.** The subject may appear either larger or smaller than normal, as shown in Figure 17-7. Try extreme angles with scenic shots, which otherwise can tend to be rather static or boring.

✔ **Changing your viewpoint can change the mood of the image.** If the photo in Figure 17-7 had been taken from a front angle, it would have been pretty dull. Taken from below, looking up, exaggerates the height and makes for a stronger and more exciting composition, making the cactus seem like nature's skyscraper.

✔ **Use direct eye contact when photographing people.** It provides a sense of realism and makes the image more intimate and warm, pulling you into the photo. But remember that children are not at the same eye level as adults. We often shoot down at them, making them appear smaller than they really are. Try kneeling or sitting on the floor and getting down to their level. You will also find that you get a less distracting background in the frame, and the lighting from your flash will more evenly cover the face. Do the same for pets and other short stature subjects, such as flowers.

Corbis Digital Stock

Figure 17-7: Shooting subjects from extreme angles can exaggerate size, resulting in a more interesting shot.

Use Light

When we think of light in regards to photography, the first thing that comes to mind are all those photos that we've taken in the past that are either overexposed (too light) or underexposed (too dark). With lighting, you have to not only consider whether you have the right amount of lighting, but also these factors:

✔ The direction of the light

✔ The intensity of the light

✔ The color of the light

✔ Whether you're shooting in natural light (outdoors) or artificial light (indoors)

✔ How to use lighting creatively to lead the eye and create a certain mood

If the light isn't right for your shot, you have quite a few choices — hurry up and wait, move yourself, move the subject, add more light with a flash, or diffuse light. Of course, which you choose depends on the circumstances of the shot and what's convenient or most productive. Here are a few tips to remember about light:

- **The best light for photographs is in the early morning and later afternoon.** The light is warmer and softer and the shadows are longer and less harsh.

- **Avoid taking portraits at midday.** The overhead sun causes ugly shadows and makes people squint. If you must shoot then, use a reflector to block some of the sunlight or fill in the shadow areas. Or you can use a *scrim* (white translucent fabric stretched across a frame) to diffuse the light.

- **Cloudy or overcast days can be great for photographing, especially portraits.** The light is soft and diffused and flatters the face.

- **Shooting subjects with *backlighting* (where the lighting comes from behind the subject) can produce very dramatic results.** Figure 17-8 shows an example. If you want to see the details of the subject, and not just a silhouette, use a fill flash to lighten the shadow areas.

- **Watch that the brightest light source isn't directed right into the lens.** This will cause *lens flare,* those strange light circles that appear in the photo.

- **Take into account the color of the light.** The light at noon is white, the light at sunset is orange, and the light at twilight is blue. The color of the light can make an image feel warm or cool.

Corbis Digital Stock

Figure 17-8: Backlighting can yield dramatic images.

- **Use a flash when necessary.** Use a flash in low-light conditions. If your built-in flash isn't cutting the mustard, you may want to invest in an accessory flash.

- **Finally, get creative with light.** Look for those unique compositions created by the interplay between light and shadow areas or how the light illuminates a particular subject. Lighting by itself can make or break a certain mood or emotion. Think of a simple beam of light coming through the roof of an old barn. Even in the lousiest weather, the most beautifully lit images can emerge. When wet objects are lit, they seem to shimmer, as shown in Figure 17-9.

Corbis Digital Stock

Figure 17-9: Lighting can create drama from the simplest objects.

Giving Direction

When you look at magazines that feature the year's best photos, they all appear as instances of pure serendipity. Sometimes that's the case, but more often than not, the photographer arranged the shot or waited for the right light or a special moment.

As a photographer, you also shouldn't be afraid to play photo stylist:

- **Give directions on where you want people to stand, how to stand, and so on.** For example, tell people to touch each other, bring their heads towards each other or put their arms around each other, as shown in Figure 17-10.

- **Designate the location.**

- **Use props, such as trees or cars, to arrange people around**

- **Use a variety of poses.** Have some people sit and others stand.

IT Stock Free

Figure 17-10: Provide direction to the people you're photographing, while also trying to capture their personalities.

- **If you are dealing with a large group of people, rambunctious kids, or excited pets, get someone to help direct.** Just make sure that the parties being photographed pay attention and look at the camera.

- **Try and get people to relax.** While spontaneity can yield great images, you can still get good photos from posed subjects if they aren't hating the experience.

Consider Direction of Movement

When the subject is capable of movement, such as a car, person, or animal, make sure you leave more space in front of the subject than behind it, as shown in Figure 17-11. Otherwise the viewer may subconsciously experience a feeling of departure or discomfort. You want to try to give the person or object room to move into the frame. Likewise if a person is looking out onto a vista, make sure you include that vista so the person is given a point of view and the scene is given context.

Brand X Pictures

Figure 17-11: Always include room for your subject to move into the frame.

Ten More Project Ideas

So you've posted all your holiday and vacation photos in a Web Gallery and made enough albums, slide shows, and cards to keep your family and friends content for months to come? Sounds like you may be ready to take a crack at some other projects. In this chapter, you'll find some ideas on how you can use your inventory of digital images to make your life more productive, more organized, and more fun. Remember, this just scratches the surface. With a little imagination, before you know it, there won't be anything left in your life that doesn't include your photos.

Wallpaper and Screen Savers

If you like an image so much that you want to gaze at it while you're toiling away at your computer, why not use that image for the background of your computer, better known as the *desktop wallpaper*. If you can't choose just one favorite image, you can use several to create a multi-image *screen saver*.

Sharing projects

Not into killing trees? Not to worry. You don't have to print every project you make. Any file you create can be left as a purely digital file and e-mailed to other users. From the Organizer or either Editor mode, you can select files that you want to send to recipients and choose File➪Attach to E-mail. A dialog box opens, similar to the Attach Creation Item to E-mail dialog box described in Chapter 16, but with some additional options.

From the Format menu, you have options for sending your file as Photo Mail (HTML), Simple Slide Show (PDF), or Individual Attachments.

The first option saves the file as HTML that might be used for a Web page design. Other options are to send the photos as a PDF file or as a file attachment to an e-mail message. Additionally, you have options for editing your address book, selecting image quality, and downsampling. You can add a message here, or you can choose to type text in your new e-mail message.

Click the Next button, and the file (according to the format you choose) is attached to a new e-mail message in your default e-mail program.

As we mention in Chapter 2, if you are serious about image editing, you really should have a neutral gray background. But as long as your wallpaper isn't showing while you do your color corrections, feel free to decorate your desktop with your favorite colorful photo. You use just two easy steps to turn a photo into wallpaper:

1. **From the Organizer, select the photo you want to use.**

2. **Choose Edit➪Set As Desktop Wallpaper.**

   That's all there is to it! Your photo has now been transformed into desktop wallpaper.

If you have two or more photos you want to use, you can create a Windows XP screen saver. Here's how to create a screen saver in Windows XP:

1. **Select the desired photos from the Organizer.**

2. **Choose File➪Export.**

3. **Choose JPEG for your file type, select your photo size, and choose a quality setting.**

   We recommend using a size that matches the resolution setting you're using for your monitor. Use a quality setting of 12 for maximum quality.

4. **Click the Browse button.**

5. **Click the Make a New Folder button and save the photos as JPEGs to that folder. Name the folder something appropriate, like screen saver.**

6. **Choose Start➪Control Panel➪Display.**

   Depending on how your computer is set up, you might have to double-click Display to open it.

7. **Click the Screen Saver tab and choose My Pictures Slideshow from the pop-up menu under Screen Saver.**

8. **Click Settings and choose the folder you created in Step 5 that contains your photos. Define the photo size and specify all your other options.**

9. **Click Preview to see how it will appear on your monitor.**

   Move your mouse or press a key to end the preview.

10. **Click Apply and then OK to close the Display window.**

Flyers, Ads, and Online Auctions

Everyone knows a picture is worth a thousand words. Whether you're selling puppies or advertising an open house, adding a photo to an ad or flyer really helps to drive your message home.

Here are the abbreviated steps to quickly create an ad or flyer.

1. **Choose File⇨New⇨Blank File.**

2. **In the New Document dialog box, enter your desired document specifications.**

   We recommend entering the final dimensions and resolution for your desired output. If you want to print your ad or flyer on your desktop printer or at a service bureau, a good guideline for resolution is 300 pixels per inch. For more on resolution and sizing images, be sure and check out Chapter 3. If you want to fill your background with color, as we did in Figure 18-1, choose Edit⇨Fill Layer and choose Color from the Contents pop-up menu. Choose your desired color in the Color Picker.

3. **Open your photo or photos and drag and drop it/them onto your new canvas with the Move tool.**

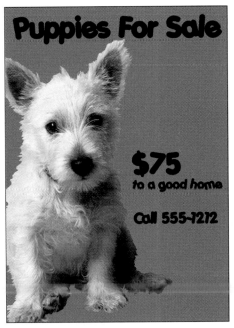

PhotoDisc, Inc./Getty Images

Figure 18-1: Quickly put together ads and flyers.

Your image is automatically put on a separate layer. For more on layers, see Chapter 8. If you want to use only a portion of the image, as we did with the puppy in Figure 18-1, then use your favorite selection method to pluck out your element. For more on selections, see Chapter 7.

4. **Select the Type tool, click the canvas, and add your desired type.**

5. **When you're done, choose File⇨Save.**

6. **Choose Photoshop (.PSD) from the Format pop-up menu, make sure the Layers option is checked, and click Save.**

   If you want to take your document to a service bureau or copy shop, like FedEx Kinko's, you should save your document as a Photoshop PDF (.PDF). That way, you don't have to worry about compatibility issues or printing snafus.

If you're preparing photos for online auction sites like eBay or Yahoo! Auctions, be sure and keep your images low resolution — 72 ppi, to be exact — and at 100% scale. Save the file as a JPEG to ensure that your file stays lean and mean while preserving colors. Be sure and check the image specifications posted on your online auction site.

CD Labels and Jewel Case Covers

If you are burning a CD of images or a creation, why not also create a custom label and/or jewel case cover that features a photo or two? There are many inexpensive CD-labeling packages, which you can purchase at computer and office supply stores, that come equipped with templates to use with a variety of programs. If none of the templates works in Elements, try this workaround:

1. **Take one of the label sheets and, with a black marker, draw around the label areas.**

2. **Scan the sheet and save it as a Photoshop (.PSD) file.**

3. **Open the file in Elements and use it as your template by dragging and dropping images onto your file.**

4. **Add your text on another layer.**

5. **When you're done, simply drag the template layer to the trash and print your file.**

Clothes, Hats, and More

Many local copy shops, retail stores, and Web sites enable you to add photos to T-shirts, hats, buttons, tote bags, ties, mouse pads, and many other items. If you can produce it, they can put a photo on it. But it is easy, and less expensive, to tackle this project yourself.

Buy plain white T-shirts at your local discount store or plain aprons and tote bags at your craft or fabric store. Then buy special transfer paper at your office supply or computer store. Print your photos on the transfer paper (be sure and flip the images horizontally first), iron the print onto the fabric, and you've got yourself a personalized gift for very little cash.

What do you get for the person who has everything? How about a blanket of memories? You can transfer photos onto patches of fabric and create unique memory quilts. What grandparent wouldn't love a quilt with photos of her children and grandchildren?

Posters

For special events, important announcements, or maybe just your favorite family photo, you can get posters and large-size prints at many copy shops and service bureaus. Call and talk to a knowledgeable rep at your copy shop or service bureau so you know exactly how to prep your file. Here are a few questions to ask:

- ✓ What file format and resolution should the file be?
- ✓ What size prints do you offer?
- ✓ Do you provide mounting and lamination services?

  In addition to printing large prints, many service bureaus will mount prints on foam core or a sturdier material called *gator board.* These service bureaus also can laminate prints to protect them from scratches and UV rays.

Household and Business Inventories

Don't wait for a natural disaster or theft to get you motivated to prepare an inventory of your household or business assets. Take your digital camera and shoot pictures of your items. Add text to describe the items in the caption section of the Organizer. Be sure and include makes, models, purchase dates, and dollar values of each piece. Then create a single PDF document from those multiple files either by creating a slide show or album, as shown in Figure 18-2. Upload the PDF to a Web storage site or burn a CD or DVD and place it off-site in a safety deposit box or other secure location. If the need arises, the PDF can be viewed by your insurance agent using the free Adobe Reader software.

Laptop, ABC Brand, Purchased Aug 2004, SN2359980, $2,200

PhotoSpin

Figure 18-2: Create an inventory of your assets.

Project Documentation

Nothing helps to document a process like images. The spoken and written word is great, but *showing* how something comes together is even more effective. Consider using your photographs to help document your projects from beginning to end. Whether it is a project involving home improvement, furniture building, crafts, or cooking, take photos at each stage to record the project. If you are taking a class or workshop and the instructors don't mind, take your camera to class. Documenting the positions or steps of that new yoga, pottery, or gardening class will help you practice or recreate it on your own later, either for yourself or to teach someone else.

Step 5

Garnish with bell, ivy, ribbon and fresh flowers.

Import the photos into the Organizer and create notes on each step of the project, either on the canvas itself or in the caption area. Output the images to a PDF slide show or a PDF of album pages, as shown in Figure 18-3.

PhotoDisc, Inc./Getty Images

Figure 18-3: Document your favorite projects for easier re-creation later.

School Reports and Projects

There's nothing like some interesting photos to jazz up the obligatory school report. Doing a botany report? Include some close-ups of a flower with text labels on the parts of the flower. Have to write a paper on the habits of the lemurs of Madagascar? Trek down to your local zoo and have a photo shoot. Create a simple collage of lemurs eating, sleeping, and doing the other things that lemurs do. In fact, buying your children their own inexpensive point-and-shoot cameras may give them a little more enthusiasm for school work.

Wait, There's More

Before we leave you to take your photos to the next dimension, here are a few extra ideas: Make fun place cards for dinner party guests, create your own business cards if you need only a few, design your own gift wrap and tags, or label storage boxes with photos of their contents. The possibilities are endless.

Index

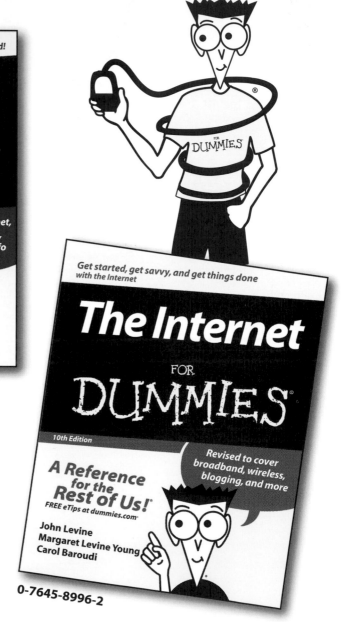